WORLDVIEWS AND THEORIES OF
INTERNATIONAL RELATIONS

Also by Jürg Martin Gabriel

THE AMERICAN CONCEPTION OF NEUTRALITY
HOW SWITZERLAND IS GOVERNED

Worldviews and Theories of International Relations

Jürg Martin Gabriel

© Jürg Martin Gabriel 1994

All rights reserved. No reproduction, copy or transmission of
this publication may be made without written permission.

No paragraph of this publication may be reproduced, copied or
transmitted save with written permission or in accordance with
the provisions of the Copyright, Designs and Patents Act 1988,
or under the terms of any licence permitting limited copying
issued by the Copyright Licensing Agency, 90 Tottenham Court
Road, London W1P 9HE.

Any person who does any unauthorised act in relation to this
publication may be liable to criminal prosecution and civil
claims for damages.

First published in Great Britain 1994 by
MACMILLAN PRESS LTD
Houndmills, Basingstoke, Hampshire RG21 2XS
and London
Companies and representatives
throughout the world

A catalogue record for this book is available
from the British Library.

ISBN 0–333–60549–7 hardcover
ISBN 0–333–60550–0 paperback

10 9 8 7 6 5 4 3 2
03 02 01 00 99 98 97 96 95

Printed in Hong Kong

First published in the United States of America 1994 by
Scholarly and Reference Division,
ST. MARTIN'S PRESS, INC.,
175 Fifth Avenue,
New York, N.Y. 10010

ISBN 0–312–10210–0 (cloth)

Library of Congress Cataloging-in-Publication Data
Gabriel, Jürg Martin, 1940–
Worldviews and theories of international relations / Jürg Martin
Gabriel.
p.   cm.
Includes index.
ISBN 0–312–10210–0 (cloth)
1. International relations—Philosophy.   I. Title.   II. Title:
World views and theories of international relations.
JX1391.G25   1994
327—dc20   93–23787
                                              CIP

To Gianina and Alex

Contents

List of Figures	ix
Acknowledgements	x
Introduction	**1**
1 Worldviews and Theories	**7**
Conventional Categories	7
Four Worldviews	12
On Theorizing	17
2 Classical Theories	**29**
Gentz: Balance of Power	29
Clausewitz: War as an Instrument	36
Bernhardi: Militaristic Imperialism	42
Kant: Perpetual Peace	51
Hobson: Social Democracy	59
Angell: Interdependence	65
Wilson: Collective Security	71
3 Contemporary Theories	**81**
Waltz: Neo-Realism	81
Gilpin: Hegemonic Change	88
Kahn: Deterrence	96
Gray: Geopolitics	106
Rosecrance: Free Trade	115
Keohane: Regimes	123
Osgood: Tension Reduction	130
Falk: Central Guidance	137
4 Worldviews: A Summary	**149**
Anarchic Idealist Theories	149
Hierarchic Idealist Theories	155
Anarchic Realist Theories	157
Hierarchic Realist Theories	162
Conclusions	**166**
Notes	169
Index	190

List of Figures

1.1	Scholarly Interests in International Relations	13
1.2	Four Worldviews	15
1.3	Idealist Transformation Theories	16
1.4	Realist Transformation Theories	17
3.1	Existing World Order System	139
3.2	Projected Growth Curves for Actors in the World Order System	142
3.3	World Polity Association	143

Acknowledgements

This study grew slowly and went through a number of stages. It originated in the typical frustrations of a graduate student trying to cope with the conceptual chaos of our field. It found its first outline while teaching Cameroonian students at the University of Yaoundé, and it matured in lectures at the University of St. Gallen. Parts of the book were written down in 1989 at the University of Virginia, while on sabbatical. A first draft was completed back home in Switzerland and then rewritten at Stanford University, where I spent two terms as visiting professor in 1991–92.

At Virginia, I had the valuable advice of Inis Claude and Whittle Johnston. At Stanford there were stimulating discussions with Stephen Krasner, and I profited from the many interesting seminars at the Center for International Security and Arms Control. Furthermore, I was very pleased that Kenneth Waltz took time to go through the manuscript and make a number of important suggestions. I would also like to thank Patrick de Souza, a Stanford graduate, who read the opening chapter critically and suggested changes.

At St. Gallen, Doris Rudischhauser, Marcel Müller and Armin Guhl helped with proofreading, producing the final draft and preparing the index. Finally, thanks go to my students whose many questions and comments have forced me to think in neat categories.

JÜRG MARTIN GABRIEL
St. Gallen, Switzerland

Introduction

A perusal of contemporary theory in international relations leaves one with a mixed impression: on the one hand there is a great outpouring of new contributions suggesting unbroken optimism about the possibilities of progress in our field; on the other hand there are indications that theorizing meets with innumerable obstacles and that some authors are highly pessimistic about the state of our discipline.

The optimists keep searching for systematic knowledge, for the causes of war, the dynamics of international change, the patterns of world order or the reasons for failure in crisis control. They ask interesting questions and try to come up with answers permitting improved understanding and possibly improved management of world politics. Some show how nuclear proliferation can be curbed; others argue that massive war is outmoded. Some predict the rise of the trading state, while others see the continued dominance of the military state. Some deplore the decline of American hegemony and fear it will lead to instability; others argue that there can be stability without hegemony. There are those who see the post-Cold War era as unipolar, and there are others who perceive a return to multipolar balance. There is no lack of new theory; on the contrary, the flow of new ideas is so copious that it is difficult to preserve an overview.

But there are also frustrations. One of the most common complaints expressed is that knowledge in our field is not cumulative, that after years of intensive research there are at best "islands of explanation." Theorists of international relations seem to turn in circles: each generation deals with the same fundamental issues over and over again whereas progress remains elusive. The reasons are partly substantive and partly methodological. Important terms like "system," "hegemony," "regime," "war" or "integration" are difficult to define precisely, and it is impossible to get agreement on techniques of observation, methods of collecting data, and standards for testing hypotheses. The complaints are familiar and need not be repeated here in detail.

Whom is one to take seriously, the representatives of hope or the representatives of frustration? The tenor of this study is on the side of optimism, not because I believe that a significant breakthrough is possible but because a careful look at the work of important theorists in our field suggests that there is a set of central questions which guides their efforts, questions that are relatively timeless and that have been asked before. Knowledge in the social sciences is repetitive more than it is cumulative.

We certainly know more today about arms races and disarmament negotiations than earlier generations did, but it is also true that each generation has to deal with a set of basic questions that change very little over time. Nuclear proliferation and arms-control verification are children of the twentieth century, but the Greeks already knew the basics about armament dynamics and threats. The task of scholarship is not only to search for more knowledge but also to deal repeatedly with fundamental issues and to do so in the light of new circumstances. We cannot expect knowledge in the social sciences to cumulate like knowledge in some of the natural sciences, but we can expect that the central questions belabored by each generation are dealt with in a self-conscious and orderly way. Flashy and impressionistic work may be stimulating, but it is not academic.

The purpose of this study is to show that there is a set of relatively permanent issues that scholars in our discipline identify with and theorize about. I do this by introducing the concept of *worldview* and by demonstrating its usefulness against the background of a number of *classical* and *contemporary* theories.

Worldviews are different from theories. Worldviews are simple devices but their very simplicity allows the isolation of a handful of terms central to describing and analyzing international relations.[1] Theories are more demanding, they are built upon worldviews but go beyond them; theories are more elaborate and contain numerous features not inherent in worldviews; theories are shaped by circumstance and have to be relevant for men acting under particular constraints. The theory of deterrence, for instance, has emerged in the nuclear age and must be useful to men acting in today's world, but the worldview on which it is based has a much more timeless character. The same holds true for theories of integration, collective security, imperialism, regimes and so on.

Worldviews and theories are not essentially different, however. Both share a number of features. Neither are objective constructs free of values and assumptions, and both exhibit a preference for rational schemes over empirical patterns, for understanding over explanation. Neither worldviews nor theories are purely descriptive but embrace a prescriptive and action-oriented component.

The ideas presented here show the influence of a number of scholars in our discipline. As a graduate student I was impressed by Waltz's *Man, the State and War.*[2] In that seminal work Waltz makes an effort to group the many theories of international relations. Based on what various authors regard as the causes of war, Waltz divides them into three broad categories, into what he calls first-, second-, and third-image theorists. I also read Aron's *Peace and War*,[3] but that experience was different. I did not appreciate the book at first because it contains too much redundant information. However, the way in which Aron presents the antinomies of war and peace is impressive, and the various levels of conceptualization on which the book is based also made a lot of sense.

When, much later, I read Waltz's *Theory of International Politics*[4] I was again stimulated. It was not the central (or neo-realist) argument that made the greatest impression on me but his treatment of such basic concepts as anarchy and hierarchy. I also liked the manner in which he ties these terms to cognitive questions, to wholes and parts, to causality and explanation. I came away from reading Aron and Waltz convinced that the antinomies of war and peace, anarchy and hierarchy were fundamental to our field.

The present study begins in Chapter 1 with a detailed account of worldviews. As already mentioned, worldviews are simple devices. They are defined along two dimensions only – the duality of war and peace on the one hand, and the duality of anarchy and hierarchy on the other. Based on these limited criteria a matrix emerges which permits the characterization of four separate and mutually exclusive worldviews. The presentation of the matrix (framework or "field") is followed by a discourse on theorizing in general. Chapters 2 and 3 demonstrate the usefulness of the framework by applying it, first, to classical and, second, to contemporary theories. Chapter 4 sums up some of the findings with reference to the various worldviews.

Given the fact that knowledge in the social sciences is repetitive as much as it is cumulative, it pays to look back at the classics. These texts, by virtue of being classics, have the distinctive advantage of dealing with important questions lucidly and without some of the modern jargon. In a number of ways, therefore, the discussion of classical authors paves the way for a more thorough analysis of contemporary authors.

Chapter 2 begins with three well-known German authors: Friedrich von Gentz, Carl von Clausewitz and Friedrich von Bernhardi. All three are exponents of *Realpolitik* but disagree on a number of important issues. They view war as a normal instrument of politics but differ widely about the context. Gentz, writing at the height of the Napoleonic domination of Europe, advocates the restoration of the balance of power,[5] but Bernhardi, a century later, calls for its abolition.[6] Gentz and Bernhardi disagree on whether war should be associated with a decentralized system, with anarchy and equilibrium, or with a degree of centralization, with hierarchy and hegemony. Their disagreement points to the fundamental realist cleavage in the study of war and peace.

Clausewitz is also a realist but not an easy one to classify.[7] He is the author of the famous dictum that "war is nothing but a continuation of politics by other means" – but he is not explicit about the nature of politics. Is war a continuation of anarchical or hierarchical international politics, is it an instrument of balance of power politics or of imperialism? The difference is important because in one case war is a restrained instrument of politics, in the other case it is unrestrained. Clausewitz is not clear on this point. Nevertheless, he raises important questions about war as an instrument, questions that are of relevance to this very day.

The chapter then turns to four exponents of classic idealism – J. A. Hobson, Norman Angell, Immanuel Kant and Woodrow Wilson. Hobson's *Imperialism: A Study*[8] is a book known for its critique of modern imperialism but which in fact contains an interesting plan for what could be called "anarchic peace through social democracy." Norman Angell in his long and active life wrote a great deal, but his most famous publication is *The Great Illusion*,[9] a book in which he becomes one of the earliest theorists of decentralized interdependence. Hobson and Angell continue to be of interest because they discuss the question of war and peace in terms of social justice, democracy, free trade, interdependence, and even integration. These are issues that motivate many contemporary theorists of international relations.

Immanuel Kant and Woodrow Wilson also deal with eminently modern topics. Kant, in 1795, wrote his famous treatise *Perpetual Peace*[10] in which he suggests that republics have the inherent ability to live in anarchic peace, in a rather informal "Federation of Republican States." Wilson, by calling for the creation of the League of Nations, transcends such informality.[11] He outlined a path that, with the founding of the United Nations, led "beyond anarchy" because that organization represents a (modest) first step in the direction of a more hierarchical world order.

Chapter 3 turns to contemporary authors, first to four realists. In view of the rich literature in this area of international relations theory, it is difficult to make a choice. After much reflection I decided to settle for Kenneth Waltz, Herman Kahn, Colin Gray, and Robert Gilpin.

Waltz, in his *Theory of International Politics*,[12] is credited with having established neo-realism, an up-to-date version of classical balance of power theory and an improvement on the kind of realism propagated most prominently by Hans J. Morgenthau. Waltz derives his theory from the innate structure of the international system, from the logic of anarchy and self-help. Neo-realism is therefore also referred to as "structural realism."

Kahn is not the most important theorist of deterrence but his *Thinking About the Unthinkable*[13] is a highly trenchant (and controversial) presentation of the logic of nuclear war. Furthermore, Kahn emphasizes the need for American superiority, a theme that transcends Waltz's balance of power

Introduction 5

theory and takes us into the realm of hierarchic realism, of hegemonic theory. Colin S. Gray and Robert Gilpin also deal with this theme, although in very different ways.

Gray is a civilian writing on military themes, and in his *Geopolitics of Superpower*[14] he calls for American superiority in the struggle against the Soviet Union. The Cold War context makes the book somewhat dated but since the theory is grounded in Halford Mackinder's axioms on geopolitics it has an importance that carries well beyond that struggle. Gilpin is a political economist who presents a theory of cyclical hegemonic change tied to rational choice.[15] From a formal point of view his work is of interest because it represents the recent tendency in our field to combine the language of microeconomics with the classical ideas of war and peace. From a substantive angle the contribution is important because it raises many of the issues that arise from hegemony and, now that the Cold War is over, from a unipolar world.

Chapter 3 then deals with four contemporary idealists – Richard Rosecrance, Robert O. Keohane, Charles E. Osgood, and Richard A. Falk. Rosecrance has become a proponent of peace through free trade because in his *Rise of the Trading State*[16] he anticipates an anarchic world in which trading nations are on the upswing. Keohane has become known as a theorist of international regimes. In his *After Hegemony*[17] he argues that following the decline of American hegemony regimes develop a measure of autonomy and help to stabilize the international system. Keohane, like Rosecrance, believes that peaceful order is possible in a decentralized world.

In the early sixties, Osgood, a political psychologist, made a case for unilateralism, for reversing escalation by unilaterally induced tension reduction and by initiating a veritable spiral of peace.[18] In the midst of the Cold War the theory appeared utopian: if tension reduction was possible at all in those years it was through bilateral or multilateral means – never unilaterally. Now that the Cold War is over Osgood's ideas are of renewed interest because unilateral tension reduction (and even disarmament) is common. Osgood has lost the image of a utopian.

Falk still has that image. In a book entitled *A Study of Future Worlds*[19] he presents what amounts to a plan for world government. Falk prefers to call it "Central Guidance" but the difference is mostly semantic. It is Falk's contention that only supranational institutions will be able to preserve peace and to handle the many other problems confronting mankind in the decades to come. Falk is an idealist with a strongly hierarchical bent.

It is impossible to do full justice to fifteen different authors. Many have written extensively on international relations, and some have endorsed more than one theory. This study deals with only one book by each author and makes no effort to discuss any one author in a comprehensive fashion. Neither is it the purpose of this study to cover all theories in our field and to provide a comprehensive overview. Important contributions are left out,[20] and the fifteen authors have not necessarily been included because they are well-known, although many are, but because they demonstrate that worldviews can provide an instrument to gain an overview of our field. Finally, no new theory is proposed in this volume. While it is true that worldviews could provide a stimulus for the formulation of theories in the future, no such effort is undertaken in this study.

1 Worldviews and Theories

CONVENTIONAL CATEGORIES

There are many different theories of international relations and they are so diverse that a cursory observer can easily get the impression of diversity overpowering unity. What, after all, does Robert Keohane's treatment of regimes have in common with Herman Kahn's ideas on deterrence? Where is there a link between Charles E. Osgood's work on unilateral tension reduction and Colin Gray's notions of geopolitics? Can there be any trace of similarity between the work of a political economist, a nuclear strategist, a psychologist and a geopolitician? It appears quite impossible to find a unifying theme among so many disparate efforts stemming from such diverse specialties.

Still, there are times when it is necessary to gain an overview of our field, to see the wood for the trees. Such occasions arise when professors of international relations have to teach survey courses on theory and are forced to make up a syllabus that structures the broad spectrum of theories; it happens when they are confronted with the request to define their discipline, to explain, in a nutshell, what the study of international relations is all about; it becomes necessary when they organize scientific meetings and have to assign priorities to topics and papers; it is the case when texts and readers are edited, books that are meant to be representative of our field. In all of these instances we are called upon to press our discipline into some organizational framework, to categorize the innumerable concepts, variables, terms, theories, paradigms, models, and approaches.

A common way of summing up the field is to distinguish between realism, pluralism, and structuralism or, more popularly, between the billiard-ball, the cobweb, and the layer-cake approach.[1] The billiard-ball approach is identified with the state-centered model of international relations, with the rather traditional notion of highly sovereign states acting in a decentralized system where conflict is endemic and security is managed by self-help. Each state has to provide for its own security, each state is forced to arm. Economic considerations are subordinate to security considerations; relative advantage is regularly more important than absolute advantage. The Prisoners' Dilemma is a fact of international life, suboptimal solutions are the rule. Perpetual peace is impossible; at best there can be stability through the adroit management of alliances that counter-balance potential hegemons.[2]

The cobweb approach is radically different. Science, technology, and economics produce interdependence and force nations to abandon some of their sovereignty and independence. In a tightly interdependent world sub- and supranational actors begin to replace traditional nation-states. The cobweb approach is not state-centered; it goes "beyond the nation-state." In such a setting security considerations are superseded by considerations of well-being. As the principle of self-help becomes less dominant the probability of war decreases while the chance of peace increases. The international system is no longer fully decentralized because regimes are necessary to coordinate the ever more powerful forces of interdependence. Large and small states, developed and underdeveloped states are members of these institutions, and all profit from cooperation. Absolute instead of relative gains are dominant, the Prisoners' Dilemma can be overcome.[3]

The layer-cake approach is different again. It rests on a highly stratified conception of international relations where economically and militarily powerful states are at the top of the state hierarchy and correspondingly weaker states are at its bottom. The international system has a strong center and a weak periphery, and exchange between the two is unequal, even exploitative. Instead of true and balanced interdependence there is one-sided dependence. Injustice is endemic, and so is revolution and war. Only self-reliance and dissociation can liberate dependent states from the unequal structure.[4]

The three approaches lay the groundwork for many interesting theories of international relations that explain and predict numerous phenomena, but there are also some gaps. The layer-cake approach, for instance, provides a basis for Marxist and Neo-Marxist theories of dependence and exploitation but cannot explain why similar hierarchic structures emerged in precapitalist days – among Greeks, Egyptians, Persians, and Romans – and under Fascism and Communism. Tendencies toward stratification have long been present in the international system. As Kenneth Waltz says, imperialism is at least as old as recorded history.[5] Is the layer-cake approach too narrow, and should it be substituted by a more broadly defined hierarchical approach?

The cobweb approach has limitations, too. It lays the groundwork for various theories of interdependence but cannot explain supranationality. Why does interdependence produce supranational institutions in Western Europe, but fail to do so in other highly interdependent regions, in North America and the Far East? Could it be useful to distinguish between coordinated cobwebs and sub- and superordinated cobwebs? The billiard-ball approach, finally, is extremely broad. It is meant to cover balance of power theory as well as hegemonic theory, the work of Gentz and Waltz as well as that of Bernhardi and Gilpin. Is it really useful to subsume such diverse conceptions of international relations under one approach? Is it helpful to characterize hegemonic and nonhegemonic states alike as billiard-balls?

This brief review of the cobweb, layer-cake, and billiard-ball approaches demonstrates that they succeed in categorizing certain theories of international relations but cannot account for others. They seem to have particular difficulty dealing with hierarchical theories, with theories of supranationality, hegemony, and imperialism, all of which go beyond the traditional decentralized and anarchic pattern.

Keith L. Nelson and Spencer C. Olin, Jr., two historians of international relations, suggest a set of categories that closely resemble the three approaches discussed above. Instead of realism, pluralism, and structuralism they speak of conservatism, liberalism, and radicalism, and instead of approaches they prefer to speak of ideologies.[6] However, the three categories face problems similar to those already discussed. The conservative ideology, like the billiard-ball approach, embraces too vast a spectrum of theories and, therefore, cannot account for the important difference between conservative theories that are anti-hegemonic (equilibrium theories) and conservative theories that are pro-hegemonic (anti-equilibrium or imperialistic theories).[7]

The liberal and radical ideologies face similar problems. Nelson and Olin identify liberalism with Locke, Smith, Kant, Bentham, Mill, Wilson, Schumpeter or Keynes and radicalism with Rousseau, Marxism, and socialism. These distinctions are useful (and common) when theorizing at the domestic level. At the international level, however, the distinction is problematic. Among the liberals, for instance, Kant and Bentham assume that republican states can coexist in peaceful anarchy whereas Wilson and Keynes go "beyond anarchy" by arguing that some degree of collective management is necessary for international peace and well-being. As already mentioned with reference to the cobweb approach, these differences are important in the theory of international relations. Today, European liberals clearly divide between those who favor coordinated cobwebs (like GATT or EFTA) and those who favor sub- and superordinated cobwebs (like the European Community). The really important divisions in international relations theory run not only between liberals and conservatives, idealists and realists – but also amongst them! Conventional categories take no account of this.[8]

Another way of categorizing theories was presented by Kenneth Waltz in the mid-fifties. In his *Man, the State and War*[9] Waltz distinguished between authors who locate the causes of war either in man, in the state, or in the state system, and he referred to them as first-, second-, and third-image thinkers respectively. Furthermore, he subdivided theorists into optimists and pessimists. The former believe that the cause of war in their particular image can be overcome, that peace is possible; the latter deny this possibility. A few examples help to illustrate his argumentation and also to show its limitations.

Morgenthau is classified as a pessimistic first-image thinker because he sees the causes of war in man and does not believe that the nature of man can be changed. Wilson, on the other hand, is an optimistic second-image thinker because he assumes that the causes of war lie in the nature of states (in authoritarian states) and that by the creation of democratic government these causes can be eliminated. Rousseau is depicted as a typical third-image thinker seeing the causes of war in the anarchic state system and remaining skeptical about the possibility of changing it.

The book still makes for good reading and represents a major contribution to theorizing in our field. If nothing else, by dealing with the three images Waltz tackled the "level-of-analysis" problem, an important issue in international relations theorizing.[10] Waltz succeeds most importantly in demonstrating that the various levels of analysis are intimately tied up with questions of values and "images." Images, as Waltz uses the term, are subjective projections originating with the theoretician, images about the subject matter of international relations, about the "nature" of man, the state, and the state system. Waltz's cognitive argumentation was doubly appreciated in the sixties when empirical and behavioral theories of international relations entered the scene and raised claims and hopes that were completely out of reach.

If cognitively Waltz's images constitute an important contribution, their substantive nature is more problematic. The three images fail to supply useful categories for ordering theories because they are wedded to one single cause, whereas many theories are multicausal. As a consequence, most theories belong to more than one image. Waltz is aware of this and admits that "so fundamental are man, the state, and the state system in any attempt to understand international relations that seldom does an analyst, however wedded to one image, entirely overlook the other two."[11] Therefore, he concludes, "some combination of our three images, rather than any one of them, may be required for an accurate understanding of international relations."[12]

Morgenthau is a case in point. He argues that the major cause of war lies in the nature of man and that peace can only be established through world government, something mankind is not ready for, however. Morgenthau then settles for the second-best solution, for a balance of power operated by skilled statesmen. But, and this is important, by arguing that world government is necessary for peace, Morgenthau admits that some causality must also lie in the international system, that in a state of anarchy there is no one to prevent war. It follows that Morgenthau is not merely a first-, but also a third-image theorist. He sees the efficient cause of war in man and the permissive cause in the anarchical state system. The same holds true for Woodrow Wilson. In the analytical part of his theory he attributes the major cause of war to the flawed nature of some types of government, but, by opting for collective security as a mechanism to preserve peace in the prescriptive part of his theory, he, too, attributes some weight to the third image. The two examples demonstrate how Waltz's images are not well-suited for categorizing theories of international relations. His scheme is too ambitious. By attempting to classify theories based on causality Waltz overreaches – and fails.

After reviewing the various efforts at categorizing theories I have come to the conclusion that the most useful distinction is still that between realism and idealism. It is true that these concepts pose problems, too, but compared to all other categories they seem minor and adjustable.

One of the problems is of an epistemological nature. The concepts of realism and idealism have cognitive connotations and are quite common in the philosophy of science. Beginners in our field, therefore, have a tendency to assume that realism suggests closeness to reality, and idealism the opposite – distance. Neither is true, of course, because both realist and idealist theories can be close to reality – or far from it. The difference between realism and idealism, as developed in this study, relates to the substance and not to the formal shape of worldviews and theories. Worldviews and theories do, of course, have an epistemological dimension but, as I will show later on, it is identical for both categories and does not separate them.

Realism and idealism, therefore, primarily refer to substance, but here there are problems as well. As shown above, the two concepts could very well be identified with conservatism and liberalism. Both are useful terms and point out many of the features typical of realist and idealist theory. The terms are common in Europe where they originated and have kept their original meaning.[13] In the United States, however, "liberal" has taken on a second meaning which creates more problems than it solves. Given this difficulty, it is best to settle for realism and idealism after all.

The main substantive problem with the two terms consists in the fact that they are enormously broad; a multitude of different theories are labeled realist or idealist. This uncertainty does not invalidate any one particular theory but it does make the terms problematic for categorizing. To remedy this flaw realism and idealism must be reduced to basics, to a restricted number of dimensions on which there is broad agreement. Worldviews, as mentioned earlier, represent such an attempt.

FOUR WORLDVIEWS

For anyone in search of basic international relations features European history is a useful laboratory. For a number of centuries the relations among European nations have alternated between peace and war on the one hand, and between an anarchic and a hierarchic order on the other hand.[14] The Treaty of Westphalia symbolizes the end of the hierarchic medieval and the beginning of the anarchic modern order. In the seventeenth and eighteenth centuries war alternated regularly with peace, and there were various attempts at hegemony, but none succeeded until Napoleon. By 1809 French imperial hierarchy had largely replaced decentralized anarchy. After the Congress of Vienna the traditional pattern reemerged and throughout the nineteenth century limited wars alternated with limited durations of peace. In the first half of the twentieth century Europe experienced two German attempts at imperial hierarchy. In the process war became total and peace became rare.

As a result of this tragic experience and in the shadow of the Soviet attempt at hegemony Europe began to move beyond conflictual anarchy and to establish peaceful hierarchy – the European Community. In the process of integration traditional sovereignty is diminishing while supranationality is growing. In recent years Eastern Europe has experienced the opposite development – a hierarchical order is dying and new nations are being born. The international relations of Europe are indeed a typical example of the alternation between war and peace, anarchy and hierarchy.

Scholars of international relations study such phenomena. Some theorists have an interest in peaceful change within a decentralized and anarchic setting, in free trade, for instance, and in how it promotes cooperation among sovereign and independent states. Others investigate peaceful change within a hierarchic setting, they ask how integration promotes cooperation among nations. There are scholars who describe warlike change in an anarchic setting, who show the workings of the classical balance of power system. Finally, some theoreticians are fascinated by warlike change in a hierarchical setting, in the cyclical and violent rise and fall of empires.

War and peace are here defined as processes, as violent and nonviolent forms of conflict management among nations. This is a minimal definition but it must suffice for the purpose of identifying worldviews. It is up to the many different theories of international relations to be more specific, to determine, for instance, the difference between legitimate and illegitimate, just and unjust wars. The distinction between violent and nonviolent forms of conflict resolution is important, however. At all levels of social reality, whether among individuals, social groups or entire nations, there is a threshold in conflict management that, when overstepped, is difficult to reverse.

Worldviews and Theories

Figure 1.1 Scholarly Interests in International Relations

	peace	war
anarchy	peaceful change in an anarchic setting	warlike change in an anarchic setting
hierarchy	peaceful change in a hierarchic setting	warlike change in a hierarchic setting

That threshold is reached when violence becomes a means of conflict resolution. There is a broad consensus that the distinction between violent and nonviolent processes of conflict is important. Of course, there is disagreement over what is probable and normal: realists assume that war is normal among nations while idealists adhere to the opposite view.

Anarchy and hierarchy, as used in this study, are structural terms, they represent two different types of social organization: horizontal coordination versus vertical super- and subordination.[15] In any social setting these terms are important. There are traditional tribes, for instance, with an anarchic or hierarchic order, and there are multinational corporations that correspond more with one pattern than with the other. There are also anarchic and hierarchic philosophies of government. Godwin, for instance, is known for his theory of (peaceful) anarchy,[16] whereas Hobbes is renowned for his theory of (conflictual) hierarchy.[17]

The same applies to theories of international relations. There are theories based on anarchy or on hierarchy, and both can be found among idealists and realists. Proponents of complete disarmament argue that states can coexist in peaceful anarchy while balance of power advocates maintain that they can coexist in warlike anarchy. Integration theorists think in terms of supranational hierarchies while theorists of imperialism conceive of hegemonic hierarchies. Of course, anarchy and hierarchy are complex terms and need to be defined in more detail. They are, for instance, intimately related to such concepts as equality and independence, sovereignty and autonomy. But, once again, it is up to specific theories to be more precise.

As Waltz shows, anarchical structures are typical of international politics while hierarchical structures are typical of domestic politics.[18] This is certainly true but should not be overemphasized: not all theories of government are hierarchical and not all theories of international politics are anarchical. There are famous philosophers of anarchical government and there are important theoreticians of hierarchical world order. Furthermore, students of international politics like to study the transition from anarchical to hierarchical orders, or vice versa. They concentrate on integration and disintegration, on the rise and the demise of nations. In all these theories the dialectic between anarchy and hierarchy is central.

Of course, nation is an important term, too. In fact, it is inseparable from the definitions given above. In the two anarchic worldviews nations are defined as fully sovereign and as either peaceful or warlike, in the two hierarchic worldviews as only partly sovereign and as either peaceful or warlike. Again, these are crude categories. Nations can and must be more carefully defined. There are nations with different degrees of sovereignty and independence, with a socialist, liberal or authoritarian character. Particular theories specify the nature of nations, and some even go "beyond" the nation-state by postulating its demise or its integration within larger units. For the purpose of outlining worldviews, however, a simple definition must suffice.

Based on the above definitions four different worldviews can be outlined. The *anarchic idealist* worldview starts from the assumption that nations coexist in a state of peace; the *anarchic realist* worldview assumes that nations coexist in a state of war; the *hierarchic idealist* worldview is premised on the conviction that nations live in a state of peaceful super- and subordination; the *hierarchic realist* worldview postulates that nations live in a state of conflictual super- and subordination.

A few examples help to illustrate the four categories. Liberal theorists of international relations have often argued that peace through free trade is possible. Such theories conform with the *anarchic idealist* worldview because they assume that free trade operates best in a decentralized world order and even contributes to its stability and peace. Of course, such theories go beyond this simple worldview. They generally assume that governments keep in the background and, at best, provide the legal framework for fair and efficient trade. Entrepreneurs and other social groupings are in the foreground and account for the bulk of relations between nations. Their dealings are by nature peaceful because human beings and commercial relations are cooperative rather than conflictual. Ultimately, such theories rest on an enlightened image of man and of society. A host of other features are identified with such theories and, as will be shown in more detail later on, Richard Rosecrance's study of the rise of the trading state is a modern version of this particular worldview. Norman Angell proposed a similar theory around the turn of the century, just prior to World War I. Immanuel Kant's conception of perpetual peace is not as explicitly Anglo-Saxon liberal in character but the loose federation of republics which he proposes rests on an anarchic idealist worldview too.

Figure 1.2 Four Worldviews

	peace	war
anarchy	anarchic idealist worldview	anarchic realist worldview
hierarchy	hierarchic idealist worldview	hierarchic realist worldview

Woodrow Wilson's theory of collective security also has an idealist orientation, but in contrast to the classical liberals Wilson has a somewhat different conception of processes and structures. He leans toward the *hierarchic idealist* worldview because he does not believe that peace in anarchy is possible, not even among predominantly rational men organized in democratic states. In his view peace has to be promoted by an institution that overcomes the decentralized international setting, and his theory therefore suggests first steps in the direction of a more centralized and hierarchical world order – collective security. Rosecrance and Wilson are both liberal theorists but their assessment of anarchic order is rather different.

Robert Keohane is not as explicit about his own position as is Wilson, but his regime theory tends in the same direction. He agrees with many realists that hegemons can help to create regimes. The continued existence of regimes "after hegemony," however, has causes that cannot be attributed to a starkly anarchic and conflictual world. Keohane, therefore, conceives of regimes as international actors with a meaningful degree of autonomy and in this sense goes beyond the highly state-centered worldview typical of realists. In his theory regimes are liberated from their status as dependent variables and begin to emerge as independent variables; international organizations begin to live lives of their own. Keohane's regime theory, therefore, has a slightly hierarchic idealist bent. Of course, it is nowhere near as hierarchical as Richard Falk's theory of world government. Falk would not reject Keohane's argumentation in favor of regimes but in his view a much more decisive step "beyond anarchy" is necessary.

Balance of power theory conforms to the *anarchic realist* worldview. The assumption is that decentralized coexistence of states is possible and that war is a rational instrument for the maintenance of an anarchic equilibrium. Friedrich von Gentz, writing in 1806, was one of the first to formulate balance of power theory systematically. He demonstrated how sovereign nation-states could coexist in a multipolar self-help system.

Kenneth Waltz, writing during the Cold War, adapted balance of power theory to bipolarity; he demonstrated the validity of balance of power theory in the age of nuclear superpowers. The theory fits neatly into an anarchic realist pattern.

Von Bernhardi was a German imperialist who wrote before World War I, and, like all proponents of *Realpolitik*, felt that war was normal among nations. In contrast to Gentz, however, he did not believe that states could coexist in warlike anarchy. In his estimation war was the expression of the "law of the strongest"[19] leading inevitably to the predominance of the most powerful state. His theory has a *hierarchic realist* penchant. The same applies to Gilpin's theory of hegemonic cycles. The "law of uneven growth" conditions the rise and decline of nations, propelling them through cycles of sub- and superordination. The beginning and the end of each cycle is accompanied by major wars.

Some theories are combinations of two different worldviews. Wilson's theory is such a case. In its analytical (and critical) part it localizes the causes of war in the anarchic realist world, in balance of power politics; in its prescriptive part, however, the theory sees the cure for war in hierarchic idealism. Many theorists embrace such combinations because it is common to locate the causes of a problem in one worldview and the solution in another. Hobson finds the cause of imperialism (and war) in hierarchic realism, in the oligarchical structures of conservative society and in the maldistribution of savings. The solution, however, is firmly embedded in an anarchic idealist worldview: Hobson expects social democratic states to coexist peacefully in a decentralized international system. Both Wilson and Hobson propose to alter the international system; they formulate transformation theories of international relations.

Lenin also formulated a transformation theory. In comparison to Hobson's theory his is more simplistic. Lenin starts with a one-dimensional and monocausal analysis of imperialism (of a realist hierarchical theory) and ends with an equally extreme prescription that fits the anarchic idealist

Figure 1.3 Idealist Transformation Theories

	peace	war
anarchy	democratic peace	balance of power
hierarchy	collective security	imperialism, hegemony

Figure 1.4 Realist Transformation Theories

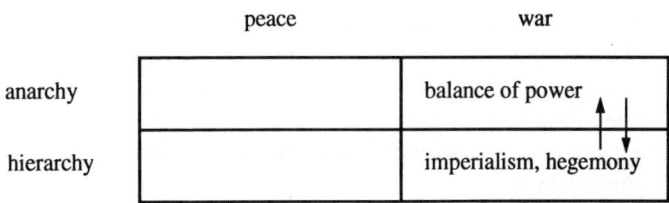

pattern. The cause of war, according to Lenin, lies in material reality, in the ownership of the means of production, and the quest for peace must begin with the redistribution of these means. The bourgeois nation-state will then wither away and the post-statist world will be peaceful and anarchic. Marxist theory clearly rests on two different worldviews and is transformational.

Some realists also formulate transformation theories. Gentz confronted the Napoleonic Empire and proposed the reestablishment of the classical balance of power. Bernhardi, on the other hand, was unhappy with the balance of power and suggested a hierarchic Europe dominated by Germany.
The urge to either maintain or transform a given international system is not the exclusive property of any one group of theorists.

Before closing this discussion of worldviews it is important to emphasize once more that theories are more specific than worldviews and shaped more by circumstance, by time and by place. Bernhardi's theory of militaristic imperialism, for instance, is a typical child of its time and had to be relevant to men living and acting in those days, just as the theory of cabinet warfare or of the classical balance of power were creations of earlier centuries and had to be useful to men acting in those very different circumstances. Lenin's theory of international relations cannot be separated from the context within which it was conceived – the era of nascent capitalism prior to World War I. And Waltz's neo-realist theory makes specific reference to bipolarity and to the Cold War context. Worldviews are simple and rudimentary – theories are elaborate and sophisticated. What is the nature of theories?

ON THEORIZING

The literature on theorizing in international relations is voluminous, and while there is agreement on some points there is disagreement on others. I will approach the issue from a very broad perspective and then relate it to our field. It is not my goal to deal exhaustively with this complex question but simply to outline the basic features of theorizing as I see them.

Deconstruction and Reconstruction

Neither worldviews nor theories represent reality; they are constructs of reality. Homo sapiens grasps reality indirectly – with the aid of mental constructs. Science is a human creation.[20] This holds true for all science, for natural and for social science. Scientific knowledge is constructed knowledge or, more precisely, science is an effort characterized by deconstruction and reconstruction.[21]

In order to understand reality we must, as a first step, take it apart, dissect the shapeless and mysterious physical and social world around us. Phenomena have to be separated from the (yet unknown) texture of which they are part. From a linguistic viewpoint this is the definitional stage of inquiry because phenomena are given names; they are, for the purpose of thinking and communication, provided with labels. The definitional stage, although part of deconstruction, has therefore a constructive side – it embraces the construction of terms. Terms are not given in nature, they are made (or defined) by men. They become then the building-blocks of theories and of science, the fundamental units of theory-building. Deconstruction, therefore, should not be confused with destruction: it is a positive step, it represents the first of two steps in the process of theory-building.

In a second operation terms have to be put together; this is reconstruction. Phenomena and terms must be recombined, must be built into a new order. New relations have to be established between them. The new constructs are conscious patterns, they represent known texture where before there was unknown texture – that is the essence of theory and of science. It is the goal of science to have a conscious image of reality, to know how phenomena are related, to know how one term relates to another term. It is also the goal of science to find relations with a high degree of generality and certainty and, if possible, to know the laws, forces and causes that bind phenomena together. Finally, science is trying to produce knowledge that is useful, that helps man in the management of his life, that assists him to improve his command over the social and physical environment. Put more simply, science is finding answers to problems.[22]

Science is problem-solving. Confronted with an intractable difficulty a theorist must first formulate the problem, that is, isolate the relevant variables, define terms, analyze the situation. This is deconstruction. The solution of the problem then demands reconstruction – finding patterns among phenomena, tracing relations between variables and terms.

The study of international relations can be seen as a form of problem-solving. Many theorists are concerned with the problem of war and they look for ways to understand and to solve it. They begin by analyzing war, by isolating a given number of factors that influence and condition war. They then suggest an hypothesis, a model or a theory with explanatory power that might be useful to remedy war. However, in the social sciences deconstruction and reconstruction encounter a number of special problems. International relations is part of the social sciences and as such confronts some of the same problems.

Difficulties in Social Science

In the social sciences it is difficult to separate deconstruction from reconstruction because phenomena (terms, variables) cannot easily be isolated from their context. Let me illustrate the problem with reference, first, to the physical sciences and, second, with reference to the social sciences. A carburetor can be defined as an object made of metal, consisting of various channels and chambers, valves and components, and it can also be defined as an apparatus that transforms air and gasoline into an explosive mixture. Because this definition is restricted to the carburetor as such it isolates the device from its context, from engines; the definition is *noncontextual*. Of course, a *contextual* definition is also possible. It defines a carburetor as a component of combustion engines, as a specific part of a wider whole, as a mechanism playing a given function within a system, as a means to a specific end, as an object with a purpose. Because this second definition is tied to the logic of engines it is not separated from reconstruction. Contextual definitions presuppose reconstruction, coincide with it and are therefore circular.[23]

As we move from physical to human affairs, the separation of contextual and noncontextual definitions becomes difficult. A European football, for instance, can be defined noncontextually as a round leather object filled with air and kicked around by human beings. For most people, however, footballs are intimately related to a context, to the notion of sports, to a specific form of interpersonal competition, to systems of action with specific rules and regulations, to human behavior with a clear purpose and an end. Who would theorize about footballs without making reference to the game and the logic of football? The temptation to subsume the context is great.

Isolation becomes virtually impossible when we move up to man himself. Of course, man can be defined noncontextually as a being with a head, two arms, a body and two legs to walk on in an upright manner. These are what we refer to as descriptive characteristics, but men also have qualitative traits. They can be defined as peaceful, aggressive, submissive or dependent. These are all contextual definitions, they refer to relations among men, they define man as part of a wider group, as a member of society.

The same applies to nations. They can be defined noncontextually, as collectivities with a government and a territory. But nations have other qualities as well; they too can be peaceful, aggressive, submissive or dependent. Again, these are contextual definitions because they refer to the context within which nations live, to international relations. These definitions too presuppose reconstruction and are circular.

Furthermore, qualitative definitions are highly contested, they rest on what are called weak or soft terms. It is easy to get consensus on definitions relating to our five senses, but it is difficult to get consensus on definitions that go beyond them. Take the example of a football. If we define it as a spherical object made of leather and filled with air the terms "spherical," "leather," and "air" are hardly contested. For the purpose of this definition it can be assumed that they are self-evident, that no further evidence (no additional definition) is necessary. The definitional process stops with these terms. Human terms, however, are difficult to get consensus on because they cannot be defined exclusively with reference to our senses. The definitional process of terms like "peaceful," "rational," "autonomous," or "dependent" does not stop with the ready availability of self-evident terms and, at some point, has to be cut off arbitrarily and without consensus. Therefore, the definitions of important terms in social science, whether contextual or noncontextual, are often arbitrary and contested. In international relations too we are regularly dealing with soft terms.

Correlational knowledge

But let us assume, for the moment, that noncontested and noncontextually defined terms are available. In such a case correlational reconstruction becomes possible. A theorist can then try to relate one set of terms to another set, to see whether they "go" together, whether they are correlated.[24] Does "outbreak of war" relate to "high levels of unemployment," does "maintenance of peace" correlate with "high per capita GNP?" A theorist may detect significant or insignificant correlations and come up with weak or strong explanations concerning these phenomena. Correlational knowledge is entirely scientific; it permits the formulation of probabilistic if–then statements, of predictions and of recommendations for action. Some correlational statements can also be tested against reality. More about these points later on.

Correlational reconstruction has advantages and drawbacks. If the correlational theorist really succeeds in operating without contextual definitions he can keep deconstruction and reconstruction apart, thereby avoiding circularity. He can credibly argue that his findings are not prejudged by the terms employed and that his results are rather descriptive and objective.[25] However, with no contextual definitions involved the correlational theorist resembles an uninitiated observer. As Raymond Aron shows with reference to sports, uninitiated observers remain outsiders, they do not know the nature and inner logic of a game, its rules and norms. All they possess is exogenous knowledge. An exogenous theorist of football may detect that "success" correlates with "X hours of training" or that "failure" goes with "alcohol consumption." However, he cannot attribute success or failure to strategies and rules, to tactics and norms. Only endogenous theorists know such phenomena, only insiders know the logic of the game.[26]

Put differently, endogenous knowledge permits understanding while exogenous (or correlational) knowledge does not; it leads at best to explanations.[27] An exogenous theorist does not worry about the inner logic of the commotion on a football field, about rules and regulations, proper means to attain specific ends, rational and nonrational moves. All of this he does not know and understand because he sees no interrelation between these phenomena – he sees correlations only.[28] And, as Aron demonstrates, the theory of football cannot be induced from correlations. To assume that it can is what Waltz calls the "inductivist illusion."[29]

In our field theorists who correlate noncontested and noncontextual terms are generally identified as empirical, behavioral or descriptive scientists. They have often found it difficult to isolate terms and to trace correlations.[30] In international relations the definitions of all important terms are soft and contested, and if correlations are discovered they tend to deal with questions of marginal importance that confirm the obvious. Furthermore, empirical and behavioral knowledge has not been cumulative as expected. The relations discovered have remained as isolated as the terms involved. Of course, correlations become more meaningful when soft terms are chosen, but then the correlational theorist abandons his exogenous position and can be accused of circularity.

Morton Kaplan, one of the early and well-known exponents of the behavioral–empirical school, is a perfect example of this dilemma. His aim is to explain "systems of action:"

> A system of action is a set of variables so related, in contradistinction to its environment, that *describable behavioral regularities* characterize the internal relationships of the variables to each other and the external relationships of the set of individual variables to combinations of external variables.[31] [emphasis added]

In order to trace "describable behavioral regularities" Kaplan has to select variables, and here his problems begin. Technically, he argues, any set of variables may be considered a system: "Napoleon, the Columbia River, and a dinosaur may be considered a system. However, it would be most difficult to find a relationship between the variables, and also that relationship would be uninteresting or useless."[32] But how can a purely descriptive theorist tell what relationships are "interesting" and "useful?" Kaplan solves the problem by proposing six different systems, all of which have a tight inner logic and specific rules. Obviously, these models contain suggestions about "interesting" and "useful" relationships! In short, Kaplan operates with two different conceptions of science, one endogenous and the other exogenous, one based on contextual, the other on noncontextual terms. Small wonder Kaplan manages to trace "describable behavioral regularities."[33]

Given these difficulties, most theorists of international relations choose to work with contextually defined and contested terms, to produce endogenous knowledge. Today, practically all of the well-known theorists opt for this path. Empirical and behavioral work is being pursued and has its place in political science, but the bulk of theorizing is "traditionalist" in nature.

Interrelational Knowledge

Traditional theorizing, as hinted at, has advantages and drawbacks. Endogenous theory permits understanding and can tackle some of the central problems of international relations. Yet, endogenous theory is circular because deconstruction and reconstruction cannot be separated. In fact, endogenous theory is built into the basic terms of a theory, it is part and parcel of contextual definitions. The traditional theorist cannot separate theories from definitions, for him theorizing is reduced to defining.

When theorizing is reduced to defining it is no longer a two-step operation. As deconstruction and reconstruction coincide theorizing is reduced to concept-building or to what Aron calls "conceptualization."[34] In the construction of concepts the definitional task occupies center stage, and anyone dealing with such theory must carefully study definitional questions. They are not, as is often argued, a marginal and purely semantic concern. On the contrary, semantics is at the heart of endogenous theory-building.[35]

Take the concept of "nation:" it is central to theories that deal with inter*national* relations, and it is also at the heart of the four worldviews outlined earlier. In the two anarchic worldviews nations are defined as sovereign and independent entities. In the idealist anarchic worldview this definition is expanded to embrace peace, in the realist anarchic worldview to embrace war. Both definitions are contextual, both contain a vision of relations among nations.

The two hierarchic worldviews define nations as only partly sovereign and independent, against the background of either peace or war. And, once more, the context is obvious: in one case nations exist in a state of peaceful (and therefore voluntary) super- and subordination (or hierarchy), in the other in a state of conflictual and involuntary super- and subordination. Again, the definition of nation is contextual and cannot be separated from the relations nations have with each other. The four definitions (or concepts) are a first and rudimentary stage in theory-building; more demanding theories of international relations rest on more sophisticated definitions of nation.

The above definitions specify the "nature" of nations. "Nature" implies reality, and for the purpose of theorizing it is assumed that nations are in reality what we define them to be. Any theorist knows that this is not true, that definitions are generalizations or abstractions, that not all nations are in fact peaceful or warlike, independent or dependent. We assume, however, that these qualities are the rule (or norm) rather than the exception, that they are more typical than atypical. Generalizations reflect the fact that the building of concepts (and of theories) is a selective process whereby "like" and "unlike" phenomena are sorted out, where certain phenomena are "selected in" while others are "selected out." The decision about what is typical, natural, normal, like and unlike is made by the creator of a concept or theory.[36]

Generalizations are at the heart of endogenous theory-building because they permit the construction of theories (or of concepts) with a compelling inner logic, with deductively arranged relations among terms. A generalization, because it excludes any deviation, allows the drawing of necessary and law-like conclusions.[37] Syllogisms represent such compelling and logical constellations. They are based on a general statement (all nations are peaceful), on a nongeneral or specific statement (A is a nation), and then permit a compelling deduction (A is a peaceful nation).[38]

A compelling logic entails necessity: if A and B are given, then C must necessarily follow. Necessity is reflected in such expressions as "force of logic" or "logical rigor." Some endogenous theories of international relations contain a completely compelling logic. Norman Angell, for instance, sees his peace logic as so strongly compelling that war, in his own words, becomes "impossible." In Angell's theory the "law of pure reason" is triumphant; men and nations cannot resist, they have no choice.

But it is also possible to assume that the "law of pure unreason" is triumphant. This occurs when nations are perceived to be driven by instinct, passion or superstition. If in such a theory mind is involved at all, it is purely mechanical. Clausewitz, for instance, discusses such theory. In his concept of "pure war" there is a tendency toward extremes in which war resembles an explosion or a burst of pure passion.

The "law of pure reason" and the "law of pure passion" rest on fairly simplistic definitions of nations. Nations are seldom driven by pure reason or pure instinct or, for that matter, by some irresistible "force of history."[39] There is usually some interference, some lack of necessity and "compellingness." Most theories of international relations, therefore, opt for a modified position – they perceive a trend or a tendency. Trend projections rest on the assumption that in the long run (or ultimately) a logic is compelling but that in the short run some deviation (resistance, interference, irrationality) is possible. Gilpin, for instance, argues that in the short run states may resist the law of uneven growth. In the longer run, however, states must adapt to the compelling logic of hegemonic cycles. Rosecrance, too, distinguishes between the long and the short run. In the long run the trading logic (or the liberal law of demand and supply) is compelling, but in the short run states have a choice and may opt for the territorial logic (or the mercantilist law of economics). The same applies to Gray's "law of geopolitics" or to Kant's perceived tendency for favoring perpetual peace.

Generalizations are the foundation of such logical rigor, but they have other qualities as well. They represent comprehensive and bounded wholes, and the terms covered by them are parts of these wholes. As Kenneth Waltz says, "a theory is a depiction of the organization of a domain and of the connections among its parts."[40] Generalizations can also be seen as systems, and the related terms as functions of systems.[41]

The parts–wholes and systems–functions perspective is typical of endogenous theorizing. Anyone steeped in the logic of engines knows the function of a carburetor within the system, anyone knowledgeable in football knows the positions of the various players, the parts (and roles) they play. The uninitiated exogenous observer is unaware of such relations. All he sees are "things" that potentially correlate. He lacks a holistic or comprehensive view of things, and consequently he does not comprehend or understand. At best he can explain.

Exogenous and endogenous theorists establish qualitatively different links between phenomena. For an exogenous theoretician two things "go" together; for an endogenous theoretician two things "belong" together: they are not merely correlated, they are interrelated. For the exogenous scientist "war" is correlated with "poor nations," but for the endogenous scientist "war" is interrelated with "poor nations."[42]

Parts and wholes, systems and functions are related to two further constellations – to ends and means and to cause and effect. A carburetor is a means to produce specific effects, an instrument to serve the end of automotion. If an engine breaks down a malfunctioning carburetor may be the cause of the unfortunate effect, and if a game of football is lost a poor defense may be the cause of the defeat. From an endogenous perspective causal relations are logical and compelling, from an exogenous perspective they are not. For the uninitiated observer it is impossible to determine necessary causality because several variables might correlate with defeat.

Ends and means, wholes and parts, systems and functions are also related to rationality. A mechanic acts irrationally if he adjusts the water pump when the carburetor is malfunctioning, and a coach is irrational if he orders his men to break the rules. In both instances means are improperly related to ends, parts are out of focus with wholes, functions are not in line with the system. Rationality, too, is a contextual quality. The four worldviews outlined earlier all have their own conception of rationality. The behavior of nations within one worldview is entirely irrational within the context of another.

Ends and means are also related to finality and purpose. A carburetor serves the purpose of automotion, and the purpose of football is to win. Winning provides football with sense and meaning. For the exogenous observer football is a behavior without sense and meaning: he is unaware of the players' motives and projections. For the endogenous observer, however, the projections are known because they coincide with his contextual definition, with his own projections. Where projections meet understanding becomes possible. The endogenous theoretician is an insider because his mental construct and the mental construct of the objects observed are one. Oneness is the essence of understanding.

Oneness stands for subjectivity. The reality on the football field cannot be separated from the definition in the mind. It goes back to what I said earlier about generalizations, about assuming for the purpose of theorizing that a certain term has a given nature while knowing full well that in reality it does not. We assume that nations are either peaceful or warlike, independent or dependent, that they follow a certain norm or rule. Now we discover that the assumption of such a norm is value-laden. Generalizations in international relations make the distinction between "is" and "ought" impossible, and they make it impossible to separate values from facts. For endogenous theorists values are facts, too.[43]

The endogenous theorist of international relations cannot fully separate himself from the matter under investigation. By working with contextual and generalized terms he becomes part of the objects he studies or, put differently, he cannot clearly separate object from subject – hence subjectivity. This is true for idealists and realists alike, although some would not admit this. As will be shown later on, a number of contemporary theorists believe that they have overcome subjectivity. This includes some political economists who adopt the language of microeconomics but it is also true of realists with a systemic or structuralist perspective. It can easily be shown, however, that their basic definitions are fully contextual. They are perfect insiders while pretending not to be! They all share a particular worldview.

The term worldview suggests that a theorist has a personal view or vision of the world. In German the term *Weltbild* is even more explicit: it suggests that theories resemble images and pictures (*Bild*) of the world (*Welt*). Pictures are not reality, they are reconstructions of reality, and in this sense theorists resemble artists who create subjective abstractions of reality, leave out many details but manage to understand it. Theorists-as-artists care more for the general features of world politics, more for the broad rules than for the deviations from the rule.

Similarities between Correlational and Interrelational Knowledge

So far I have emphasized the differences between endogenous and exogenous theories. They are important but, before closing, it is necessary to also point out some of the similarities. Both types of theory allow the formulation of if–then statements and of predictions, they can provide guidance in action and, under certain conditions, they permit testing in the real world.

Although if–then statements appear in both types of theory they have different structures. Endogenous–logical theories are premised on the assumption that "if" a generalization is correct "then" certain compelling consequences follow. Idealists, for instance, would reason that "if nations are democratic, then disarmament is possible." Exogenous–correlational theories, however, are premised on the assumption that "if" phenomenon A is fully isolated (if other factors do not interfere, are kept stable), "then" it correlates (or varies) with phenomenon B in a certain way. For example, if the definition of "one-sided dependence" is truly noncontextual and uncontested, then it can be shown that it correlates with "rising international tension."

The "ifs" in both statements stand for an assumption. In the case of correlational theories the assumption is that the term can be isolated from its context, and in the case of logical theories the assumption is that the generalization comes close to reality. Neither type of theory can do without assumptions.

In addition, both types of theory produce predictions. They inhere in the if–then statements just cited. True theory is always predictive. Of course, a prediction is only as valid as the underlying assumption, as the "if" in the statement. It follows that when a prediction fails it is not the prediction as such that is faulty but the underlying assumption. If democracies are not generally peaceful then they will not disarm, and if one-sided dependence cannot be isolated then it will not be tied to rising international tension.

Furthermore, prediction cannot be separated from prescription, and that is why both types of theory are prescriptive, both contain recommendations for action and control.[44] If we want to disarm, then democracies must be installed; and if we want to lower international tension, then one-sided dependence must be reduced. Of course, the exogenous theorist will claim that his prescription is value-free while the endogenous theorist must admit that his prescription is value-laden. From a methodological viewpoint this is certainly true.

The fifteen theories discussed later on are all action- or control-oriented. Of course, some are more obviously so than others. Actually, some authors may not realize the prescriptive nature of their theory, and some may even deny it. But there is no such thing as a purely descriptive or purely analytical theory – it is a contradiction in terms. This is not to say that action presupposes theory. As Waltz has shown lucidly, action-oriented knowledge must not necessarily be tied to theory. We know how to fight fires, and in an emergency the fire department acts without knowing exact causes. The same is true of medical therapies that lack a proper explanation of the illness's roots. People wore glasses for generations before optometrists understood the biological, chemical, and physical causes of deteriorating eyesight.

The argument, once more, is not that action must be based on proper theory but that proper theory implies prescription. Or, put differently, it is not necessarily the aim of the man of action to have perfect theoretical knowledge before he decides on a move, but it is the aim of the theoretician to search for that knowledge. The ideal of the scientist is to link the realm of knowledge to that of action, and that is why physicists, chemists and biologists continue the search for the true causes of eye problems until they have found them. The situation of the scholar in international affairs is no different: he, too, perseveres in searching for the causes of war and peace so that the handling of these phenomena can be improved.

But what about astronomy? Is this not a purely contemplative science? Can man ever hope to control the movement of the heavenly bodies, and does it not prove that purely contemplative knowledge exists? The point is valid to the extent that man is indeed in no position to move the planets and the stars, but the argument fails when it comes to the usefulness of such knowledge for man's existence on earth. Since time immemorial astronomy has helped man to manage everyday problems – and it has also helped him to get to the moon!

Control-oriented knowledge is necessary if man wants to solve problems and to live comfortably.[45] To assume otherwise is fatalistic. Fatalism is an entirely valid philosophy of life but it is incompatible with social science. Science has arisen from human curiosity, from asking questions about man's existence and about the problems associated with it. Furthermore, in the social realm a fatalistic philosophy of nonaction is in itself a type of action – it amounts to permissiveness or, in the theory of international relations, to a theory of appeasement.[46]

Finally, there is the question of testing endogenous and exogenous theories. Controlled experiments in laboratories are ideal testing grounds. In international relations such experiments are impossible: there is no laboratory to test graduated nuclear response, imperialism or regime theory. Simulation games are a substitute for controlled laboratory situations, but they are so far removed from reality that they are more useful as teaching devices than as testing grounds.

The most common laboratory for testing international relations theories is the real world. If a given theory predicts the formation of trading blocs, then "history" can be used as a testing ground. Past or future events may be used to falsify or verify the theory.[47] Historians seek evidence in documents, social scientists tend to seek evidence in future events. Both methods may work but they are also problematic because the interpretation of past and future events is complicated. What one observer sees as positive evidence, another sees as negative evidence: clear-cut cases are rare. In legal proceedings a jury will weigh the evidence, but who is performing this role in world politics? Finally, some theories cannot even be tested in the real world because they predict a nonevent. The effectiveness of deterrence theory, for instance, is extremely difficult to verify or falsify.

2 Classical Theories

GENTZ: BALANCE OF POWER

Friedrich von Gentz's *Fragments upon the Balance of Power in Europe*[1] is a classic because it is the first book to deal explicitly with balance of power theory and, as any classic should, to raise fundamental questions about war and peace. Can sovereign and independent states coexist or is there an inevitable trend toward preponderance? Is anarchical balance the normal state of affairs or is hierarchical domination? Is self-interest (or national interest) a sufficient precondition for equilibrium or is more needed? What is the relation between domestic and foreign politics in a balance of power system, and what is the role of war (intervention), diplomacy and law?

Gentz is the first author to answer these questions systematically, to construct a theory. It is not a perfect construction; formally and methodologically the theory is not as sophisticated as contemporary balance of power theory, but substantively it raises issues that modern theorists often overlook. Gentz's theory fits neatly into the anarchic realist worldview but, as is to be expected, goes well beyond it.

Circumstances helped Gentz perceive matters clearly. In 1806, when he published the book in St. Petersburg, Europe was under French domination and Gentz, along with many other Germans, lived in Russian exile. The old anarchic order had been replaced by a hierarchical one. The former balance was gone because the various anti-French coalitions and alliances had failed. But people like Gentz (or Metternich) were unwilling to give up and did all they could to organize another counter-alliance in order to reestablish the old order. Publications were one means of pursuing this objective. Only three years later, A. H. L. Heeren, professor of history at the University of Göttingen, wrote a treatise on the history of the European state system[2] in which he also dealt with the balance of power in some detail. Balance of power thinking was the antidote to French imperialism, and it expressed the mood of the day – Gentz's work was an immediate bestseller translated into a number of different languages.[3]

The study has five chapters, the last of which is the least relevant because it is excessively long (two-thirds of the book) and because it deals with the complex history of Franco-Austrian relations. The other chapters, however, are predominantly concerned with theory.

30   Worldviews and Theories of International Relations

The first chapter explains "The True Concept of Political Equilibrium," and Gentz demonstrates that the true concept, in contrast with several false ones, is premised on a limited notion of equality. All states, small and large, have an equal right of existence, but no more. He rejects what he calls the bourgeois concept of equality which goes beyond the mere right of existence. Gentz favors an international system in which a great variety of states coexist, small and large states with all kinds of rights.

Such a system existed between 1648 and 1800, from Westphalia to the advent of Napoleonic predominance. During that first balance of power era there were great and small powers, and certain rights (and responsibilities) went with size. Great powers carried more responsibility for the maintenance of balance than small powers, and sea powers, for instance, were able to play a more flexible role than land powers.[4] "One became aware that relative to the power of each component part within the whole certain ground-rules existed without whose influence the order could not be secured."[5]

The rules embraced four maxims:

1. no participant in the system is ever permitted to become so strong as to coerce all others jointly;
2. to avoid system-wide conflicts it is desirable that not all but only a few states have to unite against a challenger;
3. to avoid constant conflict it is even more desirable that a challenger is stopped merely by threats;
4. a challenger has to be opposed irrespective of whether his power has been acquired in accordance with international law or not.[6]

These maxims specify the balancing mechanism that is built into the theory. It rests on the assumption that hegemonic ambitions disturb an existing balance and that these ambitions must be opposed to preserve the right of all states to sovereign and independent existence (Maxim 1). The formation of (temporary) alliances is the normal means to achieve the end, and in most cases an alliance of only a few (large) states should be sufficient for the task (Maxim 2). War is the *ultima ratio* but ideally the threat of war will do (Maxim 3). The criterion for determining imbalance (or hegemony) is power and not international law (Maxim 4).

The maxims emerged slowly over several centuries and they functioned well:

It is a wondrous phenomenon that in the course of three eventful centuries, with so many awesome wars, with so many important negotiations, so many shifts in power, such great and general revolutions, such active fermentation in social, civil and religious matters *not a single independent state was destroyed by violent means*.[7] [emphasis added]

The maxims provided the system with a common bond. In Gentz's view the bond was so strong that he often refers to the system as a community (*Gemeinwesen*), a confederation (*Staatenbund*) or even a federation (*Bund*).[8] The classical European balance of power system, from this perspective, was characterized not only by conflict and war but also by a minimal and very important sphere of cooperation.

The system functioned successfully because states began to realize that their self-interest (their national interest) was identical with the general interest, that of Europe as a whole, and they became accustomed to playing a given role within the system, to fulfill a specific function. It shows that Gentz defines states contextually: states are sovereign entities with an equal right of existence and with an ability to play by the rules that the context (the system) demands. If states no longer conform with this definition then balance of power politics fails.

That is what happened after 1800. According to Gentz the system broke down for two reasons: "abuse of form" and "apathy of spirit." Balance of power logic was formally abused in the various divisions of Poland, and it failed substantively when, in the face of revolutionary dynamics, the European states lost spirit and became politically apathetic.

By political apathy Gentz means the unwillingness of European statesmen to live by the old rules of international politics. It is symbolized by the rise of narrow self-interest, a weakening of the spirit (*Erschlaffung des Geistes*) and a spread of fatalism. Many a statesman began to believe that

> the balancing of power among states was a crazy idea [*Hirngespinst*] because in history the stronger had always dictated the law to the weaker, and whether some geographic area was dominated by one or by twenty was immaterial to those who had to obey.[9]

Gentz regrets that so many European states have lost their will to survive in independence, and he is particularly saddened that in Germany the loss of political willpower has gone further than anywhere else.

In Gentz's theory states have a dual nature. On the one hand they are assumed to be capable of rational action, to have the willpower to survive and to choose the appropriate means. On the other hand states are also irrational. It shows in one of two ways: either they lose their will to survive, thereby creating a power vacuum, or else they opt for power expansion and hegemonic ventures, thereby threatening the existence of other states. Both situations represent a cause of war. Vacuum invites attack and constitutes a permissive cause of war; hegemony engenders attack and constitutes an efficient cause of war.

The formal abuse of balance of power theory took place when Prussia, Russia, and Austria formed alliances to eliminate Poland. Alliances are instruments to counterbalance a hegemon but are not meant as tools to eliminate a player. The latter happened in the various divisions of Poland and, not surprisingly, it blinded the conservative powers to the real danger – France. By eliminating Poland, these powers acted once more irrationally: they pursued an issue of narrow self-interest and lost sight of their true self-interest, the prevention of French hegemonic ambitions.

Gentz also devotes an entire chapter to the Revolution in France and in doing so touches upon another important aspect of balance of power theory – the relation between foreign and domestic politics. Noninterference in the internal affairs of states is an important principle of the theory, although often violated in practice. It assumes the separation of foreign and domestic politics or, at the very least, that domestic politics does not interfere with international politics. But what if a revolution occurs within a state, as it did in France, which first creates a power vacuum (thereby attracting potential conquerors) and then produces a veritable explosion rendering the formation of a counter-alliance impossible? Is interference then not called for?

Gentz answers in the affirmative. He is reluctant to abandon the principle of noninterference but argues that in cases of revolution the separation of domestic and international politics is impossible.[10] Liberal revolutions do not fit into the classical balance of power theory because they clash with one of the important assumptions of the theory – the nature of the state.

Gentz adheres to a conservative state image. The movement to reverse French hegemony, led by Metternich, initiates an era in European history called Restoration. The term refers to the reestablishment of the former balance between states but also to the *anciens régimes* within states. It is a return to a conservative, if not a reactionary, conception of politics. Most representatives at the Congress of Vienna believe that the balance of power system cannot rest on liberal foundations, and so they establish the European Concert, a semi-permanent conference of the major powers to coordinate assistance (through intervention) to conservative regimes in danger of being overthrown. Until about 1823, intervention becomes an institutionalized part of the European balance of power.[11]

Why the fear of liberal régimes? There are economic, social, religious, and other reasons but at the root is a skeptical image of man. From a conservative perspective, man is imperfect and does not possess the potential for improvement that the liberals assume. The masses are incapable of self-government and of guaranteeing peace. They need strong government, and

Classical Theories 33

peace has to be imposed. As the French Revolution shows, liberal regimes are unstable and end in imperial adventures undermining the European order. The libertarian virus is so infectious that scores of states lose their will to exist. As Gentz says, there is a "weakening of the spirit" and a spread of fatalism. Proud and independent states are all of a sudden willing to accept a higher authority, a hierarchical and hegemonic order, and the former European "freedom" is gone. Of course, by freedom the conservatives mean the independence of states and not the independence of the individual. Gentz adheres to a skeptical image of man and of society.

For the conservatives the spread of liberal ideas also means the intrusion of domestic into foreign politics. With ideological concerns determining foreign policy, states are no longer free to enter into alliances the way they want in order to preserve the balance. The "authoritarian Prussians," for instance, are judged to be the wrong allies for the "free French." Such considerations interfere with the balance of power logic because the primacy of domestic policy challenges the all-important primacy of foreign policy.

The clash between the primacy of domestic policy and the primacy of foreign policy reflects a clash between two conceptions of international politics. The primacy of foreign policy is dictated by the need of nations to act in accordance with the rules of an anarchic and conflictual international system. The primacy of domestic policy, however, is dictated by the needs of constitutional, democratic and peaceful states. It is a clash between a liberal and a conservative theory of international relations. Realist theories of international relations, such as von Gentz's, emphasize the primacy of foreign policy; idealist theories, as will be shown later on, emphasize the primacy of domestic policy.

Quite obviously, Gentz has no intention of formulating a transformation theory of international relations, a theory that abolishes war and possibly even the anarchical coexistence of nations. His is a nontransformational theory – he wants to restore the classical balance that existed before Napoleon. If Gentz's theory has a transformational aspect at all then it is the desire to transform hegemony back to anarchy.

The focus of Gentz's theory, therefore, is not on war and peace but on states. His topmost interest is the survival of sovereign and independent nation-states. And, as is typical for a conservative, his concern is state order and stability. The German term *Ordnungstheorie* is very suitable to describe his effort. War is taken for granted, it is a normal form of conflict management among states.

Gentz outlines an endogenous theory. It rests on a contextual definition of state (he does not speak of nation yet), on a generalization that lays the foundation for a rigorously logical theory. States are conservative and only partially rational: at times they aim for sovereign independence, at other times they do not; at times they act in accordance with the basic rules of balance of power politics, but sometimes they fail to do so. The situation is precarious but solidly conservative statesmen who know the logic of balance of power politics can, if they are given an opportunity, promote rationality among European statesmen.

The theory fits neatly into a functions–systems logic. Gentz himself uses the term "system" and demonstrates that states have specific functions "relative to the power of each component part within the whole." Important powers have an important function, minor powers have a minor function. The management of the system is oligarchic, and imbalances occur primarily when important powers fail to fulfill their function, when they do not set counterweights quickly enough by allying themselves with other important powers.

Balance of power theory also fits into a whole–parts logic. As Gentz says, "each component part within the whole" has a role to play. Europe is the whole, the states are the parts. It is characteristic of Gentz and of his times to emphasize the whole almost more than the parts because his generation had witnessed the disintegration of a European consensus. It explains why he speaks so respectfully of the whole as *Gemeinwesen* or *Bund*. These terms do not imply that Europe is an organized community with a higher authority; as Gentz uses the terms they simply mean that for the functioning of the balance of power Europe has to be more than an area of conflict – there has to be a minimal consensus about the nature of the whole and the role the parts have to play in it.[12]

In addition, Gentz's theory conforms to the ends–means logic. The primary aim of international politics is the preservation of all nation-states, the means are contained in the four maxims. Any state conforming with this logic acts rationally, any state acting counter to the logic acts irrationally. Gentz formulates an endogenous theory. He knows the logic of the "game" that is unfolding before his eyes, he is an initiated observer. He never pretends to be an uninitiated observer who objectively describes the given "laws of nature and of history." Gentz is too much the active and committed diplomat to engage in such cognitive self-deception.

Furthermore, Gentz's theory contains if–then statements: "if alliances are not formed flexibly enough (cause), then balance does not result (effect)," or "if nations aim at preserving their sovereign independence (end), then certain maxims are logical instruments (means)." Cause and effect, ends and means, system and function, wholes and parts – all of these expressions of logic are intimately related in endogenous theory. It goes without saying that these constellations permit prediction and prescription.

And, Gentz would argue, they can all be tested in reality, in the laboratory of history.

Gentz expresses his theory also in terms of interest. He distinguishes between narrow and true self-interest or, as modern realists prefer to say, between narrow and true national interest. The European balance is never the sum of national interests narrowly conceived because narrow self-interest is detrimental to the maintenance of community and balance. Narrow self-interest resembles zero-sum reasoning where one loses what the other wins, or the Prisoners' Dilemma where solutions are suboptimal. When true national interest is pursued, however, all win because there is a convergence of interest, because all states manage to maintain their sovereign independence. True national interest is enlightened national interest and coincides with the community interest, with the *Bund*; true self-interest is the "invisible hand" guaranteeing that violent competition ends in equilibrium.

Classical international law is the expression of true self-interest and of a minimal consensus among nations. Gentz does not refer in detail to international law, but others do.[13] International law rests on the convergence of national interest and represents a set of rules to guide statesmen in their dealings, in times of peace and of war. It is based on the principle that in peace states should do their utmost to help each other, and in war the utmost not to hurt each other. The classical international law of war defines the ground rules of the contest, the manner in which war is initiated, fought and terminated, and it restrains the use of force.

Balance of power politics, therefore, is not a pure Hobbesian state of war or an unlimited Darwinist struggle for survival. These assume the unrestrained use of force; balance of power politics does not. Napoleon reintroduced the unrestrained use of force; balance of power advocates like Gentz did not. To be sure, balance of power politics embraces a conservative image of the state, and the political style is oligarchic, but to identify classical European politics with the Hobbesian state of war, as some theorists do, is to misunderstand at least portions of European history.

As I will show later on, theorists who adopt the Hobbesian point of view produce highly "compelling" theories because the logic of a perfect state of war leaves very little room for free will. Von Gentz's balance of power theory is different. It contains a dualistic image of states and consequently allows for a certain amount of choice.

For our discussion of contemporary balance of power theory later on in this study it is also important to realize that Gentz does not define the whole (the *Bund*) in isolation from the parts (the conservative states). They form an inseparable unity. There is no system "as such," no "systemic perspective," just as there are no states "as such;" the system cannot survive without conservative states, and the conservative states cannot survive without the system. As is typical of endogenous theory, the central term is contextually defined.

In conclusion a word about the concept of power. Although Gentz deals with the idea of balancing power it is dangerous to identify him with "power politics." He does not propose that states maximize power but merely that they balance it. The supreme goal of states is not the search for power but the search for the preservation of sovereignty and independence of all. Power is only a *means* of attaining this end. It needs emphasizing because some modern authors have a confused notion of "power politics," and consequently of balance of power theory.[14]

CLAUSEWITZ: WAR AS AN INSTRUMENT

Clausewitz's *On War*[15] is famous not because it is a military handbook but because it deals with general questions of war and of politics. The book contains the well-known dictum that "war is nothing but a continuation of politics by other means," but this statement is not part of a systematic theory. Although a contemporary of Gentz, Clausewitz does not clearly reject imperial politics and endorse balance of power politics. On the contrary, he tries to deal with them both. It is his intention to develop a unified theory integrating the pre-Napoleonic tradition, in which he was trained, with the Napoleonic tradition, to which he was exposed as an officer.

Clausewitz vacillates inconclusively between two worldviews. Therefore, his writings are contradictory, reflecting the tensions of the age in which he lives. Clausewitz's work is a classic not because it is clear and systematic but because it makes the reader think about the relation of war and politics. As Bernard Brodie, the foremost American expert on Clausewitz, says, *On War* is not an easy book to read. It gives the impression of an author engaged in "intensive rumination," and to keep up with his rambling mind the reader "should be prepared to tarry, to pause frequently for reflection."[16] Clausewitz makes us think but that does not mean that he himself thinks clearly.

Unlike Gentz's study, Clausewitz's work had no impact in its day; it was not even published in his lifetime. The manuscript was found after his death, and an accompanying note said that, except for the first part, it was incomplete – nothing but a loose collection of ideas.[17] Experts agree: the book gives an orderly impression at first sight, but when read carefully it is exactly what Clausewitz says it is.[18]

Most treatments of *On War* are consequently limited to the first and completed part of the book. It begins with a discussion of abstract or pure war, which Clausewitz compares to a duel: "Each [of the opponents] tries through physical force to compel the other to do his will...War is thus an act of force to compel our enemy to do our will."[19] The clash, looked at abstractly, ends in an extreme, and Clausewitz distinguishes three different "cases of interaction" that lead up to the extreme. The first deals with war as an "act of force:"

> War is an act of force, and there is no logical limit to the application of that force. Each side, therefore, compels its opponent to follow suit; a reciprocal action is started which must lead, in theory, to extremes. This is the first case of interaction and the first "extreme" we meet with.[20]

The second "case of interaction" results from the fact that the two opponents try to disarm each other. Unless one of them finds himself without weapons there is fear "that he may overthrow me."[21] The third "case of interaction" has to do with the means and the will involved. Each of the opponents wants to mobilize a maximum of material and mental strength "and, in pure theory, it must again force you both to extremes. This is the third case of interaction and the third 'extreme'."[22]

Clausewitz then leaves the world of abstract ideas and of extremes. He shows that in the real world war is modified by a number of factors: it is not an isolated act, never consists of a single blow and is not the product of a perfect political decision. War is never isolated because "neither opponent is an abstract person;" on the contrary, the opponents tend to know each others' "history," their personal predilections and habits. War is never a single blow because of the enormous physical, geographical, technological and economic hindrances put in its way. Real war consists of a succession of blows and "the interaction of the two sides tends to fall short of the maximum effort."[23] In the end the probabilities of real life dominate the scene of war, and the political decision reemerges. At first, the law of extremes overshadows politics,

> but as this law begins to lose its force and as this determination wanes, the political aim will reassert itself. If it is all a calculation of probabilities based on given individuals and conditions, the political object, which was the original motive, must become an essential factor in the equation.[24]

Clausewitz also shows that there are interruptions in war caused by a lack of strategic polarity. Defense confronts offense, and in his judgment the defense is the stronger form of war.[25] If the offense were the stronger form there might be fewer interruptions, but things being what they are, "frequent periods of inaction remove war still further from the realm of the absolute and make it even more a matter of assessing probabilities."[26]

Inasmuch as war is a matter of assessing probabilities it resembles a gamble. A gamble is determined by objective and subjective factors, and the theory of war, in Clausewitz's estimation, should account for the objective factors without neglecting the subjective ones – such as courage and self-confidence:

> Courage and self-confidence are essential in war, and theory should propose only rules that give ample scope to these finest and least dispensable of military virtues, in all their degrees and variations.[27]

But war is ultimately more than a gamble, it is a serious business and as such an act of policy. At this point Clausewitz returns to his central theme and introduces the dictum that "war is merely the continuation of politics by other means."[28] The statement is followed by a discussion of the relation between war and politics, and because the question is so important it is necessary to quote Clausewitz at some length:

> If we keep in mind that war springs from some political purpose, it is natural that the prime cause of its existence will remain the supreme consideration in conducting it. That, however, does not imply that the political aim is a tyrant. It must adapt itself to its chosen means, a process which can radically change it; yet the political aim remains the first consideration. Policy, then, will permeate all military operations, and, in so far as their violent nature will admit, it will have a continuous influence on them...War in general, and the commander in any specific instance, is entitled to require that the trend and designs of policy shall not be inconsistent with these means. That, of course, is no small demand; but however much it may affect political aims in a given case, it will never do more than modify them. The political object is the goal, war is the means of reaching it, and means can never be considered in isolation from their purpose.[29]

In this important passage Clausewitz is not entirely clear about the proper relation between war and politics. On the one hand, politics should "permeate all military operations," "have a continuous influence on them" and remain "the supreme consideration" in the conduct of war, even in the choice of means. On the other hand, policy "must adapt itself to the chosen means," a process "which can radically change it." A commander can also be "entitled to require that the trend and designs of policy shall not be inconsistent with the means."

One wonders: does policy modify war, or does war modify policy? Depending on the answer, either war is a function of politics or politics a function of war. The question is so important because in one case war is an instrument of politics whereas in the other politics is an instrument of war, thereby reversing the famous dictum. Where does Clausewitz really stand on this crucial issue?

To find out it is necessary to take a close look at Clausewitz's definition of the central terms, of war and of politics. In the two sections that follow the famous dictum Clausewitz declares explicitly that "all wars can be considered acts of policy" – large wars, approximating his definition of absolute war, and small wars, at the opposite end of the spectrum. Not even in a veritable explosion of passion is policy absent. Clausewitz states clearly that policy permeates both types of war: "While policy is apparently effaced in the one kind of war and yet is strongly evident in the other, both kinds are equally political."[30] It follows that there are two kinds of war covered by two kinds of policy. The following passage makes this clear:

> If the state is thought of as a person, and policy as the product of its brain, then among the contingencies for which the state must be prepared is a war in which every element calls for policy to be eclipsed by violence. Only if politics is regarded not as resulting from a just appreciation of affairs, but – as it conventionally is – as cautious, devious, even dishonest, shying away from force, could the second type of war appear to be more "political" than the first.[31]

There is a type of policy "where every element in the state's brain is eclipsed by violence," and there is another type of policy "where caution and deviousness dictate a path away from violence." War is a continuation of both types of policy, of what we might call "grand policy" and "petty policy."

A closer look at Clausewitz's writings suggests that by "grand policy" he means the imperial politics of Napoleon, and by "petty policy" the balance of power politics of the statesmen before and after Napoleon. In his life, Clausewitz experiences them both, and in his theory of war and politics he wants to unify them. He is trained in the pre-Napoleonic era, in an age where cabinet warfare is still the rule, a type of war characterized by clumsy and geometrically arranged maneuvers whose primary aim is conflict avoidance. Then he is confronted with the dynamic and brilliant generalship of Napoleon, a type of war that makes the old rules obsolete. Like many a contemporary, Clausewitz is at first bewildered but then tries to come to terms with both phenomena. He tries to fit the experience of his life under one theoretical roof – but that is impossible. There can be no unified theory of war.

Clausewitz's writings reflect the contradictions he experienced, the dilemma of his age, but by not dealing with the contradictions explicitly and systematically, his writings have given rise to much confusion and misinterpretation. Over the past 150 years, interpretations have varied widely. Militaristic Germans have tended to see in him an advocate of massive warfare, of decisive battles (*Entscheidungsschlacht*) guided by "grand policy." To them war is a continuation of imperial and hegemonic politics by other means.[32] They see in Clausewitz the general–theoretician who has properly interpreted the French military genius that humbles Prussia and that many later want to best. These interpreters find enough material in *On War* that, taken out of context, prove their case. Clausewitz's discussion of abstract and pure war contains passages like the following that fit neatly into nationalistic publications prior to World War I and World War II:

> Kind-hearted people might of course think there was some ingenious way to disarm or defeat an enemy without too much bloodshed, and might imagine this is the true goal of the art of war. Pleasant as it sounds, it is a fallacy that must be exposed: war is such a dangerous business that the mistakes which come from kindness are the very worst. *The maximum use of force is in no way incompatible with the simultaneous use of the intellect.*[33] [emphasis added]

There are a number of such passages where massive and unrestricted war is felt to be compatible with the use of intellect and policy. Even Bernard Brodie must admit that at times Clausewitz "is describing total war, which today would be nuclear, but the acceptance of such a state of affairs is still policy."[34]

Of course, Clausewitz lends himself to different interpretations as well. There have always been Germans who argued that the maximum use of force was in no way compatible with the simultaneous use of the intellect. Force, to be a rational instrument, had to be constrained by the intellect, they maintained. Bismarck was famous for the restrictions he placed upon the use of force. The Iron Chancellor saw war largely as a continuation of balance of power politics, and there are important German interpreters of *On War* who argue that Clausewitz is more than a simple proponent of massive battles, of schemes like the Schlieffen Plan or, for that matter, of unrestricted submarine warfare.[35]

Today, in the nuclear age, Clausewitz is generally interpreted as an opponent of unrestricted war. The Neo-Clausewitzians, as they are called, fully appreciate the nefarious meaning of absolute war and of the three different "cases of interaction" leading to an extreme. Clausewitz's remarks on pure or abstract war read like a modern account of nuclear escalation and of the forces that determine it: (1) the effort to disarm the opponent, (2) the maximum use of force and (3) the maximum exertion of will. In the nuclear age the result is mutual annihilation. Depending on the expectations strategists place on the possibility of controlling an exchange, different assumptions exist about "modifications in reality." Some theorists feel that even such an encounter is (a) never a wholly isolated act, (b) does not consist of a single decisive blow, and (c) is not based on one political decision. Clausewitz's concepts are quite relevant to "thinking about the unthinkable" in the nuclear age. Small wonder that he has been quoted widely again in recent years.

Much of the confusion and misinterpretation could have been avoided had Clausewitz been more explicit about the tensions between unrestricted war (and imperial politics) on the one hand, and restricted war (and balance of power politics) on the other. In Clausewitz's time, it means the difference between Napoleon and the statesmen before and after him. For the Germans of a later generation, it means the difference between Bismarck, William II, and Hitler. The difference is important.

Had Clausewitz been more explicit on this point he could have shown that generalship is torn between two logics: in one war is a means to the end of balancing power, in the other it is a means to the end of maximizing power. In one logic it is part of an anarchic worldview, in the other it is part of a hierarchic worldview. In one system a particular type of war is functional, in another system the same war is dysfunctional.

Clausewitz fails to make the dichotomies explicit because, in sharp contrast to Gentz, he never defines the central actor in international politics – the state. With a fully developed contextual definition of the state Clausewitz would have clarified matters. He would have told us whether it is the nature of states to balance or to maximize power, to be conservative or hegemonic (and revolutionary), to fight restrained or unrestrained wars. Gentz drew that distinction, Clausewitz did not. His unsuccessful attempt to develop a general theory of war is accompanied by a very general and uncertain conception of the state.

This uncertainty reflects Clausewitz's own experience with the state. He confronted various types of states – the conservative, the revolutionary liberal, and the early national state. He served conservative rulers, but for a while was also identified with the Prussian reformers, although they were neither liberals nor democrats. We do not know what he thought of Kant's treatise on perpetual peace, but we do know that Clausewitz, unlike Kant, lacked a liberal penchant.

If any German philosopher had an influence on Clausewitz it was Hegel. There are indications that Clausewitz heard of Hegel's dialectic, but it cannot be shown that he actually applied the method.[36] If Hegel had any influence on Clausewitz it was general and indirect. Both share a fundamentally conservative philosophy of life typical of the age they lived in.

BERNHARDI: MILITARISTIC IMPERIALISM

Friedrich von Bernhardi, German general and military author, published his *Germany and the Next War*[37] in 1912, two years before the outbreak of World War I. The book was an immediate sensation, was translated into various languages and seemed to prove what many feared – that Germany was intent on starting a major war to establish its hegemony on the continent, and perhaps worldwide. As it turned out, Bernhardi was right – war came and developed, in the beginning at least, as he predicted. Retrospectively, therefore, the book was for many incontrovertible evidence that Germany, and particularly the German military, wanted this war and did everything to make it happen.

Apart from its historic importance, the book represents an interesting contribution to the theory of international relations because it portrays with utmost candor a hierarchic realist worldview. War is normal, it is the central phenomenon of history and evolution, and because it is the expression of the law of the strongest it leads not to a state of balance but to a state of domination, a situation quite natural in history. The balance of power established at the Congress of Vienna and the relatively peaceful century that followed were, from this perspective, a transient and abnormal period in history. The equilibrium in Europe was artificial, possible only because Germany was weak and underdeveloped. Also, there never existed an equilibrium at the global level where the British Empire was dominant. With Germany on the rise, things were about to change.

Bernhardi was not the only German to present such arguments: his book was representative of the thinking in nationalistic, militaristic and imperialistic circles and, unfortunately, it also reflected the mood at the court of William II. Nor was Bernhardi the first German to voice such ideas. Heinrich von Treitschke expressed similar thoughts a generation earlier, and he is an authority that Bernhardi frequently quotes.[38] Treitschke was equally unhappy with the balance of power, but while Bismarck was chancellor the idea still enjoyed a modicum of respectability, and Treitschke did not yet openly advocate its overthrow. What unites the two authors, however, is their reckless militarism and their glorification of war.

Germany and the Next War contains fourteen chapters, but only the first five are of interest to the theoretician of international relations; the remaining chapters deal with relatively practical matters, such as the organization of armed forces, education and training, finances and economics. It is the beginning of the book that has attracted so much attention, particularly the chapters on "The Right to Make War," "The Duty to Make War," "Germany's Historical Mission" and "World Power or Downfall."

The book opens with a critique of Kant and his *Perpetual Peace*. Ever since that tract was published, so Bernhardi complains, people regard it as an established fact "that war is the destruction of all good and the origin of all evil."[39] Peace movements and peace leagues have sprung up, and there are even governments proclaiming that peace is their top priority. Peace Congresses are held at The Hague, and to promote peace the American government sponsors courts of arbitration. In Bernhardi's opinion, all of these aspirations are "directly antagonistic to the great universal laws which rule all life,"[40] and these laws have their origin in war.

Bernhardi sees two justifications for war: one in material reality, in biology, the other in moral reality, in what he calls idealism.

> War is a biological necessity of the first importance, a regulative element in the life of mankind which cannot be dispensed with, since without it an unhealthy development will follow, which excludes every advancement of the race, and therefore all real civilization. 'War is the father of all things.' The sages of antiquity long before Darwin recognized this.[41]

War is the central phenomenon in nature and in history, its dynamics determine all life and evolution. Darwin expresses it well when he speaks of a struggle for survival and of the survival of the fittest. Bernhardi says repeatedly that "the law of the strongest holds good everywhere," among animals, individuals, groups, and nations.[42]

A difference, however, exists between the struggle at the intra- and at the extra-societal level: at the intra-societal level the law, backed by the power of the state, stands over and above the rivalries of individuals and groups. That power is used "not merely to protect, but actively to promote, the moral and spiritual interests of society."[43] Beyond the states, at the extra-societal level, no agent exists to promote order and morality, so that "between states the only check on injustice is force, and in morality and civilization every nation must play its own part and promote its own ends and ideals."[44]

I shall return to Bernhardi's view of the state as a moralizing agent later on. What matters for the moment is that between states, where no higher authority is effective, the laws of biological necessity work without restraint, war at that level is normal, natural, rational and necessary. And, as Bernhardi shows, the struggle has a demographic and economic dimension as well:

Strong, healthy, and flourishing nations increase in numbers. From a given moment they require a continual expansion of their frontiers, they require new territory for the accommodation of their surplus population. Since almost every part of the globe is inhabited, new territory must, as a rule, be obtained at the cost of its possessors – that is to say, by conquest, which thus becomes a law of necessity.[45]

The right of conquest is universally acknowledged, and Bernhardi adds to it the right of colonization. Vast stretches of land are occupied by "uncivilized masses" that "higher civilizations" have a need for.[46] A civilized state without colonies "runs the danger not only of losing a valuable part of its population by emigration, but also of gradually falling from its supremacy in the civilized and political world through diminishing production and lessened profits."[47] Production diminishes because industries in a civilized state depend heavily on exports, but because industrialized countries in the long run cannot buy from each other and are forced to erect tariff barriers, colonial outlets are the only alternative.

Bernhardi then turns to his idealist explanation of war. Man is not a materialistic being satisfied with consumption and production alone; man is also a moral being endeavoring to develop its spiritual and intellectual faculties. Only a strong state can promote these values. A materialistic state, such as the Anglo-Saxon state, based on egotistic individualism and conceived of as no more than "a legal and social insurance office"[48] will not do. The materialistic state is a weak state and therefore has to make the pursuit of peace its highest value. The strong state is different. It does not shy away from the necessity of going to war, and in the process it raises man to a higher level of moral and spiritual perfection:

> War, from this standpoint, will be regarded as a moral necessity, if it is waged to protect the highest and most valuable interests of a nation. As human life is now constituted, it is political idealism which calls for war, while materialism – in theory, at least, repudiates it.[49]

To a reader raised in the liberal tradition, these are unusual definitions of idealism, individualism and materialism. Idealism is identified with a strong and martial state "calling for war." Liberal individualism is put on the same footing as materialism, egoism, weakness and peace. For Bernhardi, individualism is identical with the pursuit of narrow and material self-interest producing a weak state not meant to interfere with the materialistic concerns of its citizens. It is a vulgar view of Great Britain and the Anglo-Saxon world but, unfortunately, quite common in Germany at the time.

The German state is different. It has its foundation not in degenerate materialism but in stark reality, in the law of nature and in a conception of history as a state of war. All else is derived from this fact, the image of the state as well as the image of man. To survive, the state must be strong, on the inside and on the outside. It must be able to organize and mobilize the masses for war, and to fight other states. When war breaks out, all individualistic and egotistic interests must be sacrificed to the higher interest of the state, all petty conflicts between parties and groups must be put aside. To underscore the point, Bernhardi quotes Treitschke, an authority on this subject:

> At the moment when the State cries out that its very life is at stake, social selfishness must cease and party hatred be hushed. The individual must forget his egoism, and feel that he is a member of the whole body. He should recognize how his own life is worth nothing in comparison with the welfare of the community. War is elevating, because the individual disappears before the great conception of the State.[50]

In this passage it becomes quite evident that man, too, is merely a function of the war logic. The individual must, when necessary, completely subordinate his personality and interests to the will of the state and the necessities of war. The highest duty of man is to realize that "his personal life is worth nothing in comparison with the state." The ultimate purpose of man is to sacrifice himself for the survival of the state. War and the state are everything, man is nothing. The cause is always war and the state (or history), man is merely the effect. Liberalism has the opposite perception of causality, of course.

It is a very skeptical image of man. Man is not self-reliant and autonomous, not able to live with other men on the basis of voluntariness and equality. He is most certainly not capable of improvement and perfection. It is the state that must promote his perfection. Bernhardi states clearly that the state is capable "of raising the intellectual and moral powers of a nation to the highest expansion,"[51] and that it is also the state "which draws the individual out of the narrow circles in which he otherwise would pass his life, and makes him a worker in the great common interest of humanity."[52] The state provides compensation for the individual's weaknesses. It is not the individual that is perfectible but the state, or, more precisely, the élite that guides the masses and acts on their behalf. The state élite exemplifies the *raison d'état* and the *volonté d'état*. When this group decides to go to war, man and the state achieve perfection.

War is so central in the thought of Bernhardi and Treitschke that it becomes a positive good – and peace a positive evil! In times of peace, individuals and nations decay, in times of war, they flourish: "All petty and personal interests force their way to the front during a long period of peace. Selfishness and intrigue run riot, and luxury obliterates idealism."[53] War, on the other hand, "brings out the noblest activities of the human nature...[and] even defeat may bear a rich harvest."[54] This is realism at its purest – and at its most absurd.

To strengthen his case, Bernhardi refers to the Bible and to legal philosophy. It is all wrong, he argues, to assume that the Bible is based on nothing but brotherly love. There has never been a religion more combative than Christianity: "Christ Himself said: 'I am not come to send peace on earth, but the sword'."[55] And when it comes to law, all is either subjective or relative. For Bernhardi, law can mean two things: a consciousness of what is right and good, and a rule laid down by society or the state, either written or sanctioned by tradition. "In its first meaning it is an indefinite, purely personal conception; in its second meaning it is variable and capable of development."[56] Justice is to him an indefinite and purely personal notion, and positive or enforceable law is variable in time and place. The same applies to international law:

> There never have been, and never will be, universal rights of men. Here and there particular relations can be brought under definite international laws, but the bulk of national life is absolutely outside codification.[57]

This concludes the first chapter on "The Right to Make War." There is nothing that stands in the way of going to war, no biological and no moral law. All speaks in favor of war; war *is* the biological and moral law.

In the second chapter, Bernhardi deals with "The Duty to Make War," and his aim is to justify aggression. It is not a simple task because no lesser German than Bismarck warned against starting wars intentionally: "Prince Bismarck repeatedly declared before the German Reichstag that no one should ever take upon himself the immense responsibility of intentionally bringing about a war."[58] These words were remembered by many Germans, and the aggressive militarists had to come to terms with them if they wanted to convince their less militant countrymen that Germany should intentionally start a war.

Bernhardi advances two arguments: first, the Iron Chancellor's admonition was quoted out of context and, second, Bismarck himself did not live up to it: "It is his special claim to greatness that at the decisive moment he did not lack the boldness to begin a war on his own initiative."[59] And, as history shows, other great statesmen also started wars intentionally, especially some British prime ministers. Bernhardi is therefore able to conclude that the appropriate and conscious employment of war as a political means has always led to happy results...[and] wars which have been deliberately provoked by far-seeing statesmen have had the happiest results.[60]

With these remarks the question is dismissed. It is now clear to Bernhardi that Germany not only has a right to go to war but also, if circumstances permit, a duty to do so. His next question is whether circumstances demand such a step, whether the moment is right. To answer that question he discusses Germany's present position, then the possibility of coming to an understanding with the British and the Americans, and finally whether Germany should rise to the status of a true world power or face a downfall.

Bernhardi distinguishes between the political and the nonpolitical development of Germany. Politically, Germany is not in very good shape: on the inside she is torn by dissent, and on the outside surrounded by enemies. The nonpolitical side of the picture is brighter. Germany's scientific, economic and cultural development has in recent decades been respectable so that materially the country is in a good position to go to war. Looking at the overall situation, the balance is positive:

> So stands Germany today, torn by internal dissensions, yet full of sustained strength; threatened on all sides by dangers, compressed into narrow, unnatural limits, she is filled with high aspirations, in her nationality, her intellectual development, in her science, industries, and trade.[61]

But what about the future? Bernhardi is convinced that merely holding on to what Germany has is not enough. The world is dynamic, the other powers are expanding, and in such an environment "we shall not be able to maintain our present position, powerful as it is, in the great competition with the other Powers, if we are contented to restrict ourselves to our present sphere of power."[62] Germany must also expand, and on such a scale that "we no longer fear that we shall be opposed by stronger opponents whenever we take part in international politics."[63] Expansion will soon appear as a necessity, and because Bernhardi is convinced that it will be opposed he concludes that "what we now wish to attain must be fought for, and won, against a superior force of hostile interests and Powers."[64] These sentences are unmistakable in their intent – Germany should fight a hegemonic war.

Before drawing final conclusions, Bernhardi deals with a question on the minds of some Germans at that time: could German interests be satisfied by a grand deal with Great Britain and America, a completely new Triple Alliance allowing for a fundamental rearrangement of the spheres of influence?

For such a union with Germany to be possible, England must have resolved to give a free course to German development side by side with her own, to allow the enlargement of our colonial power, and to offer no political hindrances to our commercial and industrial competition. She must, therefore, have renounced her traditional policy, and contemplate an entirely new grouping of the Great Powers in the world.[65]

He rejects the idea as impossible: British pride and self-interest would not permit it. But in discussing the idea Bernhardi reveals his true intentions: he wants Germany to overcome its continental confines and to join Great Britain (and America) in a new club and a new class of world powers. Because he knows that Great Britain would never agree to such a change voluntarily, he is ready to go to war and to force the British out of their present position. It is bound to be a hegemonic struggle with worldwide implications. The immediate interest of Germany is to consolidate its position on the continent, but its wider interests lie in challenging the British Empire.

Bernhardi is particularly outspoken about eliminating France as the first obstacle along the road: "France must be so completely crushed that she can never again come across our path."[66] Once France is no longer a Great Power, Russia stands alone and can be dealt with separately. Germany can then proceed to form what Bernhardi calls a "Central European Federation," an enlargement of the existing Triple Alliance between Germany, Austria–Hungary, and Italy. It means reducing France, Russia, Austria–Hungary, and Italy to the rank of second-rate powers completely at the mercy of Germany.

Bernhardi is fully aware that the scheme clashes head-on with the traditional conception of a European balance of power. In his opinion, that concept is an anachronism and must be discarded. The principle, which since the Congress of Vienna has led "an almost sacrosanct but entirely unjustifiable existence, must be entirely disregarded."[67] The concept served the purposes of Metternich and Bismarck but in the last few decades it has had the effect of paralyzing the continental powers:

> It can only have the disastrous consequences of rendering the forces of the continental European States mutually ineffective, and of thus favouring the plans of the political powers which stand outside that charmed circle. It has always been England's policy to stir up enmity between the respective continental States, and to keep them at approximately the same standard of power, in order herself to remain undisturbed to conquer at once the sovereignty of the world.[68]

Once more, Bernhardi's vision focuses on Great Britain and on challenging its position as the sole power with a truly global reach. He proposes setting up a new and truly global balance of power: "It is now not a question of a European State system, but of one embracing all the States of the world, in which the equilibrium is established on real factors of power."[69]

Not once does Bernhardi ask whether the British would feel secure with an "imperial partner" such as Germany, a state that believes in the law of the strongest while denying human rights, a state that regards peace as evil and war as the supreme civilizing force. Logic tells us that coexistence with such a state is impossible and that sooner or later the final struggle will break out over the issue of worldwide hegemony. There are indications that Bernhardi has a cyclical conception of history, that he believes in the inevitable ups and downs of hegemonic powers. If Great Britain is at the top now, why not Germany next? Against this background his words about "establishing an equilibrium on real forces of power" sound rather hollow. Cyclical conceptions of international politics were common at that time. It was particularly fashionable to personalize the life of nations, to think of them as having been born, then reaching maturity and manhood, and finally growing old and beginning to decline. Such ideas prevailed in many countries and were not a specifically German invention.

Bernhardi's image of the state system is clear – he has a negative image of anarchy and a positive image of hierarchy. Bernhardi rejects an anarchic system based on balance not because it outlaws war, which it does not, but because it is incompatible with the dynamics of war. Equilibrium puts restraints on war and constrains the life cycle of nations, it interferes with their normal growth and decline. The most vital nation must get a chance to run the international system. The normal and rational management of the system is neither universalistic nor oligarchic – it is monistic.

One nation defines the nature of the international hierarchy, all others have to play subordinate parts. The lesser states are imperfect and weak, the hegemon is wise and strong: his superiority compensates for their inferiority. Some of the lesser states accept the restrictions imposed on their sovereignty voluntarily, others do not. Italy and Austria belong to the former category, France, Russia and Great Britain to the latter. Dependence, inequality and involuntariness are normal in the life of nations. In the prevailing state of war some powers win, some lose – zero-sum reasoning prevails.

Absolute conflict is at the core of Bernhardi's theory. War dominates all, it represents ultimate causality and the driving force of history. War is the foundation of rationality and is identical with the logic of politics; war is a process that determines structure. In contrast to Gentz, Bernhardi sees no convergence of enlightened national interest: his theory is war-centered, not state-centered.

Bernhardi's image of the state is a function of the international system. Given the international state of war and the primacy of foreign policy, state structures have to adapt themselves – states must be of the hard variety. Conservative and authoritarian states are better adapted than liberal and democratic states, and the most successfully adapted state is the hegemon itself. It represents the system; it and the system are inseparable. The two cause each other: the nature of the system determines the nature of the hegemon, and, conversely, the nature of the hegemon determines the nature of the system.

In Bernhardi's theory the average state does not count, and neither does man. Man is a pawn of history, a means to other ends. Within the overall system it fulfills a given role and function. The ultimate causes of human success or failure lie outside man. Only a handful of individuals can escape this fate – they are the true leaders of mankind. They are "world historical personalities" embodying the *Zeitgeist*, as Hegel would say. But even these supermen are unable to stop the rise and decline of empires.

Bernhardi's theory of international relations is a mixture of Hegelianism, Social Darwinism and raw Hobbesian power politics.[70] The various "laws of nature" determine the development of all life, of human history and of each individual. The theory contains a highly deterministic conception of science, a conception not necessarily shared by other realists. Gentz's balance of power theory, for instance, is built on a much less compelling vision of social science. In that world states have a choice between being (conservatively) rational or irrational but in Bernhardi's world there is no room for choice. The imperialist logic imposes itself with great inevitability and necessity.

The theory fits neatly into the hierarchic realist worldview. Conflict among nations is normal, even central. If Gentz's theory is state-centered, Bernhardi's is war-centered. The law of the strongest dominates all and provides the generalization on which a highly compelling and deterministic logic is based: it determines the (contextual) definition of nations; it defines rationality, the relation of wholes to parts, systems to functions, ends to means and causes to effects; it allows for rigorous if–then statements, for predictions and prescriptions. It is also a transformational theory of international relations because balance of power politics has to give way to imperialist politics. Finally, the theory will be tested in history. Bernhardi's theory of militarist imperialism is fully developed and inherently consistent.

KANT: PERPETUAL PEACE

Kant's *Perpetual Peace*[71] appeared in 1795, at a time when the Wars of the French Revolution had not yet spread across the face of Europe and when Bonaparte was not yet in charge. It was a time when there was still hope that with the advent of the French Revolution, and with the American Revolution completed only a few years earlier, permanent peace might finally become possible among the more enlightened nations. It would mean the end of frivolous wars started by absolutist monarchs over what were mostly dynastic issues.

Kant's treatise sold well, it was in harmony with the spirit of the times. What made it attractive, however, was not its content alone but also the concise and clear manner in which it was written. While some of Kant's other works are philosophically much more important they are also ponderous and difficult to read. *Perpetual Peace* covers all of 90 pages, and the core of the argument is contained on no more than 30 pages. Small wonder that it has become by far the most widely read Kantian tract.

The plan is presented as a treaty consisting of nine articles with a supplement and an annex. The articles are extremely short: most of the 90 pages are taken up by commentary. At first sight, therefore, the booklet gives the impression of a legal treatise, but it is not. It cannot be compared to Abbé de Saint Pierre's *Projet pour rendre la paix perpétuelle en Europe*, published in 1713.[72] Saint Pierre drafted a complete charter for an international organization, which was one of the reasons why the proposal was so much ridiculed. Furthermore, Saint Pierre's project is highly conservative, of dubious origin and meant to serve the narrow dynastic interests of France. Kant's plan is different in every respect.

It was not submitted to a ruler, not meant to serve the purposes of any one power, and did not even aim at abolishing war immediately. But it does contain some of the most progressive and enlightened ideas published at that time in Prussia. Kant stands unambiguously for peace, something that distinguishes him so remarkably from other Germans, from contemporaries like Hegel or from successors like Treitschke.[73]

Kant is optimistic about the ultimate fate of man but does not expect to change the world overnight; he is no revolutionary. He believes in progress but his conception of change is measured and evolutionary. He does not expect nations to adopt all articles at once but, as he explains in his *Critique of Practical Reason*, statesmen and ordinary citizens alike have the ability and the duty to act morally.[74] If enough of them take his suggestions to heart, some progress can be made.

The nine articles are divided into two groups: six are preliminary, three are definitive. The preliminary articles indicate what should be avoided, they represent the negative conditions for peace; the definitive articles indicate what must be done and constitute the positive conditions for peace.[75] Some of the preliminary articles can be applied immediately while all the definitive articles take time to grow and mature.

The Preliminary Articles

Article 1: No treaty of peace shall be regarded as valid, if made with the secret reservation of material for a future war.[76]

Secret clauses were common in the peace treaties of those days, often constituting causes for another war. What was meant to bring peace established no more than a truce, "a mere suspension of hostilities" between two inevitable wars.[77] Eliminating secret reservations strengthens peace because open clauses promote openness and transparency in diplomacy and legal dealings, and it constitutes a step away from the realist conception of international politics where peace is but an interlude between wars. In Kant's opinion this article could be implemented immediately.

Article 2: No state having an independent existence – whether it be great or small – shall be acquired by another through inheritance, exchange, purchase or donation.[78]

This article challenges the custom of absolutist rulers to dispose of entire countries and provinces as if they were personal property. In Kant's view, the citizens of every country must have a say in what happens to their state, or else the notion of "original contract" has no meaning.[79] By original contract he means the right of every people to enter into a constitutional agreement with their ruler. Kant actually postulates the right of self-determination which, of course, runs counter to the tradition prevailing at that time. This is a big step and consequently Kant does not include this article among those that could be instituted immediately.

Article 3: Standing armies shall be abolished in the course of time.[80]

For Kant, standing armies are a threat to peace: constant military readiness creates insecurity. Furthermore, standing armies "incite the various states to outrival one another in the number of their soldiers, and to this number no limit can be set."[81] In modern parlance, standing armies lead to arms races, promote escalation and destabilize the system. Kant also considers professional soldiers as immoral "killing machines" difficult to reconcile "with the right of humanity in our own person."[82] But he does approve of citizens organizing as militias to secure their country from outside attack.

Standing armies are costly and, in true mercantilist fashion, associated with the "accumulation of treasure" by the state. For Kant, this is another source of war.[83] Mercantilist habits, however, are difficult to break, which is why Kant does not include this article either among those that could be implemented soon.

Kant does not call for disarmament; he rejects pacifism and does not argue that arms create war. As will become more evident later on, he sees social organization as the chief source of war. If perpetual peace is to be established it is more important to change the nature of states than to eliminate weapons.

Article 4: No national debt shall be contracted in connection with the external affairs of the state.[84]

Kant approves of incurring debts for the economic improvement of a country but he rejects them for the financing of armed forces. Public borrowing for war had become a favorite mercantilist instrument and appeared to be limited only by a country's ability to raise taxes to pay interest on loans. As Kant shows, the limitation on borrowing "will long be kept off by the very briskness of commerce resulting from the reaction of this system on industry and trade."[85] Defense-oriented deficit spending as a mechanism to stimulate the economy has a long history and, as Kant argues, went hand in hand with more public borrowing, higher interest rates, inflation and the regular collapse of public finance. Kant intends to break the vicious circle. Not only does he believe that the mechanism helps to promote war, it also entails unsound habits of public finance and the occasional bankruptcy of the state. Having few illusions about changing such ingrained economic practices rapidly, Kant does not include this article either among those that should be applied immediately.

Article 5: No state shall violently interfere with the constitution and administration of another.[86]

This is a reference to one of the most basic principles of international law – nonintervention. Intervening in the affairs of another country is an act of "lawlessness,"[87] and Kant believes that the practice should be abandoned immediately. He recommends that this article be written into one of the next peace treaties. Kant is willing to admit the necessity of intervention in only one case – civil war: "Here the giving of assistance to one faction could not be reckoned as interference on the part of a foreign state with the constitution of another, for here anarchy prevails."[88]

Article 6: No state at war with another shall countenance such modes of hostility as would make mutual confidence impossible in a subsequent state of peace: such are the employment of assassins or of poisoners, breaches of capitulation, the instigating and making of treachery in the hostile state.[89]

Such acts are "dishonourable stratagems" because "some kind of confidence in the disposition of the enemy must exist even in the midst of war."[90] If the conduct of war is completely unrestricted, it resembles progressively an effort at extermination, and the conclusion of peace becomes all the more difficult. Kant demands the creation of a modern law of war that puts some limitations on its conduct and renders it more humanitarian. In the nineteenth century, such a body of international law did develop, and it was ultimately codified in the various Hague and Geneva Conventions (*ius in bello*).

Limiting the conduct of war serves a humanitarian purpose but excludes the explicit condemnation of war. It is impossible to condemn an aggressor, to label his cause unjust, and at the same time to accept him as a legal partner to regulate the conduct of hostilities. Kant is aware of this: "In circumstances like these, neither of the two parties can be called an unjust enemy, because this form of speech presupposes a legal decision."[91]

This neutral conception of war creates a problem: it entails the acceptance of war as a normal and rational instrument of conflict management and is incompatible with any effort to condemn or outlaw war. How can Kant adopt such a conception of law while attempting to eliminate war and to establish perpetual peace? Is Kant the idealist falling into a realist trap?

The answer is no. Kant stops short of the outlawry of war and does not distinguish between just and unjust wars (*bellum iustum*). He assumes that perpetual peace will result from the inherently peaceful nature of modern states. International law of war (*ius in bello*) is a temporary device until perpetual peace is established. Similar laws already exist among nations and Kant, therefore, includes this article among those that can be implemented forthwith.

By outlawing the most barbarian acts of war Kant also intends to promote civilized government. The employment of assassins, poisoners and spies is often self-defeating because they undermine the state itself. He shows that especially spying habits can "not be confined to the sphere of war"; they carry over into the sphere of peace "where their presence would be utterly destructive to the purpose of the state."[92] Clandestine activities are particularly destructive of constitutional government.

The Definitive Articles

Kant then turns to the core of his plan for perpetual peace, to the three definitive articles. They contain the positive factors, the dos rather than the don'ts. These are the articles that are generally known and have made the study so famous.

Article I: The civil constitution of each state shall be republican.[93]

A republican constitution has its origins in the original contract which, as already mentioned, entails a number of basic rights. Kant now spells them out in detail:

> It is a constitution, in the first place, founded in accordance with the principle of the freedom of the members of society as human beings; secondly, in accordance with the principle of the dependence of all, as subjects, on a common legislation; and, thirdly, in accordance with the law of the equality of the members as citizens.[94]

But a republican constitution creates more than a state based on the rule of law. It is also a particular form of government: "Republicanism is the political principle of severing the executive power of the government from the legislature."[95] Republicanism stands for the separation of powers, for constitutional government and, in his perspective, must not be confused with democracy. Democracy involves the direct participation of the people, and for Kant this threatens the separation of powers: "Democracy, in the proper sense of the word, is of necessity despotism."[96] Kant favors indirect and representative government: "Every form of government in fact which is not representative is really no true constitution at all."[97]

Finally, Kant thinks that the ideal executive is monistic, consisting of a monarch or a president: "We may therefore say that the smaller the staff of the executive – that is to say, the number of rulers – and the more real, on the other hand, their representation of the people, so much the more is the government of the state in accordance with a possible republicanism."[98]

To sum up Kant's view of republicanism: it is a state based on the rule of law, on the separation of legislature and executive, on representation and, ideally, on a single ruler. Power is divided and limited in numerous ways and cannot be misused. This imposes self-discipline upon the state and promotes peace. Consent of the governed is particulary crucial:

> If, as must be so under this constitution, the consent of the subjects is required to determine whether there shall be war or not, nothing is more natural than that they should weigh the matter well, before undertaking such a bad business. For in decreeing war, they would of necessity be resolving to bring down the miseries of war upon their country. This implies: they must fight themselves; they must hand over the costs of the war out of their own property; they must do their poor best to make good

> the devastation which it leaves behind; and finally, as a crowning ill, they have to accept a burden of debt which will embitter even peace itself, and which they can never pay off on account of the wars which are always impending.[99]

This passage shows how much Kant believes in the potential for reason in man: people are able to weigh the costs and the benefits of war, and they come to the conclusion that peace is rational while war is not. If they have a voice in government their views will prevail and wars will end. Kant does not assume that in his time many a nation would reach such a degree of enlightenment, but he is firmly convinced that man has the potential to get there, assisted by Providence. Furthermore, as Kant sees it, wars have a tendency to become progressively more destructive – and self-defeating. At a certain point it will become evident to everyone that war is not a rational means for conflict resolution.[100] Only an absolutist ruler will never learn because he

> is not a citizen, but the owner of the state, and does not lose a whit by the war, while he goes on enjoying the delights of his table or sport, or of his pleasure and gala days. He can therefore decide on war for the most trifling reason, as if it were a kind of pleasure party.[101]

Article II: The law of nations shall be founded on a federation of free states.[102]

Such a federation, for Kant, is not a supranational organization or a world state. A world state would contradict the basic objective of his plan, which consists not only in achieving perpetual peace but also in maintaining the sovereignty, independence and liberty of all republican states.[103]

> Hence, instead of the positive idea of a world republic, if all is not to be lost, only the negative substitute for it, a federation averting war, maintaining its ground and ever extending over the world may stop the current of this tendency to war and shrinking from the control of law.[104]

A world state cannot guarantee peace, only a loose and informal alliance of republican states can. He speaks of a "covenant of peace" that will put "an end to war forever,"[105] but he never calls for the creation of an international organization, and he certainly does not use the term "League of Nations." This term originates with Saint Pierre, not with Kant.

Another idea, however, is typical of Kant: he assumes that a loose federation of republican states will have its origins in one enlightened nation and spread throughout the world, thereby gradually extending the zone of peace and narrowing the zone of war:

If Fortune ordains that a powerful and enlightened people should form a republic, – which by its very nature is inclined to perpetual peace – this would serve as a centre of federal union for other states wishing to join, and thus secure conditions of freedom among the states in accordance with the idea of the law of nations. Gradually, through different unions of this kind, the federation would extend further and further.[106]

There is little doubt that Kant is thinking of two countries when he speaks of enlightened and powerful nations – France and the United States.[107] Both soon disappoint him: France turns into a warlike and imperialist state, and the United States withdraws into isolation. It took over a century for the idea to materialize. Woodrow Wilson, who knew Kant's plan for perpetual peace, identified strongly with the idea that an enlightened and republican state could lead the world to peace.

Article III: The rights of men, as citizens of the world, shall be limited to the conditions of universal hospitality.[108]

Men, as "citizens of the world," have rights. These do not include the right of citizenship in every country, but they do embrace the right of hospitality. This right "belongs to all mankind in virtue of our common right of possession of the surface of the earth" and entitles us "to take advantage of our common claim to the face of the earth with a view to a possible intercommunication."[109] In this manner "distant territories may enter into peaceful relations with one another" whereby "the human race may be brought nearer the realization of a cosmopolitan constitution."[110]

These are indications that Kant believes in the beneficial effects of interdependence, of international communication and trade.[111] And, as is typical of anarchic idealists, he sees no tension between political independence and functional interdependence; on the contrary, the two combine to promote peace and well-being in a decentralized world order.

Kant says little about economics and does not explicitly praise the virtues of free trade, but by denouncing the evils of mercantilist commerce he leaves no doubt about his conviction. He severely criticizes the "commercial states of our continent," the barbarian methods of slavery, colonialism and imperialism.[112] He delights in the plight of mercantilist companies: "The worst, or from the standpoint of ethical judgment the best, of all this is that no satisfaction is derived from all this violence, that all these trading companies stand on the verge of ruin."[113] There are moments when Kant sounds almost like Adam Smith and Jeremy Bentham.[114]

Naturally, Kant is not an Anglo-Saxon liberal but in his *Perpetual Peace* he propagates ideas that are part of that tradition. The centerpiece of his scheme is an enlightened state image. He places great faith in the inherent peacefulness of republican government, and in this respect is a typical second-image theorist.[115] Unlike some of his contemporaries in Prussia (Hegel comes to mind), Kant does not want a strong state that compensates for human weakness, a state in which men risk becoming functional cogs in the great machine of "history." Kant's image of man is optimistic but the human potential for improvement can only be developed in close relation with republican government. The two are inseparable and represent the foundation of rationality.

Kant's image of the state system is a consequence of his image of the state. Given the benevolent nature of republican government, the lives of such states are peaceful and order in anarchy becomes possible. Domestic politics determines international politics, the primacy of domestic policy is assured. Republicanism produces a convergence of national interests that guarantees perpetual peace.

The theory fits neatly into the anarchic idealist worldview and rests on an explicit contextual definition of nations. The generalization lays the foundation for a rigorous and logical theory complete with if–then statements, predictions and prescriptions. It is also a transformational theory because it shows how nations can work themselves out of the zero-sum war logic typical of realism, out of the Prisoners' Dilemma with its suboptimal outcomes. Kant does not foresee a quick transformation of world politics. Unlike such contemporaries as Jeremy Bentham and Thomas Paine he argues that the transition will be slow and painful. Only in the long run is Kant's logic compelling. This injects a note of caution into his theory and creates a certain (although tenuous) affinity with the evolutionary conservatism of Burke.[116]

Furthermore, Kantian peace will be perpetual only among the select group of republican states, not between republican and nonrepublican states. If a republic has absolutist neighbors it is tempted to intervene in their affairs to promote liberal causes: to stop violations of human rights, protect private property, support liberal allies against nonliberal regimes. As Michael Doyle has argued convincingly, liberalism carries a dual legacy: peace among liberal states, and interventions of liberal in nonliberal states.[117]

Kant also distinguishes between the "law" and the "state" of nature. The law of nature prevails among republican states and stands for peace; the state of nature (or the natural state) characterizes the original situation among men and stands for war. "A state of peace among men who live side by side is not the natural state, which is rather to be described as a state of war," and in a footnote he explicitly refers to Hobbes.[118]

The subtle linguistic distinction between a state of nature on the one hand and the law of nature on the other can lead to false interpretations of Kant. Because he assumes that the origins of man can be traced back to a state of nature it is tempting to argue that he has a realist conception of man and an affinity with Hobbes. Nothing could be further from the truth.

Although both theorists begin their interpretation of the origins of man with a skeptical image, the fact is that Hobbes can imagine a state of peace only once man has turned over his rights to a Leviathan, whereas Kant argues that man has the potential (although in a long evolutionary process) to assume these rights and to establish a state of peace based on liberal principles of law, nationally and internationally. Ultimately, therefore, Kant's image of the nature of man is optimistic. Optimism is one of the hallmarks of his political philosophy, and it is buttressed by his distinction between Pure Reason and Practical Reason, and by his strong (religious) belief in Providence.[119] Kant's philosophy of the lives of men and of states is certainly not a tragic or pessimistic one. However, he is not as optimistic as Norman Angell who, as will be shown, has an exceedingly compelling notion of theory and of progress. Kant did not underestimate man's ability to resist the logic of liberal rationality and consequently conceived of slow and evolutionary change.

HOBSON: SOCIAL DEMOCRACY

Two facts are commonly known about Hobson's *Imperialism: A Study*[120] – that it represents an important contribution to the modern discussion of imperialism and that it had a direct influence on Lenin.[121] It is therefore often assumed that Hobson was a Marxist and an anti-imperialist. Only the second part of this assumption is true – Hobson was indeed an outspoken anti-imperialist, but he was no Marxist, not even a dogmatic socialist. As Philip Siegelman points out, he never advocated the abolition of capitalism.[122] Hobson favored an interdependent world and functioning markets but, and this is where he parted company with many liberals at that time, functioning markets had to be compatible with democracy and social justice.

Hobson was an early social democrat who occupied a difficult position between British imperialists, liberals, and Marxists. The imperialists to him were élitist and authoritarian, the liberals overly wed to *laissez-faire*, and the Marxists too doctrinaire about abolishing the private means of production. Hobson went his own way, and in doing so was ahead of his times: his ideas (in part) anticipate those of Keynes and what today is sometimes referred to as demand-side economics. Whatever the validity of Hobson's economic reasoning, and some of it is contested, it is his overall treatment of imperialism and the proposed remedies that are of continuing interest.[123] Finally, Hobson's book is rewarding to read because it is a comprehensive critique of imperialism as propounded and practiced at that time. He criticizes a hierarchic realist worldview and proposes a transformation theory grounded in anarchic idealism.

Hobson's study has two parts, one discussing "The Economics of Imperialism," the other dealing with "The Politics of Imperialism." In the first part, he explains the nature and cause of modern imperialism; in the second, he deals with various other aspects of imperialism, loosely labeled as "politics." The first part is generally considered to be the core of the book but there are some interesting portions in the second part as well.

In the introductory chapter Hobson distinguishes between genuine and perverted nationalism. Genuine nationalism is peaceful and goes hand in hand with internationalism; perverted nationalism is aggressive and ends in imperialism. The old nationalism of the early nineteenth century was peaceful, the new nationalism of the latter part of the century is aggressive. In the older nationalism

> there was no inherent antagonism to prevent nationalities from growing and thriving side by side...and the politicians of Free Trade had some foundation for their dream of a quick growth of effective, informal internationalism by peaceful, profitable intercommunication of goods and ideas among nations recognizing a just harmony of interests in free peoples. The overflow of nationalism into imperial channels quenched all such hopes.[124]

Hobson's wish is to find a way back to genuine nationalism and to true internationalism, but imperialism obstructs the path. He sets out, first, to describe imperialism and then to analyze it. He hopes that by finding its true causes he can recommend reforms that take nations back to true internationalism and peaceful coexistence.

On the basis of trade figures, Hobson depicts three important characteristics of British imperialism. First, foreign trade constitutes a small and diminishing part of overall industry and trade, of what we call the GNP today. Second, external trade with British possessions has diminished relative to external trade with such important nations as France, Germany, Russia, and the United States. Third, of British imperial trade with (1) self-governing colonies (Australia, Canada, etc.), with (2) India and with (3) "other possessions" (Africa, West Indies), that with the last group is "the smallest, least progressive, and most fluctuating in quantity, while it is the lowest in the character of the goods which it embraces."[125] Yet it is exactly in these "other possessions" that British imperialism has recently been most expansive. What accounts for this "new imperialism?" Given these figures, it makes no sense to argue that it results from trade. Some other force must be at work, someone else must profit – and Hobson argues that it is the investing class:

> To a larger extent every year Great Britain has been becoming a nation living upon tribute from abroad, and the classes who enjoy this tribute have had an ever increasing incentive to employ the public policy, the public purse, and the public force to extend the field of their private investments. This is, perhaps, the most important fact in modern politics, and the obscurity in which it is wrapped has constituted the gravest danger to the State.[126]

The reason private investment flows abroad so abundantly is that at home there is overproduction tied to underconsumption: "It is admitted by all businessmen that the growth of the powers of production in their country exceeds the growth in consumption."[127] Hobson calls this "the taproot of Imperialism": "It is evident that the consuming power, which, if exercised, would keep tense the reins of production, is in part withheld, or in other words is 'saved' and stored up for investment."[128] It is not industrial progress that demands the opening up of new markets in the tropical regions but a maldistribution of consumptive power: it prevents the absorption of commodities and of capital at home.[129]

Hobson has found the cause and proceeds to outline the cure: if maldistribution of consumptive power is the taproot, then redistribution is the remedy. He suggests that the excessive income of the few be diverted into the hands of the many, "either to the workers in higher wages, or to the community in taxes, so that it will be spent instead of being saved, serving in either of these ways to swell the tide of consumption."[130] There will then no longer be a need for "pushful imperialism," and the cause of social reform has won a great victory.[131]

The mechanisms of social reform are trade unionism and what Hobson calls state socialism. Unions want to redistribute income at the working-place through wages, pensions, and insurance, while state socialism wants to promote the general welfare via taxes and the exchequer.[132] Hobson is convinced that redistribution would stimulate domestic consumption "because every working-class family is subject to powerful stimuli of economic needs."[133]

In the second part of his study Hobson turns to the "political" or more general aspects of imperialism, to militarism, government, psychology, science, and society. In the first chapter he demonstrates that imperialism is closely tied to militarism and that both are the mortal enemies of economics, of democracy and of peace. Militarism is ruinous for the economy because it brings "a great and limitless increase of expenditure of national resources upon armaments."[134] It is the foe of democracy because the administrative institutions of imperial government "are not, and cannot be, controlled directly or effectively by the will of the people."[135] The subordination of the legislative branch to the executive and the concentration of executive power in an autocracy "are necessary consequences of the predominance of foreign over domestic politics."[136]

Besides corrupting politics imperialism warps the minds of people. In separate chapters he investigates the malicious effect Social Darwinism has and the tendency of some scholars to employ it in a "scientific" defense of imperialism,[137] shows how "moral and sentimental factors" are tied up with imperialism when the churches get involved,[138] and points out the nefarious impact of imperialism upon racism.[139] He also adds two chapters on the British Empire. One is about imperialism in Asia and the other deals with the question of whether an Imperial Federation (Commonwealth) could be formed.[140]

In the concluding chapter of his study Hobson returns to the opening theme, to the hope that genuine nationalism will lead to peaceful internationalism. He conceives of a functionalist world characterized by interdependence and regimes:

> The genuine forces of internationalism, thus liberated, would first display themselves as economic forces, securing more effective international cooperation for postal, telegraphic, railway, and other transport services, for monetary exchange and for common standards of measurement of various kinds, and for the improved intercommunication of persons, goods, and information. Related and subsidiary to these purposes would come a growth of machinery of courts and congresses, at first informal and private, but gradually taking shape in more definite and more public machinery.[141]

Other paths to internationalism Hobson rejects. He is against a possible Anglo-Saxon alliance or a pan-Teutonic empire: "The economic bond is far stronger and more reliable as a basis of growing internationalism than the so-called racial bond or a political alliance constructed on some short-sighted computation of a balance of power."[142] Hobson rejects alliances as a foundation for peace.

He also rejects the idea of an all-European alliance embracing the great powers of Europe. It would constitute "a gigantic peril of a Western parasitism, a group of advanced industrial nations, whose upper classes drew vast tribute from Asia and Africa."[143] The scheme reminds Hobson more of the imperialism of Rome than of a truly internationalist world built upon democratic nations.

Let me now turn to a systematic analysis of Hobson's theory and begin with a formal point. More than any of the theories dealt with so far, this one exhibits two fully developed components, an analytical and a prescriptive one. Hobson provides a very specific description, analysis and critique of imperialism but, and this is often overlooked, he develops an equally specific prescription of how it should be changed. His theory is strongly action-oriented and contains direct recommendations for policy and for reform. It is a fully developed transformation theory.

Furthermore, the two components of the theory belong to separate logics: the analytical component rests on a hierarchic realist worldview, the prescriptive component on an anarchic idealist worldview. None of the theories discussed until now contains two so sharply separated logics. The division is typical of many idealist theorists and particularly of critics of imperialism. Lenin, Galtung, Senghaas, and Wallerstein come to mind.[144]

At first sight Hobson's theory is economic – the taproot of imperialism is said to reside in oversaving and underconsumption. At heart, however, it is political because the distortion between savings and consumption is produced by politics, by the undemocratic, conservative and oligarchical nature of British politics. If Britain were truly democratic and if Labour and the unions were in power the distortion would vanish, and so would imperialism. The result would be social peace at home and international peace abroad. The following passage is ample evidence of this:

> Just in proportion as the substitution of true national governments for the existing oligarchies or sham democracies becomes possible will the apparent conflicts of national interests disappear, and the fundamental cooperation upon which nineteenth-century Free Trade prematurely relied manifest itself. The present class government means the severance or antagonism of nations, because each ruling class can only keep and use its rule by forcing the antagonisms of foreign policy: intelligent democracies would perceive their identity of interest, and would ensure it by their amicable policy.[145]

Put differently, both the analytical and the prescriptive sides of Hobson's theory rest on a specific definition of nation. The analytical side is characterized by conservative nations and the prescriptive side by social democratic nations; conservative nations are identified with social injustice and war, social democratic nations with social justice and peace. Both definitions are contextual, both allow endogenous understanding. The generalizations permit Hobson to construct a perfectly coherent transformation theory.

In its prescriptive component the theory adheres to an optimistic conception of man. This becomes apparent in the realm of economics and of politics. Once the British economy is properly structured the average producer and consumer are capable of rational behavior, of maximizing utility. Hobson is not opposed to markets, he is merely opposed to unrestrained *laissez-faire*. And if the politics of Great Britain is no longer dominated by the conservative, mercantile and imperial classes the common man, by virtue of his representation in Parliament, has a healthy influence on politics. Through the Labour Party and through trade unions the individual can express his will and influence British politics.

A more democratic Great Britain guided by a truly representative Parliament will conduct a peaceful foreign policy. The primacy of domestic politics restricts the influence of imperialist and militarist circles who claim that foreign policy has its own logic and must be in the hands of a strong executive independent of Parliament. More democracy weakens oligarchy and thereby eliminates the central cause of war. More democracy converts perverted and aggressive nationalism back to genuine and peaceful nationalism, to cosmopolitanism.

Hobson's state expresses the wishes of the working man, it is a means to fulfilling human ends, a whole serving the interests of the laboring parts. It is not allowed to become an end in itself, a power for its own sake. It is an institution which helps man overcome his imperfections and assists him in reducing barriers of all types: commercial protectionism, nationalistic stereotypes, racial prejudices and cultural misconceptions.

If Britain takes the lead and others follow, the result is a state system in which peace is normal and natural. Social democratic states guarantee justice and have no serious security problem; they manage to overcome zero-sum reasoning and the suboptimal outcomes typical of the Prisoners' Dilemma. Among social democratic states there is a convergence of national interests or, in Hobson's own words, there is genuine nationalism that produces cosmopolitan internationalism. The nature of the parts is identical with the nature of the whole.

Theorists on both the left and the right questioned Hobson's ideas. Imperialists argued that he underestimated the inherently conflictual nature of international anarchy and that he had an overly favorable image of the nature of man and of his ability to build peaceful societies and states. Marxists attacked Hobson from a socioeconomic angle: where the ownership of the means of production rests in private hands no peace is possible, either among men or among nations. Conflict is natural in a capitalist society and only a complete restructuring, a complete change in the ownership of the means of production, will bring peace and well-being.

To Hobson the Leninist dogma was unacceptable because it rests on a skeptical view of man and an optimistic view of élites. Lenin assumes that an avant-garde of the proletariat (a conspiratorial party) equipped with perfect knowledge will lead the masses to communism. In the final phase of the process, in Utopia, man will be free, and so Marxism ends with a favorable image of the nature of man, but at what price? If men have first to be conceived of as manipulable masses (and treated accordingly) so that ultimately they can be seen as true human beings then the cost is too high for an idealist like Hobson. Lenin's mixture of operational realism and residual idealism does not appeal to him. There is no room in Marxism–Leninism for a democratic route to freedom and peace. On the contrary, for Hobson the doctrine paves the way for a new type of imperialism.

Compared to Marx Hobson is also less deterministic. Marx's conception is founded on a strongly compelling law of society whereas Hobson's conception is more voluntaristic. The Marxist law implies the inevitable triumph of communism, yet there is no inevitability in Hobson. To be sure, Hobson's logic is also "compelling" but much less so than that of Marx. Hobson is a reformer, Marx is a revolutionary, and the difference between the two rests ultimately in a different conception of theory and of science.

ANGELL: INTERDEPENDENCE

Norman Angell lived to be over 90 (1872–1967), witnessed important changes in international relations and wrote a great deal. Small wonder that he proposed more than one theory. Before the outbreak of World War I he argued that economic interdependence alone made war among industrialized nations impossible, but later on he felt that more was needed, that anarchy had to be overcome by international organizations. Norman Angell ultimately became an ardent advocate of collective security and of the League of Nations.[146] But he did not start out that way.

His fame rests on a book entitled *The Great Illusion*,[147] published in 1911. It was an instant success and was translated into over a dozen different languages. Before the appearance of this study Norman Angell was a little-known journalist, afterward he became an important (and controversial) expert on peace and war. The central tenet of the book is economic: national improvement among industrialized states can no longer be promoted by conquest. The belief that it can is a great illusion, or, as the title of the German translation implies, an erroneous calculation.[148] With this argumentation Angell challenged imperialists at home and abroad who still argued that wars of conquest helped to promote national wealth.

The book has two major parts. In each Angell deals with an argument commonly advanced to explain war: first, that wars are fought for economic advantage and, second, that they are caused by the unchangeable and evil nature of man. He deals in detail with both points, but most commentators focus on the first while neglecting the second.

In the introductory chapter he discusses a fear common at the time – that the arms race raging between Germany and England will inevitably lead to war unless there is disarmament. Angell rejects both options: he does not believe that war is inevitable and sees no need for disarmament. Pacifists call for disarmament and their appeal is moral; Angell appeals to self-interest.[149] His preferred audience is not the churches or the many peace societies existing at that time but the business community in general and the financiers of the City of London in particular.

In the first substantive chapter, Angell shows that one of the unquestioned axioms of modern statecraft rests on the conviction that national wealth and prosperity are related to political power and can be increased by war. The belief is widely held in Germany and in England, not among liberal businessmen but in nationalist–imperialist circles and, unfortunately, among a large section of the general public. Angell cites the example of a certain Mr. Frederic Harrison who expressed such ideas in a letter to *The Times* of London. Angell's argumentation is in part a rejoinder to Mr. Harrison's letter. The following seven points are an example:

1. An extent of devastation, even approximating to that which Mr. Harrison foreshadows as a result of the conquest of Great Britain by another nation is a physical impossibility. No nation can in our day by military conquest permanently or for any considerable period destroy or greatly damage the trade of another, since trade depends upon the existence of natural wealth and a population capable of working it...

2. If an invasion by Germany did involve, as Mr. Harrison and those who think with him say it would, the "total collapse of the Empire..." German capital would, because of the internationalization and delicate interdependence of our credit-built finance and industry, also disappear in large part, and German credit also collapse, and the only means of restoring it would be for Germany to put an end to the chaos in England by putting an end to the condition which had produced it...

3. For allied reasons in our day the exaction of tribute from a conquered people has become an economic impossibility...

4. Damage to even an infinitely less degree than that foreshadowed by Mr. Harrison could only be inflicted by an invader as a means of punishment costly to himself...

5. For the reasons of a like nature to the foregoing it is a physical and economic impossibility to capture the external or carrying trade of another nation by military conquest...

6. The wealth, prosperity, and well-being of a nation depend in no way upon its political power...The populations of States like Switzerland, Holland, Belgium, Denmark, Sweden are in every way as prosperous as the citizens of States like Germany etc. ...

7. No nation could gain any advantage by the conquest of the British colonies, and Great Britain could not suffer material damage by their loss.[150]

Angell sums up the seven points by arguing that today a conqueror can no longer carry wealth away but has to leave it "in the complete possession of the individuals inhabiting the territory."[151] By invading the territory, he unsettles the economic conditions of a people which not only prevents him from making a gain but will guarantee a loss. The Romans may have enriched themselves by conquest, the British and the Germans no longer can: "The cause of this profound change, largely the work of the last thirty years, is due mainly to the complex financial interdependence of the capitals of the world."[152]

Angell illustrates how the occupation of London would affect the international financial markets:

> The first effect, of course, would be that, as the Bank of England is the banker of all other banks, there would be a run on every bank in England, and all would suspend payment. But, simultaneously, German bankers, many with credit in London, would feel the effect; merchants the world over threatened with ruin by the effect of the collapse in London immediately call in all their credits in Germany, and German finance would present a condition of chaos hardly less terrible than that in England.[153]

The effects on Germany would be so disastrous that the influence of the entire German financial community would be brought to bear on the German government, which would be forced to occupy England without harming private property and bank reserves.[154] Conquest, as Angell demonstrates, is not only self-defeating, it is pointless.

Angell also argues that reparation payments have become futile. Although in 1870 Prussia did exact indemnities from France over the conquest of

Alsace–Lorraine, the situation today is very different: "German trade in 1870 was not in any way dependent upon French money – dependent, that is, upon being able to secure French credit."[155] Today Germany is dependent on British credit, and that source would be eliminated by conquest.

The situation is no different when it comes to conquering British colonies. These are no longer a source of tribute or economic profit but constitute a heavy economic burden. Through conquest Britain would gain while Germany would lose. The loss of the North American colonies was a case in point. Before independence Britain paid for their security, after independence it acquired profitable trading partners.

Angell then turns to the nature of man. He devotes four chapters to the question, each dealing with one of the following arguments:

1. That the alleged unchangeability of human nature is not a fact, and all the evidence is against it...;
2. That the warlike nations do not inherit the earth;
3. That physical force is a constantly diminishing factor in human affairs; that this involves profound psychological modifications; and
4. That the increasing factor is co-operation, and that this factor tends to attenuate state divisions which in no way represent the limits of that co-operation.[156]

For Norman Angell human nature has improved greatly in the course of history. To emphasize his point he draws vivid pictures of this change: Palaeolithic man "ate the bodies of his enemies and of his own children," but who would expect a London city clerk "to brain his mother and serve her up for dinner?"[157] Angell is optimistic; in his estimation man has become more civilized, and especially through "the forces of mechanical and social development" man's pugnacity has been transformed from wasteful and destructive ends to efficient and constructive purposes.[158]

> How can modern life, with its overpowering proportions of industrial activities and its infinitesimal proportion of military, keep alive the instincts associated with war as against those developed by peace?[159]

Given such progress it is not surprising that, contrary to common argument, the peaceful, not the martial, nations "inherit the earth." Angell conducts a survey of the most bellicose countries in America, in Europe and in North Africa and concludes that they are also the least prosperous and the least civilized ones. Typical cases are Venezuela and Nicaragua for the Western Hemisphere, and Morocco, Montenegro, Armenia, Albania, and Arabia for the Eastern Hemisphere. At the opposite end of the list are the United States and Great Britain, together with such countries as Holland,

Belgium, Denmark, Norway, and Sweden.[160] Germany is part of this prosperous and peaceful group!

Angell goes on to demonstrate that physical force is a diminishing factor in human history. He admits that even in the most advanced nations physical force is present in the existence of police forces, but the context is a completely different one: "Force employed to secure more complete co-operation between the parts makes for advance; force which runs counter to such co-operation...makes for retrogression."[161] In the process of modernization the use of physical force is substituted by the use of mental force. The same applies to the accumulation of wealth:

> The wealth of the world is not represented by a fixed amount of gold or money now in the possession of one power, and now in the possession of another, but depends on all the unchecked multiple activities of a community for the time being.[162]

This is a traditional liberal argument against mercantilism. That theory starts from the assumption that the total wealth of mankind consists of a limited amount of resources and that nations, in order to increase their wealth, have to conquer part of it. Liberals reject this argumentation. They maintain that the wealth of nations is unlimited (and growing) if only states decide to cooperate based on relative advantage and the most efficient allocation of resources. Economic activity need not be a zero-sum game. If labor is divided and goods are exchanged then economic activity is a nonzero-sum proposition.

At the end of his study Angell, once more, rejects pacifism; the problem with war is not armaments, the problem is false economic reasoning. As long as major nations believe that conquest will bring material advantage there is a need to arm, even for those who would prefer not to: "On this ground alone I deem that we or any other nation are justified in taking means of self-defense to prevent such aggression. This is not, therefore, a plea for disarmament irrespective of the action of other nations."[163] When war broke out in 1914, Norman Angell stuck by his convictions and supported the British cause. Still, he was traumatized by the event because he was truly convinced that war would never come.[164]

Norman Angell was an early proponent of the cobweb paradigm and of the theory of interdependence. He realized that with the advent of the Industrial Revolution national independence had become an anachronism, and he was particularly impressed by the interdependence of financial markets. The City of London had become the hub of a worldwide, complicated and extremely vulnerable net of financial transactions. Financial markets, however, were but a manifestation of forces that lay deeper, of science, technology and economics – the so-called "forces of modernity." These, for Angell, were the true driving forces of history.

In Angell's estimation the Industrial Revolution has a dual impact on international relations: on the one hand it makes war more devastating, on the other it makes it less profitable. War is more devastating because entire nations are now equipped with the most modern means of destruction, but war is also less profitable because industrial development and interdependence make countries extremely vulnerable. Norman Angell is one of the first theorists to develop the vulnerability thesis.[165]

Interdependence and vulnerability weaken the traditional nation-state, they undermine sovereignty. Subnational actors are taking the place of national actors; banks, stock-markets, trading and shipping companies are becoming as important as foreign and defense ministries; the private sector is starting to encroach upon the public sector. In this sense Norman Angell is one of the first to go "beyond the nation-state," to deal with the obsolescence of the nation-state. Angell develops a transformation theory of international relations but, and this is very important, it does not (yet) carry him "beyond anarchy." Norman Angell is not a theorist of integration and of supranationality; if anything, his Great Illusion is a theory of subnationality.[166] His worldview is idealist and truly anarchic. He conceives of the international system as a complex and pluralistic entity where various types of actors coexist. Their interests converge peacefully and central management is unnecessary because the system is robust and largely self-steering.

Angell is not very specific about the exact nature of the new international system, and in this respect his theory is not fully developed. Modern theorists of interdependence are more specific about structures and processes, actors and functions.[167] Still, he alludes to a new definition of wholes and parts, ends and means, systems and functions. There is a new rationality among nations, and the definition of nation is contextually consistent. Traditional definitions of sovereignty and independence are being challenged. This is a new theme in the theory of international relations. Neither Kant nor Hobson go beyond the nation-state; both regard states as central actors. Kant believes in "peace through republican states," Hobson in "peace through social-democratic states." For both the driving force of international relations is political, it rests on the governmental structure of nations. For Angell the driving force inheres in science, technology and economics. The dissolution of traditional international relations is beginning to take place.

However, for Norman Angell the forces of modernity cannot be separated from the nature of man. After all, in the final analysis man himself is the source of science, of technology and of economics. The root of interdependence and peace, therefore, is man. Norman Angell has an exceedingly optimistic conception of man, and it penetrates and conditions his entire theory. The conception provides the theory with a strongly compelling logic and enables Angell to declare war an "impossibility." Expressed in Waltz's categories, Angell is a radical and optimistic first-image thinker, a theorist who believes that both the cause and the remedy of war lie primarily in man. The nature of states and of the state system, the second and the third images respectively, are of secondary importance.

This makes the theory so neat – and so utopian. When war broke out in 1914 Norman Angell began to realize that he had overestimated the positive development of man, of science, technology, and economics; and he also began to realize that he had underestimated the third image, the fragile nature of anarchy. As a result, Norman Angell took a step "beyond anarchy" and called for the establishment of a universal international organization. He looked to America for the creation of such a body. As early as 1915 he published a book entitled *America and the New World-State: A Plan for American Leadership in International Organization*.[168] He became a strong supporter of Wilson's plans for collective security, and there is evidence that Wilson was influenced by his publication.

With this step Norman Angell departed from his earlier views. He was still an idealist but no longer a purely anarchic one. From now on his ideas had a slightly hierarchic bent. He rejected the thought that interdependence alone would lead to peace and began to argue that some kind of organized collectivity was needed. It was a major step in the evolution of his thinking about war and peace, but for realists like E. H. Carr, one of his staunchest critics, he was still a hopeless utopian.[169]

Norman Angell's theory was premature. In 1911 Europe was not as interdependent as it is today, and Europeans had to go through another ordeal before they learned that war did not pay. They should have listened to Norman Angell. Had they done so the Versailles Treaty would not have contained such massive and punitive reparations. Already in 1919 Europe was too interdependent for such measures, and no lesser figure than John Maynard Keynes said so at that time.[170] But his words, too, were largely spoken in vain – and the consequences were once more tragic. Finally, after another terrible war, Jean Monnet and Robert Schumann picked up the same theme – and finally Europe listened.[171]

WILSON: COLLECTIVE SECURITY

Woodrow Wilson never wrote a treatise on collective security; there is no one coherent text to refer to.[172] Wilson was a statesman, a man of action, but he was also an academic, a professor of government whose addresses were often more like university lectures than political speeches. Wilson had a gift of expressing himself clearly, of putting profound philosophical ideas into words that everyone could understand. He was extremely explicit about his fundamental values, so much so that many of his opponents disliked him for exactly that. For the analyst of international relations the lucid and systematic language of Wilson is a great advantage; one is not forced to read between the lines.

Wilson's greatest contribution to international relations (besides helping to win the war against Germany) was the founding of the League of Nations, the first universal international organization dealing with security issues. Whatever his performance as a diplomat in Paris, and some of it is open to criticism,[173] he unquestionably made a great effort to set up the new organization and strongly identified with it. In practical and in theoretical terms Wilson made a lasting contribution to move the international system "beyond anarchy."

While it is true that the League of Nations had many different origins, Wilson's contribution was considerable and the organization can hardly be separated from his own conception of politics and of international relations. As an academic, Wilson developed a systematic body of knowledge, a personal worldview which later on guided him both in domestic and in foreign affairs. Wilson knew the workings of American government in theory and in practice and, as I will show, applied some of that knowledge to international politics and to the League. To understand Wilson's conception of collective security, therefore, it is vital to first investigate his conception of domestic politics.

Wilson developed an early interest in public affairs. Already as a professor he spoke out on public issues, and in 1902, when he became President of Princeton University, he began to address issues of national importance. This carried him into public office: from 1910 to 1912 he was Governor of New Jersey, and in 1912 he was elected President of the United States.[174]

As Governor and as President, Wilson was identified with the Era of Progressivism, a period in American history when some of the excesses of rapid industrialization were corrected. Economic power had become concentrated in the hands of a relatively limited number of large corporations (or trusts) which used it to influence politics through the Republican Party. Democrats like Wilson fought this concentration of economic and political power, they demanded economic and political reforms.

As President, Wilson promulgated the New Freedom, a program that called for social legislation but also for a reduction of import tariffs protecting big corporations and for the creation of the Federal Reserve Bank to loosen the corporations' grip on credit and banks. In the initial years of his presidency, Wilson obtained legislation in all these areas. His first term was a success for Progressivism.

Wilson's commitment to these bills was very personal, which showed in the speeches he gave: they reveal aspects of his philosophy of politics that are important to understand his conception of government and, later on, his views on diplomacy and international organization. The ideas emerge lucidly from Wilson's defense of antiprotectionist legislation.

The tariff question had been on Wilson's agenda for some time. As Governor of New Jersey, Wilson spoke out forcefully in favor of tariff reductions. He argued that high tariffs protected the very groups of society (large companies and monopolies) that needed no protection and hurt those (like the average consumer) that needed it most. High tariffs meant relief for the rich and taxation for the poor. But what angered the professor of government equally were the politics of protectionism – the lobbying of the various "interests" in Congress:

> The methods by which tariff bills are constructed have now become all too familiar and throw a significant light on the character of the legislation involved. Debate in the Houses has little or nothing to do with it. The process by which such a bill is made is private, not public; because the reasons which underlie many of the rates imposed are private... What takes place in the committees and in the conference is confidential...The debates which the country is invited to hear in the open sessions of the Houses are merely formal. They determine nothing and disclose very little. It is this policy of silence and secrecy...that makes it absolutely inconsistent with every standard of public duty and political integrity.[175]

Policy-making was dominated by only a few of the elected representatives, and it was closed instead of open. The same was true of nominations for public office: they were characterized by patronage[176] and by machine politics.[177] Small wonder that the private interest prevailed over the public interest. The political system needed reforming and democratizing. America used to have real democracy and healthy competition but it now suffered from the the "spirit of monopoly:"

> It is a very different America from the old. All the recent scandals of our business history have sprung out of the discovery of the use those who directed these great combinations were making of their power: their power to crush, their power to monopolize. Their competition has not stimulated, it has destroyed.[178]

Wilson envisioned a return to true competition or, as he preferred to say, he wanted to "set the people free." When he signed a new tariff bill in October 1913, he declared that this was the first step "in setting the business of this country free."[179] A second step followed in November 1914 when the Federal Reserve banks opened for business. He then wrote his Secretary of the Treasury that "credit had been set free."[180] Wilson meant to restore a healthy, competitive spirit in economics as well as in politics. The country needed a functioning market, pluralism, and transparency in politics.

Wilson did not care for interest groups. Personally, he disliked the atmosphere of smoke-filled conference rooms in which the typical wheeling and dealing took place. And philosophically, he believed that intermediary groups did not contribute to the public good. He rejected *laissez-faire* pluralism and the notion that large numbers of private interest groups balance each other and thereby contribute to the public interest. For Wilson interest groups were selfish, and the sum total of selfish interests he considered incompatible with the true public interest. To balance the nefarious influence of interest groups, democracy needed enlightened leadership – and he saw himself as capable of it. Wilson believed strongly that he was unselfish and disinterested, that, as he once declared, he was able to look at things from "outside the interests."[181]

He said so publicly on various occasions. In June 1916, for instance, he addressed the Associated Advertising Clubs, a public-relations interest group. Wilson did not say much about advertising but had a great deal to say about his personal public philosophy: "I am not interested, and I beg that you will believe me when I say that I never have been interested, in fighting for myself, but I am immensely interested in fighting for the things I believe in."[182]

Wilson was obviously "lecturing" the audience, and the message was clear: there is a distinction between interested politics and disinterested leadership, between lobbyism and true service to the country. Wilson labored the point further when, in the same speech, he presented the three principles of his personal philosophy of politics:

> In the first place, I believe, and I summon you to show your belief in the same thing, that it is the duty of every American in everything that he does, in his business and out of it, to think first not of himself or of any interest which he may be called upon to sacrifice, but of the country which we serve...I believe, in the second place, that America, the country that we put first in our thoughts, should be ready in every point of policy and of action, to vindicate at whatever cost the principles of liberty, of justice, and of humanity...Then, in the third place, touching ourselves

more intimately, my fellow citizens, this is what I believe: If I understand the life of America, the central principle of it is this, that no small body of persons, no matter how influential, shall be trusted to determine the policy and development of America. The principle of the life of America is that she draws her vitality...from the great body of thinking and toiling and planning men.[183]

This is an excellent summary of his convictions: (1) service above interest, (2) liberty, justice, humanity, and (3) people over cliques. These ideas also guided Wilson in international affairs.

When America entered the war in 1917 the country was not interested in joining the existing international system, and Wilson personally was unwilling to play power politics among small groups of self-interested men intent on pursuing their private (or national) interests. Such diplomacy would once more end in nationalist quarrels, in imperialistic expansion and finally in war. It was his intention to look at the world "from outside the interests," to be a true and unselfish servant of the universal interest, a mediator and a leader keeping in touch with the common people of the world, with the opinion of mankind guided by the principles of liberty, justice, and humanity.[184]

Before taking a closer look at his ideas about a lasting peace, let me point out what Wilson rejected, what he wanted to overcome once and for all. It is summed up by the term "balance of power politics": autocratic government, secret diplomacy, entangling alliances, arms races, wars of aggression, violations of international law, punitive peace treaties, maintenance of a precarious equilibrium. Wilson wondered in one of his speeches what had started the war in Europe: "Nothing in particular started it, but everything in general...mutual suspicion...an interlacing of alliances and understandings, a complex web of intrigue and spying."[185] Or, in speaking about the proposed League of Nations:

> No autocratic government could be trusted to keep faith within it or observe its covenants. It must be a league of honor, a partnership of opinion. Intrigue would eat its vitals away; the plottings of inner circles who could plan what they would and render account to no one would be a corruption seated at its very heart.[186]

He wanted no second Congress of Vienna,[187] no punitive settlement, but only a peace without victory. A peace forced upon the loser would provide a poor foundation for a stable peace and a new international organization: "Only a tranquil Europe can be a stable Europe. There must be, not a balance of power, but a community of power; not organized rivalries, but an organized common peace."[188]

What would a community of power look like? It had to rest on the pillars of equality, independence, self-determination, and democracy. In his famous 14-Points Address of January 8, 1918, Wilson spelled out in detail what he understood by self-determination. It entailed important rearrangements in parts of Europe, changing boundaries and setting up new countries, all in accordance with the wishes of the people and nationalities concerned. Outside Europe, it included "a free, open-minded, and absolutely impartial adjustment of all colonial claims...[in which] the interest of the populations concerned must have equal weight with the equitable claims of the government whose title is to be determined."[189]

Two of Wilson's 14 Points dealt with the economic dimension of a community of power. He demanded "absolute freedom of navigation upon the seas, outside territorial waters, alike in peace and in war...[and] the removal, so far as possible, of all economic barriers and the establishment of an equality of trade conditions among all the nations consenting to the peace."[190] Wilson wanted to create a framework for free world trade. He now repeated for the world what he had earlier done for America – "setting business free."[191]

Wilson did not assume, however, that trade alone would lead to peace. He was not a radical liberal advocating "peace through free trade." A fully decentralized international system, to him, was no guarantee for peace and well-being. To attain these goals a universal international organization was necessary. The specifics were contained in the first and the last of the 14 Points:

I. Open covenants of peace, openly arrived at, after which there shall be no private international understandings of any kind but diplomacy shall proceed always frankly and in the public view.

XIV. A general association of nations must be formed under specific covenants for the purpose of affording mutual guarantees of political independence and territorial integrity to great and small states alike.[192]

Democratic nations had to form the nucleus of such an organization: "A steadfast concert of peace can never be maintained except by a partnership of democratic nations."[193] America, the greatest democracy of all, was expected to assume the leading role. It fought the war "to make the world safe for democracy"[194] and within the League it would enter into a general alliance (and not an entangling one) to guarantee the peace.[195]

Diplomacy would be taken out of the hands of small groups of self-interested statesmen; it would no longer take place in dark and secret places but in the bright daylight of public conference halls. Wilson placed great emphasis on world public opinion. When talking at Paris about the future organization, he stressed the need for "the eye of nations to keep watch upon the common interest, an eye that does not slumber, an eye that is everywhere watchful and attentive."[196] And he told the gathering of select (and largely élitist) diplomats and statesmen: "Gentlemen, the select classes of mankind are no longer the governors of mankind. The fortunes of mankind are now in the hands of the plain people of the whole world."[197]

This is pure Wilson: the public good, whether national or international, cannot be entrusted to "select groups" and "interests," it must be watched carefully by the people from below and guided by unselfish leaders from above. Very much like Kant over a hundred years earlier, Wilson was convinced that an enlightened and great people would eventually lead other democratic nations to peace. He knew America was such a great nation, and he was sure that it would henceforth play a leading role in world affairs.

He was also convinced of the values America stood for: "We are the trustees for what I venture to say is the greatest heritage that any nation ever had, the love of justice and righteousness and human liberty."[198] Furthermore, that heritage was multiethnic, and America can consequently think and speak for all:

We are compounded of the nations of the world; we mediate their blood, we mediate their traditions, we mediate their sentiments, their tastes, their passions; we are ourselves compounded of those things. We are, therefore, able to understand all nations; we are able to understand them in the compound, not separately, as partisans, but unitedly as knowing and comprehending and embodying them all. It is in that sense that I mean that America is a mediating Nation.[199]

Wilson used these words in 1915 when, as a neutral, America offered to mediate between the belligerents. But the words acquired more meaning yet once America became the leader of the peace and of the prospective League of Nations. Here was the country that could understand all nations and was by definition impartial, unselfish and just. It was the country capable of looking at world affairs "from outside the interests."

What was true of America was true of its leader, of Wilson – he was also free of bias. As he told the Senate in January 1917, three months before declaring war on Germany: "Perhaps I am the only person in high authority amongst all the peoples of the world who is at liberty to speak and hold nothing back."[200]

With this perspective of himself, of America and of the world, Wilson went to Europe, and the masses were excited about the enlightened leader from the New World. But in the smoke-filled negotiating chambers of Paris, Wilson felt ill at ease and his performance was uneven. Europe was not ready for the farsighted idealist from overseas.

Wilson failed, and to this very day few theorists of international relations want to be known as Wilsonians. A theorist may embrace liberal values and he may even study collective security – still, he would most probably not want to be identified with the former president. It is fashionable to be neo-liberal but it is quite unfashionable to be neo-Wilsonian. There are many reasons for this rejection, but maybe it was Wilson's explicit moralism that makes modern theorists feel especially ill at ease. Wilson was very explicit about his basic values, and some would argue that it was the Calvinist theologian in him that made him such a crusading missionary.[201] Today's theorists of international relations have abandoned the crusading spirit but, unfortunately, they have also abandoned explicitness about basic values and assumptions. On this score, Wilson is a shining example.

His conception of man is clear for everyone to see – it is very optimistic. Man is capable of rational behavior and, given the proper institutional context, justice, well-being and peace are attainable. His conception of society and of government is evident, too. True and uncorrupted government is possible if special-interest groups are restrained. Good government can guarantee conditions for the proper functioning of markets in a pluralistic society. The result is justice and well-being for all. The parallel with Hobson is evident. Wilson is not a European socialist; but progressivist Democrats in America are relatively close to European social democrats.

As a true liberal, Wilson sees no basic distinction between domestic and foreign politics, between the standards applying to individuals and to nations. It is obvious to him that "nations must in the future be governed by the same high code of honor that we demand of individuals."[202] The primacy of domestic policy prevails but, in contrast to Kant, Hobson and Angell, Wilson draws a stricter analogy between the two realms: if the rule of law needs to be backed up by organized power at the domestic level then the same must happen at the international level. Wilson is willing to transcend anarchic idealism; his internationalism has a hierarchic dimension.

This throws light on his conception of the state system. For Wilson, there is no automatic and spontaneous order in anarchy; self-help leads to war. The whole, the international system, if it is to remain peaceful, cannot be identical with the parts, it must be more than the mere sum of its parts. There is a universal interest standing above all particular or national interests. The interest is identical with that of humanity, with the basic rights of man. For it to prevail, it must be enforced against occasional violators. The universal interest is the end, the League of Nations the means. Wars fought for the national interest narrowly perceived are no longer normal, natural, and rational. Within the new international order rational and natural wars must be fought for the universal interests of mankind. The result is a new definition of nation and of sovereignty, a definition conditioned by universal standards of morality.

For such standards to prevail, selfless and enlightened leadership is necessary. Wilson believed in the necessity of such leadership at the national and the international level. He thought that America was predestined to assume such a role and that he personally was particularly capable of disinterested leadership.

Wilson, unlike Angell, did not believe that political change occurred spontaneously, by the quiet spread of reason. He was convinced that leadership was necessary. To be sure, Wilson believed in the compelling nature of the liberal logic but he also knew of the human potential for unreason and for resisting enlightened rationality. He knew that the world had a security problem and was ready to transcend anarchy. At the very least, there had to be a forum to discuss questions of war and peace and, if the need arose, to organize for the defense of peace collectively. The League of Nations was a first step in this direction.

Compared to the United Nations, the League was a modest body. There was no institution comparable to the Security Council where binding and authoritative decisions were made, and there were no provisions for joint enforcement mechanisms. The sovereign independence of its members was in no way restricted, there was no trace of supranationality.

The League did not create a body of truly universalistic law and failed to outlaw war. The Covenant laid no foundation for the definition of just and unjust violence, it was not based on a *bellum iustum* philosophy. From a legal standpoint war was still a possibility. The League did not satisfy those who wanted to see a truly hierarchical organization.

It was merely a mechanism to postpone war. There was much reliance on dialog, on investigating and publishing facts. Given the proper information and the necessary time, a learning process was expected to set in and rationality was expected to emerge victorious. The peoples of the world would peer over the shoulders of the assembled diplomats; world public opinion would make itself felt. Open diplomacy was meant to promote the convergence of national interests and to help overcome situations like the Prisoners' Dilemma. The League would build trust among nations by reducing psychological barriers; it was intended to remove stereotypes and misunderstandings.

Should reasoning fail because a state remains recalcitrant, the Covenant obliged nations to impose economic sanctions. Military sanctions were voluntary, and the hope was that ultimately a majority of states would stand for the defense of peace. Only informally did the management of the international system acquire a somewhat hierarchic and majoritarian character. By any standard, the League was a modest step in the direction of democratic world institutions.

3 Contemporary Theories

WALTZ: NEO-REALISM

Realism is dominant among contemporary theoreticians of international relations, and has been so for decades. Some of the most prominent authors identify themselves as realists. Contemporary realism, however, has mostly been presented in an unsystematic manner. Hans J. Morgenthau and Stanley Hoffmann, two of the chief representatives of the school, have never developed an orderly version of realism.[1] Kenneth Waltz is different. In his *Theory of International Politics*[2] he makes a serious effort to put balance of power theory on a disciplined and modern footing. To build on a sound foundation, Waltz starts out with a full chapter on scientific method and on theory. He then tackles substantive issues and does so in an innovative spirit and with unusual rigor.

However, when applying his own conception of science to the formulation of what he considers to be a "systemic" theory of the modern balance of power, Waltz violates his methodological convictions. This weakens the effort although it still constitutes a vast improvement over past endeavors. One can only agree with John G. Ruggie that this book "is one of the most important contributions to the theory of international relations...it enhances in a fundamental manner the level of discourse in the field."[3]

As mentioned, the book begins with a chapter on theory and on scientific method. Waltz argues that theories are qualitatively different from laws. Laws express probabilistic relations between variables and can be inductively attained, but theories explain laws by making them parts of creatively constructed wholes, interconnected components of entire systems of knowledge. Waltz gives an example from physics:

> The formula for the acceleration of a freely falling body does not explain how the body falls. For the explanation one looks in classical physics to the whole Newtonian system – a package of interconnected concepts, an organization of the physical world in which the pertinent happenings become natural or necessary.[4]

Theories in the social sciences have the same inner structure as theories in the natural sciences but they rest on concepts (variables, phenomena) that are less clearly and less empirically definable. The central variables in international politics, as Waltz shows, have so many different meanings that our theories "turn out to be weak ones."[5] But they do not change the fact that theories of international relations conform to orderly patterns of wholes and parts: the whole is the international system, the parts are the actors within it.

Waltz distinguishes two different types of theories: one he calls reductionist, the other systemic or structural. Reductionist theory begins with the parts and moves to the wholes, systemic theory does the reverse; reductionist explanations rest on the inner nature of the parts, systemic explanations on the structure among the parts, the structure of the whole. Alliances, for instance, are explained by reductionist theories with reference to the nature of the states and by systemic theories with reference to the structure of the international system.[6]

Waltz regrets that in international relations so many theories are reductionist and locate the cause of war at the state or human level. Or, as he argues in his *Man, the State, and War*, too many theories adhere to the first and second image and not to the third.[7] He mentions Hobson, Lenin and Galtung as examples. Elsewhere he includes a number of other theorists, most of them idealists.[8]

Waltz goes on to argue that a theory of international politics, if it is to be truly systemic, must completely separate the systemic from the unit level or, as he puts it: "Definitions of structures must omit the attributes and the relations of the units."[9] He regrets that such separation is rare, that major figures like Richard Rosecrance, Stanley Hoffmann and Morton Kaplan fail exactly on this score. Waltz argues that reductionist approaches rely excessively on economic, psychological and sociological explanations and therefore fail to get at the essence of politics. He wants to build a theory of international relations that is truly political, essentially different and "pure."

He then constructs his personal systemic theory. When surveying the long history of international relations Waltz is struck by its constancy: "The texture of international politics remains highly constant, patterns recur, and events repeat themselves endlessly."[10] From the Peloponnesian War to the Cold War, states have come and gone, altered their internal make-up and advocated different ideologies – but the overall pattern of interaction has remained the same. At first sight, the lives of nations are varied and turbulent, but at closer scrutiny there is great regularity. What is the explanation?

As can be expected, Waltz's answer lies at the systemic level – it is the anarchic character of the international setting which accounts for the sameness. Domestic politics is hierarchically ordered, but international politics is not. In domestic politics, the arrangement of the parts conforms with the principle of super- and subordination, in international politics with that of coordination. In a hierarchical setting, security is provided for centrally; in an anarchical setting, each part must provide for its own security. States live in a state of war governed by the principle of self-help. To assure their own security and survival, states must acquire the necessary power.

Power is a means, not an end: the attainment of secure independence is the highest end.[11] One of the most common ways to multiply power and maximize security is to combine with others against a potential challenger: "Secondary states, if they are free to choose, flock to the weaker side, for it is the stronger side that threatens them."[12] Counterweights are set and a balancing mechanism begins to function – hence balance of power theory. According to Waltz, states do not seek to maximize power (as some realists claim) but merely to balance it.

The international system, besides being anarchic, also manifests crass differences in power. And, because the system is based on self-help, "the units of greatest capability set the scene of action for others as well as for themselves."[13] In other words, there are great and small powers, and the former call the tune: "A general theory of international politics is necessarily based on the great powers."[14] The essence of balance of power theory, therefore, is the balancing of power among the major states.

Traditionally, it has been assumed that a perfect functioning of the mechanism requires at least three great powers, preferably more.[15] Europe had such a multipolar system for several centuries. Many scholars therefore argue that the balancing mechanism cannot function in a tight bipolar system as it existed for some time during the Cold War. Waltz disagrees. To make his case he draws on investigations indicating that small-number systems are more stable than large-number systems, and that the stability of pairs is particularly high. In economics duopolies prove to be very stable, and Waltz concludes that "smaller is more beautiful than small." He then transfers the experience to international politics and argues that, contrary to conventional wisdom, a bipolar system is more likely to produce balance than a multipolar system.[16] The introduction of this idea into traditional balance of power theory accounts for what is called neo-realism.[17]

According to Waltz, a bipolar system is more likely to produce balance because there is less uncertainty: "In great-power politics of bipolar worlds, who is a danger to whom is never in doubt."[18] There is a lower probability of miscalculation and overreaction, two phenomena that, for instance, accounted largely for the outbreak of World War I. In the Cuban missile crisis, Kennedy and Khrushchev knew exactly whom they were dealing with – each other. That simplified matters. Furthermore, balancing becomes a matter of internal rather than external politics, it is managed by acquiring more arms rather than more allies. Bipolarity, therefore, has the additional advantage of simplifying alliance politics.

Waltz adds that "the simplicity of relations in a bipolar world and the strong pressures that are generated make the two great powers conservative."[19] Should war break out after all, always a possibility in a balance of power system, conservative great powers fight "power-balancing wars."[20] The aim of such a struggle is to keep the other great power from establishing hegemony, which produces a positive side-effect for minor states because predominance is not in their interest either. Or, as Waltz puts it, the great powers, "fighting in their own interest...produce a collective good as a by-product, which should be appreciated by states that do not want to be conquered."[21] Hegemonic wars are functional, they produce a collective good. The good is identical with the purpose of balance of power theory – the preservation of sovereign independence for all states. Of course, the collective good also represents the convergence of national self-interest.

It hardly needs emphasizing that Waltz's neo-realist theory conforms largely with the anarchic realist worldview. The fit is particularly neat because Waltz is so explicit about the cognitive nature of theory, about wholes and parts, ends and means, cause and effect. The whole is identical with the anarchic system, an order dominated by uncertainty, risk, insecurity, self-help and the constant search for survival in balance. The behavior of the parts is a function of the whole rather than of domestic concerns, hence the primacy of foreign policy. War is normal and rational, it serves a positive function by contributing to the maintenance of balance and by promoting the survival and coexistence of all units of the system. The logic also explains the unchanging nature of world politics over the ages: the regular occurrence of war, the constant shifting of alliances, the relative irrelevance of ideologies.

At a general level, Waltz's neo-realism is a definite improvement over earlier versions of balance of power theory. On closer scrutiny, however, the theory has a flaw. One of Waltz's most basic methodological assumptions is that in the construction of his own theory he has succeeded completely in separating the systemic from the reductionist level, that his is a purely systemic theory with no reductionist attributes. This cannot be.

It is impossible to separate the systemic from the reductionist level of analysis because it is impossible to separate wholes from parts, ends from means, causes from effects. As Waltz explains so lucidly in his chapter on theory, explanations are derived from the interrelation of parts and wholes. When the interrelation is removed, so is the power of explanation. There is no such thing as a pure whole or a pure part. It is a cognitive–epistemological impossibility!

Waltz's effort to define international relations without reference to the nature of nations is like defining combustion engines without reference to the nature of parts, to valves, plugs and pistons. Such a definition of engines would be "systemic" and avoid reductionism, but it would be noncontextual and exclude endogenous knowledge. An endogenous theory of engines must rest on a contextual definition of parts just like an endogenous theory of international politics must rest on a contextual definition of nations. How can Waltz hope to grasp the logic of international politics without interrelating parts and wholes, how can he expect to arrive at true understanding, how can he ever be an initiated insider?

Waltz's theory is in fact endogenous and it does interrelate parts and wholes, the nations and the system but, unfortunately, the interrelations are implicit rather than explicit. Waltz is a tacit reductionist and this has a number of unfortunate consequences. By denying the importance of parts he attributes qualities to the system that it does not possess, adopts a monistic view of causality, hides his image of the state, arrives at a simplistic definition of national self-interest and underestimates the importance of rules, particularly the rules of war. Let me deal with these points one by one.

Waltz's tacit reductionism shows when he describes the structure of the international system. By his own standards structure must be defined purely and solely with reference to the system, not with reference to the units. But he violates that instruction when he defines structure in terms of the units' capabilities, in terms of state power. In an anarchic system military and economic capabilities inhere in the units; only in a hierarchic system with a supranational actor could such capabilities lie elsewhere. An anarchic international system is in every respect subsystem-dominant; this includes capabilities. It is simply impossible to describe structure without reference to the power of the parts.

Waltz seems aware of the problem and admits that "defining structure partly in terms of the distribution of capabilities seems to violate my instructions to keep unit attributes out of structural definitions."[22] Why does it merely "seem" to be a violation? It "is" a violation, and its origins lie in the impossible attempt to formulate a purely systemic or structural theory of international politics.

By not explicitly dealing with the units, Waltz adopts a simplistic notion of causality. He argues that the cause of war lies primarily in the system, not in the parts. In a decentralized and anarchic order security can only be provided by self-help, but self-help (or armaments and national defense) increases the insecurity of all thereby producing the well-known security dilemma. The assumption that anarchy and self-help causes war is typical of third-image thinkers, but it holds true only when the parts are seen as imperfect. With perfect parts peace in anarchy is entirely conceivable.

Kant's republics coexist in anarchic peace and have no security dilemma. Waltz tacitly assumes imperfect parts.

Once imperfect parts are assumed, however, the cause of war is no longer located exclusively at the systemic level – it is shared with the units. The anarchic system (and self-help) is at best the permissive cause of war, while the units represent the efficient cause. Anarchy does not prevent war but it alone cannot cause it. Waltz attributes qualities to the system that reside at least partly in the units. It is a simplified conception of causality, a monistic or one-dimensional one. It would be more correct to say that war in an anarchic system is caused partially by the nature of the units and partially by the system itself. As Waltz himself admits in his *Man, the State, and War*, the cause of war is often explained by more than one image; image combinations are the rule.[23] His own systemic theory partakes of the second and of the third image. The lives of his nations are violent because the system does nothing to prevent war but also because the nations themselves unleash it. Waltz likes to think of himself as a third-image theorist but in reality he is also a second-image and a state-centered pessimist!

As can be expected Waltz adheres to a conservative image of the state. Given the permanent international security problem Waltz cannot possibly emphasize the virtues of an open world society, human rights and democracy. The rights of nations are more important than the rights of individuals. His theory is state-centered, not man-centered: in the relations of nations individuals play subordinate roles. Individuals are organized in collectivities, and these collectivities dominate the international scene. The harsh realities of the international state of war and the primacy of foreign policy force states to be hard rather than soft. A state may not necessarily be authoritarian, but it must at the very least have a tough outer shell. Gentz, in contrast to Waltz, is very explicit on this point. For a state-centered theorist this is important.

From a democratic and constitutional standpoint neo-realism raises a number of questions. What is the relation, for instance, between a tough outer shell and a soft inner core? How much of a voice is the public (or its representatives) allowed to have in foreign policy without interfering with the innate logic of the balance of power? What are some of the inevitable tensions between the requirements of the "state of law" on the one hand, and the "state of war" on the other? A fully developed and modern balance of power theory meant to be useful in a country like the United States should deal with these issues. Waltz avoids them because his theory is purely systemic.[24]

Obviously, Waltz pays little attention to subnational actors, to individuals, to private organizations, and to multinational corporations. He concedes that their dealings are of increasing importance in a modern world but in his judgment they do not matter in determining the issues of war and peace. Free trade and international communication do not prevent the outbreak of war, and interdependence, in the words of Waltz, is a myth.[25] More than once, Waltz ridicules "today's transnationalists and interdependers."[26] He obviously does not believe that economic and technological development promotes peace and weakens state sovereignty and independence. National interests are in the foreground, subnational interests in the background.

National self-interest also produces balance:

> States strive to maintain autonomy. To this end, the great powers of a multipolar world maneuver, combine, and occasionally fight. Some states fight wars to prevent others from achieving an imbalance of power in their favor. Out of their own interest, great powers fight power-balancing wars. Fighting in their own interest, they produce a collective good as a by-product, which should be appreciated by states that do not want to be conquered.[27]

Gentz would agree, he also believes that great powers, fighting in their national self-interest, can produce balance, but he distinguishes between true and narrow self-interest. True self-interest engenders a collective good that Gentz calls federation or community. Narrow self-interest, however, does not result in convergence, in balance or community – it entails the loss of sovereignty for some, the establishment of hegemony for others. Balance and convergence is the result of national interest broadly defined, of enlightened self-interest. Such a definition embraces some consensus between states, an agreement about rules which turns the competition into a "game of war" rather than a "state of war."

At the very least, the consensus has to include the right for all states to exist. Bernhardi shows what happens when there is no such consensus, when no such right is acknowledged. National interest narrowly defined converts competition into a Darwinist struggle for survival dominated by the law of the strongest, a struggle that leads not to balance but to the establishment of a hierarchical order. Gentz's four maxims are meant to prevent such an outcome, they represent the rules governing the balance of power "game."

The rules are necessary because, as Gentz demonstrates, states have a dualist nature. On the one hand they are capable of pursuing their true self-interest and maintaining the balance, but on the other, states are prone to undermine it by either becoming indifferent or aiming for hegemony, thus pursuing their narrow self-interest. Gentz assumes that in the long run the balancing logic (or interest) is compelling but he is quite concerned that in the short run states are capable of irrational behavior. Gentz experienced the precarious nature of the European balance and wrote his book to persuade statesmen of their true self-interest.[28] He does not assume that balance is the spontaneous and automatic product of a general self-interest or, in Waltz's terms, of "structure" and of "system."

Both Waltz and Gentz have a moderate conception of the state of war but Waltz is not explicit enough on the conditions for moderation. Moderation is the product of conservative states following conservative maxims. There is nothing wrong with structural attributes typical of duopoly and small group dynamics but these cannot be separated from the nature of states and the rules they follow. It is not merely "the simplicity of relations in a bipolar world and the strong pressures that are generated which make the great powers conservative." By neglecting this factor Waltz's theory is uncomfortably compelling, it attributes causality too lightly to structural "interests," "pressures," and "forces."

By not spelling out his own (neo-conservative) rules and maxims Waltz fails to deal in detail with an important phenomenon in balance of power theory – war. Are all types of war compatible with balance, conventional and nuclear wars? What are the rules of war? As I have shown, Clausewitz also remains unclear on this score. He intends to formulate a general theory covering all types of war: pure and practical war, abstract and real war, restricted cabinet war and unrestricted Napoleonic war, war dominated by petty policy and war dominated by grand policy. Can neo-realism afford such a general and vague conception of war? Neo-realism is meant to be relevant in the nuclear age where some kinds of war are most certainly incompatible with balance – but Waltz never addresses the point. For a meaningful reformulation of balance of power theory in our age, for a truly new realism, it is vital to come to terms with this question. Any theorist who regards war as normal must state openly what types of conflict he still considers rational in the nuclear age. Some realists do,[29] Waltz does not.

GILPIN: HEGEMONIC CHANGE

Robert Gilpin is also a realist but he is not identified with balance of power theory and with neo-realism. Gilpin is a traditional realist with a hierarchic bent – his theory deals with the rise and fall of empires and hegemonies. There is nothing terribly new about the theory except that it is couched in the language of microeconomics and of rational choice. Gilpin succeeds, however, in presenting the theory in a disciplined and scholarly fashion and in making explicit what in so many other discussions of hegemony remains implicit.

The theory was developed against the backdrop of a steady decline in American economic preponderance in the 1970s. Theorists of international relations were particularly worried about the consequences of "lost hegemony" for international stability. Would international trade and finance suffer? Would regimes like the GATT disintegrate? Would there be a return to neo-mercantilist economics, protectionism, regional block-building and trade wars?

The answers varied. Richard Rosecrance, as I will show in one of the following sections, feels that the decline is natural and will have no serious consequences because the international system, helped by free trade, is robust and capable of steering itself. Robert Keohane is somewhat less optimistic. As the discussion of his theory of regimes will demonstrate, he is not sure whether order in anarchy is natural. He attributes some merit to hegemonic stability and points out how it has promoted the establishment of regimes. In the period "after hegemony," regimes remain important for the management of the international system; it is Keohane's contention that they will survive and make a positive contribution toward international order and stability.

Robert Gilpin is skeptical.[30] He interprets the relative decline in American economic preponderance as the end of a cycle in international politics and, at the same time, as the advent of a new one.[31] Such transitions are generally accompanied by large-scale war producing a new hegemon. Regimes cannot stabilize the system, nor can free trade.

Rosecrance, Keohane and Gilpin differ in their interpretation of "lost hegemony" but they all avoid a purely systemic approach. They opt for an actor-oriented perspective couched in the language of microeconomics. Such a perspective does not fully disregard the system but its starting point is different. Gilpin, in comparing himself with Waltz, is very specific on this point:

> Waltz starts with the international system and its structural features in order to explain aspects of the behavior of individual states. My *War and Change in World Politics* emphasizes the opposite approach, namely, that of economic or rational choice theory: I start with individual state actors and seek to explain the emergence and change of international systems.[32]

Political economists tend to look at international politics through the eyes of individual actors and end up developing theories that combine systems and actors, wholes and parts. Gilpin's theory is a case in point. It postulates that international politics are cyclical[33] and that a cycle is characterized by five different systemic phases:

1. An international system is stable (i.e., in a state of equilibrium) if no state believes it profitable to attempt to change the system.
2. A state will attempt to change the international system if the expected benefits exceed the expected costs (i.e., if there is an expected net gain).
3. A state will seek to change the international system through territorial, political, and economic expansion until the marginal costs of further change are equal to or greater than the marginal benefits.
4. Once an equilibrium between the costs and benefits of further change and expansion is reached, the tendency is for the economic costs of maintaining the status quo to rise faster than the economic capacity to support the status quo.
5. If the disequilibrium in the international system is not resolved, then the system will be changed, and a new equilibrium reflecting the redistribution of power will be established.[34]

The international system moves from a state of equilibrium to one of disequilibrium, to a resolution of the ensuing tensions and back to a state of equilibrium.[35] Equilibrium is not identical with balance: any system is in equilibrium (and stable) as long as no state believes it profitable to change it. According to Gilpin, history shows that in modern times the most stable systems have been hegemonic. But even hegemonies are eventually challenged, and although peaceful change is not impossible "the principal mechanism of change throughout history has been war, or what we shall call hegemonic war (i.e., a war that determines which state or states will be dominant and will govern the system)."[36]

When discussing Propositions 1 and 2, Gilpin analyzes the various factors producing change. He distinguishes environmental factors (transportation, communication, economic or military technology), factors inherent in the structure of the international system, and factors located within the actors of the system. The discussion of the factors takes up a sizeable portion of the study,[37] but it is inconclusive – the various factors are not very helpful in explaining change. Hence Gilpin's somewhat sobering conclusion: "Whether or not change will in fact take place is ultimately indeterminant."[38]

The discussion of Proposition 3 bears more fruit. It deals with the expansionist phase of the cycle and the establishment of a new equilibrium. Gilpin distinguishes between pre-modern cycles of empire and modern cycles of hegemony. The pre-modern cycles (Persians, Romans, Turks and so on) last until the end of the Religious Wars when, with the Treaty of Westphalia, a modern international system begins to take shape. The new order coincides with the triumph of the nation-state, the breakthrough of economic growth, the creation of a world market economy and a succession of hegemonies – but not of empires. Most prominent among the modern hegemonies have been the Pax Britannica and the Pax Americana.[39]

The modern era is also characterized by the emergence of the balancing mechanism, a mechanism that is compatible with hegemonies but not with empires. The reason, once again, is economic. Pre-modern imperial cycles are accompanied by massive territorial conquest whereas modern hegemonic cycles rely more on the market mechanism.

Imperial expansion remains a possibility, however. In two World Wars Germany and Japan tried to revert to the pre-modern pattern but did not succeed. There is no guarantee that other attempts will not be made so that "the succession of hegemonies of the nineteenth and twentieth centuries (like the Greek city-state system) will be seen as merely an interlude in the more universal pattern of unifying imperialisms."[40] The two hegemonies, the Pax Britannica and the Pax Americana, would then be the exception, not the rule.

Proposition 4 deals with the phase of decline. This phase sets in because "once an equilibrium between the costs and benefits of further change and expansion is reached, the tendency is for the economic costs of maintaining the status quo to rise faster than the economic capacity to support the status quo."[41] There are internal and external economic factors influencing costs and capacities. Domestically, the hegemon confronts unfavorable structural changes, a tendency for the most efficient military techniques to rise in cost, and, as his society becomes more affluent, a tendency for both private and public consumption to grow faster than the gross national product.[42] Among the external factors influencing the decline there is the increasing cost of political dominance and the loss of economic and technological leadership.[43] Gilpin summarizes the situation as follows:

> Once a society reaches the limit of its expansion, it has great difficulty in maintaining its position and arresting its eventual decline. Further, it begins to encounter marginal returns in agricultural or industrial production. Both internal and external changes increase consumption and the costs of protection and production; it begins to experience a severe fiscal crisis. The diffusion of its economic, technological, or organizational skills undercuts its comparative advantage over other societies, especially those on the periphery of the system. These rising states, on the other hand, enjoy lower costs, rising rates of return on their resources, and the advantages of backwardness. In time, *the differential rates of growth* of declining and rising states in the system produce a decisive redistribution of power and result in disequilibrium in the system.[44] [emphasis added]

Decline is halted when a new equilibrium is reached. But the establishment of a new equilibrium involves some agonizing choices. They are dealt with in Proposition 5. Gilpin distinguishes three basic alternatives: preventive war, reduction of costs by further expansion, limitation of foreign commitments.[45] Most of these alternatives entail war. Throughout history, Gilpin argues, "the primary means of resolving the disequilibrium between the structure of the international system and the redistribution of power has been war, more particularly what we shall call a hegemonic war."[46]

Hegemonic wars are a contest between the dominant power and the rising challenger, and the issue at stake is the nature and the governance of the system. The wars are characterized by the unlimited means employed and by the general scope of the struggle.[47] Hegemonic wars have been an integral part of all systemic changes: "Every international system that the world has known has been a consequence of...such hegemonic struggles."[48] Hegemonic war represents the end of one full cycle, and at the same time

> the beginning of another cycle of growth, expansion, and eventual decline. The *law of uneven growth* continues to redistribute power, thus undermining the status quo established by the last hegemonic struggle. Disequilibrium replaces equilibrium, and the world moves toward a new round of hegemonic conflict.[49] [emphasis added]

Gilpin is aware that in the nuclear age hegemonic war is potentially disastrous. In his final chapter he wonders whether mankind will develop a mechanism of peaceful change – and remains skeptical. After pondering some of the developments characterizing our age (nuclear weapons, greater interdependence, a global society), Gilpin concludes that their impact is ambiguous[50] and that "war and violence remain serious possibilities as the world moves from the decay of one international system toward the creation of another."[51]

Gilpin is particularly distressed about man's potential for progress and improvement. He admits this freely and argues that pessimism is the hallmark of the realist philosophy in international politics: "Unlike its polar opposite, idealism, realism is founded on a pessimism regarding moral progress and human possibilities."[52] Gilpin is doubtful whether man, confronted with an unfavorable cost–benefit calculation in the nuclear age, will learn to change and opt for peace, for a type of rationality different from the past. Man is capable of acting in accordance with the rationality of war but not with the rationality of peace.

The rationality of war is at the center of Gilpin's theory. After all, the title of his book is *War and Change in World Politics*. War is intimately related to change; it produces it. War is an expression of the law of the strongest, hence the strongest state emerges from it. War, as Gilpin argues, produces hegemons. This is clearly a war-centered theory; war is at the heart of hierarchic realism.

This is not the case with anarchic realism. The overriding purpose of balance of power theory is the survival of all sovereign and independent states, and war is but a means to achieve that end. The theories of Gentz and Waltz are state-centered, not war-centered. In those theories equilibrium is the rule, hegemony the exception, whereas for Gilpin hegemony constitutes the rule and equilibrium the exception.

Bernhardi would agree. For him the European balance of power was a momentary phenomenon, the brainchild of Metternich and a reflection of the power realities as they existed at the Congress of Vienna – but no more. Britain then distanced itself from the continent, Italian and German unification followed, and the balance died. Toward the end of the century Germany found itself in Phase 2 of Gilpin's hegemonic cycle, a time when the cost–benefit calculation of war appeared attractive. In that phase it was natural and rational for the German leadership to contemplate the overthrow of the existing European order and to put its economy on a war footing. For Bernhardi, Germany had the power, the will and the right to go to war and to initiate a cycle of empire.

Of course, there are differences between Gilpin and Bernhardi. Gilpin adheres to a fully cyclical theory of international relations while Bernhardi does not. There are merely hints that Bernhardi adheres to a cyclical notion of history but he is not explicit about this. In addition, Gilpin uses the language of microeconomics; Bernhardi does not. Also, Bernhardi's language is nationalistic and chauvinistic, which leads him to glorify war.

And, unlike Gilpin, Bernhardi is a Social Darwinist. Today it is no longer fashionable for a theorist to speak of the survival of the fittest and of natural selection. But Gilpin's cycle can easily be put in Darwinist terms. In Phase 1 war does not select because of a negative cost–benefit calculation; during Phase 2 war becomes attractive and begins to select; in Phase 3 the fittest is selected and rewarded; in Phase 4 the fittest is punished instead of rewarded, and in the final phase the selective power of war reverts to indifference. Gilpin comes close to promulgating an economic version of Social Darwinism. His use of rational choice and microeconomics is purely formal. Substantively he promulgates an imperialist–mercantilist theory of economics dominated, as he says, by the law of uneven growth.

The contrast to liberal economics is evident. Market economics resemble a positive-sum game, and in the long run there is a leveling effect conforming with the "law of even growth." Thanks to free international markets Europe and Japan recovered quickly after 1945 and have reached a level of development comparable to that of the United States; thanks to liberal economics developing nations in the Far East are "catching up" with the developed nations. Liberal economics have a leveling effect. It is a Marxist and an imperialist argument that uneven growth results, that capitalism polarizes peoples and nations.

This leads me to surmise that at its core Gilpin's law of uneven growth is not economic but political, that it is part and parcel of the law of the strongest reflecting the dynamics of a permanent state of war. In the Hobbesian situation economics becomes a function of war, and the law of uneven growth is in fact the "law of war economics."

There is plenty of evidence for this. In Phase 4 of the hegemonic cycle the rising cost of empire begins to hurt. The cost is said to be economic, but in fact it is military and relates to war: domestically, the hegemon confronts a tendency of the most efficient *military* techniques to rise in cost, a tendency of *defense-related* investment to drive out private investment, and finally a tendency for public (that is, *defense-oriented*) spending to grow in excess of the gross national product; abroad the hegemon faces the rising costs of *military occupation* as well as a loss of economic and technological leadership affecting his ability to be victorious on the *battlefield*. The hegemon's capacity for maintaining the status quo decreases and decline sets in. Quite obviously, the "law of war economics" is at work.

Gilpin's worldview is truly Hobbesian and he is quite explicit on this point. He cites Hobbes' famous remark to the 2nd Earl of Devonshire: "It's the jungle out there!"[53] In a state of relentless conflict balance is but a transitional stage between two situations of hegemony – and it is identical with instability. Small wonder that his critique of Waltz is rather lengthy.[54] Waltz and Gilpin have a completely different reading of history. When looking at Europe since the Treaty of Westphalia, they see the same phenomena but interpret them in opposite ways. As shown earlier, since 1648 Europe has witnessed constant alternations between hegemony and balance, and sometimes hegemony and balance coexisted, as when Britain kept the balance on the continent while maintaining an empire around the globe. In the interpretation of these events Waltz is impressed by one side of the picture, Gilpin by the other. Waltz emphasizes events that relate to balance, Gilpin highlights phenomena linked to hegemony. They both look at the same reality but perceive it in a different light.[55]

What Gilpin can explain best are pre-modern cycles of empire. Increasing the wealth of nations through territorial conquest conforms most typically with the Hobbesian state of war. Modern cycles of hegemony, however, cannot be deduced from the Hobbesian model alone. Why are

Anglo-Saxon hegemonies liberal in nature? Why do they rely on the market mechanism more than on conquest?

Gilpin argues that cost–benefit calculations explain the difference, that in modern times the market mechanism has turned out to be more efficient. This may very well be true but liberal efficiency rests, among other things, on the recognition of basic rights – property rights, contractual rights, and so on. Can these (and regimes like the GATT) be deduced from the Hobbesian model? Or is the Lockean model more relevant? Is Gilpin tacitly introducing idealist arguments? I shall return to this argument later on when dealing with Keohane's theory of regimes.

Hedley Bull is more helpful when it comes to distinguishing between different forms of empire. He differentiates between dominance, hegemony and primacy. Dominance is crude imperialism characterized by the habitual use of force; hegemony is imperialism "with good manners," and primacy is leadership freely conceded by the lesser states.[56] America exercised primacy during the Cold War when the European states sought protection under its wings. American predominance was freely conceded; when the French objected to some of its features they were free to quit – and they did. Britain, in the nineteenth century, established hegemonies "with good manners," and the Soviets imposed primacy when they conquered Eastern Europe like an imperialist with "bad manners." For Bull the difference between different forms of predominance has to do with "freedom" and "manners." Gilpin's theory cannot account for such qualities. The distinction between cycles of empire and cycles of hegemony remains unexplained.[57]

Gilpin's image of the state and of man is also conditioned by the Hobbesian state of war. Man is a pawn of history and needs a strong state to compensate for his weakness. The central actors are states, not individuals. As Gilpin says, homo sapiens is a tribal species, and the modern tribe is the nation.[58] In any tightly organized tribe, the individual is a subordinate part of the collective, a means to the fulfillment of collective ends. Such men are dependent variables and have no basis for rationality and free will.

Gilpin's definition of the state is not explicit. But in Phase 2, when the cost–benefit calculation indicates that war pays off, Gilpin says that states "will" attempt to change the system. This implies a penchant for aggression. Actually, the efficient cause of war lies in the states themselves because Gilpin, in contrast to Waltz, rejects systemic and structural causes. The anarchic international system is at best a permissive cause of war. Gilpin's definition of nations is fully contextual – warlike nations are part and parcel of a warlike system.

Nations have no real choice, although Gilpin argues that at times they do. In the downturn phase nations can choose between (1) limiting foreign commitments, (2) preventive war or (3) progressive expansion.[59] The first option is peaceful, the others are not. In Gilpin's mind it is very unlikely that they will opt for the peaceful route. The law of uneven growth is highly compelling. A hegemon would have to abandon war politics and war economics – something he may not even do in the nuclear age. As shown, Gilpin ponders the question of nuclear war and wonders whether man, faced with total destruction, will learn and change. He remains pessimistic. He has good reason for being so because optimism would undermine his theory.

KAHN: DETERRENCE

Deterrence theory is a modern offspring of realism. From a realist point of view threats of war are as normal as war itself, they are part and parcel of traditional international conflict management. With the advent of nuclear weapons, however, deterrence has become such an important matter that a separate body of theory has emerged, accompanied by a massive literature. Some of it is quite intriguing because nuclear weapons highlight the basic issues of deterrence in a most dramatic way and force theorists to think with utter clarity. Deterrence theory permits a valuable insight into the logic of enmity and war.

Herman Kahn is not the most important theorist of deterrence. Thomas Schelling and others have made more basic contributions, but Kahn has a gift of expressing himself lucidly and dramatically. His *Thinking About the Unthinkable*[60] exemplifies these qualities like no other book. To facilitate entry into the somewhat complex terminology of deterrence, I have decided to begin with some remarks of my own and a short historic background.

As long as the United States enjoyed a nuclear monopoly and did not have to expect retaliation, there was no great controversy over the use of atomic weapons. Once the Soviet Union had its own nuclear capability, however, and once the United States became vulnerable, two schools of deterrence emerged. Some specialists argued that the very awesomeness of the weapons forced the United States to emphasize a reluctant ultimate or finite use. But others took the opposite view: just because the weapons were so awesome and their ultimate (or massive) use was so catastrophic, it was necessary to think through all possible phases of a nuclear war and to prepare for the use of the weapons at various levels of conflict.

Representatives of both schools agree that war avoidance is the topmost aim of nuclear strategy and that the threat potential is the real issue, hence the centrality of the term "deterrence." But deterrence is an inherently contradictory concept because a credible and successful deterror must at once give the impression that he is both willing and unwilling to use force. If the deterror is perceived as being unwilling to use force (because he conveys a totally peaceful image), deterrence fails. If, on the other hand, he is perceived as being completely willing to use force (because he conveys a totally belligerent image), deterrence fails as well. Successful (or credible) deterrence must consist of a subtle mix of both images, of a combination of willingness and unwillingness to use force.[61] Theorists can in all honesty disagree on how to weigh the mixture. Those who consider nuclear weapons as an "ultimate" means emphasize unwillingness more than willingness, whereas those who propose to "think through its use" put more emphasis on willingness than unwillingness.

As far as the United States is concerned, its present nuclear posture, and the theory behind it, exhibits a combination of both views. At the core of official deterrence doctrine stands the concept of assured destruction, which reflects the "ultimate" willingness to fight an all-out nuclear war. There is also room, however, for nuclear war-fighting, for using nuclear weapons in a careful move through various stages of escalation in the hope of terminating an encounter short of mutual destruction. Because war-fighting aims at preventing an all-out war as long as possible it is often also referred to as damage limitation. The United States can adhere to both schools of thought simply because it has a sufficient variety of weapons systems.[62]

To some extent, therefore, the division exists on paper more than in reality. But when it comes to nuclear disarmament, for example, it matters a great deal whether weapons are dismantled that are part of a finite or part of a war-fighting strategy. The same is true in weapons acquisition. The division is therefore more than just academic.

It was most acutely felt in the late fifties and the early sixties when, under the impression of Russian predominance and a supposed missile gap, nuclear strategy was for the first time discussed in public, when academics became involved and important decisions on new weapons systems had to be made. Most prominent at that time was a group of specialists working for the RAND Corporation, a think-tank associated with the U.S. Airforce. It included such well-known names as Bernard Brodie, Albert Wohlstetter, Morton Halperin and Herman Kahn.[63] Many of these took up important positions in the Kennedy administration and acquired influence.

Kahn, because of his ebullient personality and his ability to write intelligibly and dramatically, became the figure best-known to the public. For many people at that time, he was the incarnation of strategic thinking, but for many others his uncanny ability to "think through" thermonuclear war was also repulsive and highly dangerous. His first major book, *On Thermonuclear War*,[64] appeared in 1960 and was meant mainly for specialists. Two years later, he published a more popular version provocatively entitled *Thinking About the Unthinkable* and thereby launched a debate that was carried far beyond the United States itself. Because the book is such a clear-cut expression of war-fighting theory, it is a good example of contemporary realism or, as some authors prefer to say, of Neo-Clausewitzian thought. Kahn himself did much to put himself into a Clausewitzian image. Not only does he quote the Prussian war theorist but the very title of his first book, *On Thermonuclear War*, suggests an affinity with Clausewitz's *On War*.

Small wonder that Raymond Aron was asked to write the introduction to *Thinking About the Unthinkable*. Aron was one of the first to investigate and to demonstrate Clausewitz's relevance to nuclear war. In his introduction, Aron shows some understanding of critics of Kahn who believe that the subtlety of the analysis has become an intellectual game and that no amount of hard thinking will change the fact that the first atomic bombs may unleash homicidal madness:

> But it is not demonstrated that it must be this way, and in differentiating the diverse kinds of thermonuclear war, in creating scenarios of possible crises and attacks, Herman Kahn, it seems to me, renders a service to everyone, civilian or military, responsible for the survival of this nation and of humanity itself.[65]

The first chapter is "In Defense of Thinking" and Kahn argues that one cannot make unpleasant facts go away or become more attractive by ignoring them and by refusing to think about them rationally. On the contrary, the advent of Armageddon can be promoted by assuming that a nuclear war will be catastrophic and represent the last of all wars – it could become a self-fulfilling prophecy. What if a nuclear weapon is fired inadvertently or by miscalculation and the powers affected have only an all-or-nothing strategy? Rational man, so Kahn says, has a duty to ask carefully how nuclear weapons could be used in a limited and controlled way. All-or-nothing theory for Kahn is irrational and premised on emotional and idealist notions about the intrinsic evil of war:

> Many people believe that the current system must inevitably end in total annihilation. They reject, sometimes very emotionally, any attempts to analyze this notion. Either they are afraid of where the thinking will lead them or they are afraid of thinking at all. They want to make the choice one between a risk [of disarmament] and the certainty of disaster, between sanity and insanity, between good and evil; therefore, as moral

and sane men they need no longer hesitate. I hold that an intelligent and responsible person cannot pose the problem so simply.[66]

The battle lines are drawn: Kahn, the realist, is on the side of reason, rationality and responsibility; his opponents, the idealists, are on the side of unreason, irrationality, emotion and irresponsibility. It looks like a familiar constellation!

Having established the right to think about the unthinkable, Kahn tackles the issue with relative discipline. At first, he analyzes the outbreak, development and termination of a large nuclear war (what he later calls the problems of Type I Deterrence). There follows a shorter chapter on the need for civil defense (one of his special concerns at that time). Next comes a presentation of American strategic doctrine, past and present, followed by a relatively loose and impressionistic discussion of various "scenarios" and "games." The culminating point is Chapter 6 where Kahn presents his famous ladder of escalation. The book is not rigidly structured; there is a good amount of overlap and repetition but the central argument, as will be shown, is crystal-clear.

To make his point against the all-or-nothing conception of nuclear war, Kahn begins by distinguishing four different possible outbreaks: inadvertent war, war by miscalculation, war by calculation, and catalytic war. The first, inadvertent war, "might occur almost unintentionally as a result of mechanical or human error, false alarm, self-fulfilling prophecy, or unauthorized behavior."[67] In Kahn's estimation the probability of inadvertent war is at that time very low. More likely is a war by miscalculation "which might result from a decision-maker's miscalculation, misunderstanding, or failure to think adequately through the consequences of his actions."[68] Kahn includes in this category wars resulting from escalation threats, a problem he discusses in more detail toward the end of the book.

Starting a war by calculation means that "after due study, a nation might decide that going to war would be the least undesirable of its choices, and it might be right in its calculation."[69] Preventive wars fall into this category. Finally, there may be catalytic wars, where "some third party or nation might for its own reasons deliberately start a war between the two major powers."[70] A minor power might want to attack the United States or the Soviet Union under circumstances which suggest a superpower attack. By unleashing a general war the smaller nation might want to improve its own position in the international hierarchy.

Under the heading of "How a War Might Be Fought" Kahn then discusses a number of targeting objectives: Countervalue, Counterforce plus Countervalue, Straight Counterforce, Counterforce plus Bonus, Counterforce plus Avoidance. Most of these terms are common today, but they were new to most readers at that time. Countervalue implies targeting an enemy's cities, counterforce the military installations necessary for retaliation. The other terms constitute combinations of the two, and Kahn explains them in some detail. It permits him to engage in one of his specialties – speculating about the human toll of nuclear war, about five, one hundred or more millions of casualties. Kahn is a physicist by training and familiar with the various effects of nuclear detonations.

This may also explain why Kahn takes such a great interest in civil defense measures, in a program for public shelters. He knows of its difficulties and pitfalls but propagates it anyway. Kahn is aware that in an all-out countervalue strike the population cannot be properly protected. But he does not believe in the probability of such a devastating first strike:

> There is good reason to believe that any all-out first-strike would be aimed at our ability to retaliate, and that cities would...not only be secondary targets but might be deliberately spared. An attack aimed at Counterforce or Counterforce plus Avoidance objectives would be the most sensible for an attacker, who would be in a better position to use the cities and the survivors as hostages to deter retaliation or to negotiate a favorable cease-fire.[71]

Kahn does not make civil defense shelters a top national priority but, as they are an integral part of his war-fighting conception of deterrence, he favors them: "Since we cannot be certain that we will succeed in preventing war, it is essential that we take moderate and prudent steps to minimize the disaster that such a failure would mean."[72]

Kahn then turns to the official deterrence doctrine prevailing at that time and shows that it seeks to achieve six broad objectives:

> (1) Type I Deterrence – to deter a large attack on the military forces, population, or wealth of the United States, by threatening a high level of damage to the attacker in retaliation;
> (2) Type II Deterrence – to deter extremely provocative actions short of a large attack on the U.S. (for example, a nuclear or even all-out conventional strike against Western Europe) by the threat of an "all-out" U.S. nuclear reprisal against the Soviet Union;
> (3) Improved War Outcome – to limit damage to U.S. (and allied) population and wealth, and to improve the military outcome for the U.S. should a war occur;
> (4) Stability – to reduce the likelihood of an inadvertent thermonuclear war;

Contemporary Theories

(5) Comprehensive Arms Control – to control and limit both the arms race and the use of force in settling disputes;

(6) Type III Deterrence – to deter provocations not covered by Type II Deterrence and provide support for the achievement of "peaceful" political objectives and for tactics such as Controlled Reprisal, other limited wars, mobilizations, negotiations, and so forth.[73]

Let me explain and comment on some of these terms. Type I Deterrence refers to threats (and to war-fighting) at the highest strategic level, that is, with intercontinental missiles. There is a large body of theory on Type I Deterrence reflecting a wide consensus among specialists in and out of government.[74]

There is less agreement about the other objectives. As far as Improved War Outcome is concerned, the idea of civilian shelters has been abandoned. Stability can be a very controversial concept, and in the sphere of Comprehensive Arms Control (and disarmament) many issues are now in flux. The most controversial concepts, however, are Type II and Type III Deterrence. They are so contested because they have had a direct connection with important issues of American foreign policy: Type II Deterrence (or extended deterrence) relates to NATO strategy, Type III Deterrence was tried in Vietnam. On both types of deterrence an enormous amount of literature exists, and disagreement is profound.[75]

Kahn intends to make a contribution to all three types of deterrence, to the whole spectrum of conflict – from nonviolent crises to guerilla warfare, to conventional war, and to various types of nuclear war. He is more than a theorist of nuclear war, he wants to be a thinker about war in general, more accurately, about manipulating the potential of war as a bargaining instrument. Of course, he is not the only theorist propagating such ideas at that time – Thomas Schelling published his *Strategy of Conflict*[76] two years earlier. It contains similar ideas.

Kahn turns to these questions in the latter part of his book and develops "Some Thoughts on International Bargaining and the Game of Chicken." Kahn quotes Bertrand Russell's description of the game:

> It is played by choosing a long straight road with a white line down the middle and starting two very fast cars towards each other from opposite ends. Each car is expected to keep the wheels to one side on the white line. As they approach each other mutual destruction becomes more and more imminent. If one of them swerves from the white line before the other, the other, as he passes, shouts "Chicken!" and the one who has swerved becomes an object of contempt.[77]

According to Kahn, the best way to win the game is to adopt a strategy of rational irrationality: to get into the car drunk, wear dark glasses and throw the steering wheel out of the window, all in full sight of the adversary. By pretending to be irrational and by making irrationality a part of a rational threat one can win the game: "It can make sense to commit oneself irrevocably to do something in a particular eventuality, and at the same time it may not make sense to carry out the commitment if the eventuality occurs."[78]

Put in terms of warfare, it can make sense to commit oneself irrevocably to a violent act although it makes no sense to carry out that act. But the result is positive – it constitutes a credible threat, it provides leverage in international bargaining. And with this instrument, with what some have called coercive diplomacy, one can move up and down the escalation ladder.

Kahn's escalation ladder has sixteen rungs:

16. Aftermath
15. Some Kind of "All-Out" War
14. "Complete" Evacuation
13. Limited Non-Local War
12. Controlled Local War
11. Spectacular Show of Force
10. Super-Ready Status
9. Limited Evacuation
8. Intense Crisis
7. Limited Military Confrontation
6. Acts of Violence
5. Modest Mobilization
4. Show of Force
3. Political, Diplomatic, and Economic Gestures
2. "Crisis"
1. Subcrisis Disagreement[79]

At each level a threat is formulated and, if it is not effective, "Chicken" is played at the next higher level. At stage 15 the reader has been led for the umpteenth time through all the lurid details of possible war, nuclear or not, until Kahn concludes that "the only rational thing for them to do at this point would be to sign a truce."[80] The reason there is such a point where intrawar deterrence becomes effective is that in the conditions of the sixties, and Kahn emphasizes this point, the United States enjoyed clear strategic superiority.

At the end of the chapter, Kahn applies the logic of coercive diplomacy to the arms race. He invents a scenario where Kennedy and Khrushchev meet at a summit and the Russian, once more, raises the Berlin issue.

Kennedy, according to Kahn, could mount a credible threat by hinting at an acceleration of the arms race: "This would be dangerous to both of us but it would be substantially more dangerous to the Soviets than to us."[81] The reason is economic – the United States enjoys a far greater economic potential than the Soviet Union:

> The least we could do would be to increase our budget by a factor of two and maybe a factor of four. We could afford to do it. World War II showed that we could spend more than 40 percent of our GNP for military products without suffering any severe hardships...Moreover, we could buy central war forces, including adequate active and passive defense, so that we would unquestionably survive an all-out war.[82]

Once more, the threat works and control (or survival) is assured because of American superiority. Superiority constitutes the heart of Kahn's warfighting theory. His realism is not founded upon balance, upon nuclear parity between the United States and the Soviet Union. It reveals Kahn's image of the state system – it is hierarchic rather than anarchic. His theory rests on a hierarchic realist worldview.

America is the strongest power in the international system, it can outproduce and outgun any other state. Given this position of predominance, the United States can determine ends and means. The end is a stable international system, the most important means is war-fighting deterrence. There is a convergence of interest, but the convergence is not spontaneous – it is enforced. The whole amounts to a rational order, to a system in which each state plays a given part. America plays a dominant part, other states play subordinate parts. In the security realm at least the management of the system is monistic. Kahn's theory contains its own rationality and is clearly endogenous.

States that share similiar visions of ends do not object to subordination because it gives them protection. This applies to NATO allies, for instance: they regard a certain limitation of sovereign independence as legitimate. States rejecting the American vision of ends object to subordination and see it as an illegitimate limitation of their sovereignty. The Soviet Union is one of these states but, given its total hostility, America has no other choice.

It shows that Kahn's conception of the state is élitist. In the nuclear age America alone can engage in rational cost–benefit calculations. It has to assume the management of the system because no other state is capable of it, all other states are either too weak, lack the necessary will, or are hostile. America is in a class by itself – no other state is comparable to it. Kahn's definition of nation is contextual, it fits the system.

America can play "Chicken" better than any other state, it has the skill to properly combine rationality with irrationality and to find the right balance between the willingness and unwillingness to use force. America has the ideal dual personality, it knows how to retain its credibility by subtly cultivating a hard and a soft image. This raises questions about the dual nature of this state, the relation between America's tough "outer shell" and its soft (or constitutional) "inner life." Kahn fails to deal with these questions.

When one takes a close look at Kahn's theory, it becomes evident that in the dilemma between a soft and a hard image, Kahn settles for the latter. Since he assumes absolute Soviet hostility he settles for an American emphasis of willingness over unwillingness in the use of force. By a strategy of war-fighting, by loudly proclaiming that America is "thinking about the unthinkable" he wants to make it clear that the United States is willing to use nuclear weapons at an early stage – although America would, of course, rather not use them at all. Anything else in Kahn's estimation is not understood by the Russians.

America has to convey a strongly belligerent image because Kahn operates with a strongly belligerent image of the Soviet Union. One image determines the other; it is the core of a self-fulfilling prophecy or a vicious circle. Once initiated, escalation takes its course and, on the assumption of symmetry of capabilities, the only logical escape is a change in images. As I will show later on, Charles E. Osgood deals lucidly with the problem. He proposes an idealist solution. Kahn's realist solution is to assume asymmetry of capabilities. Because America is stronger, escalation can be terminated with a successful threat, with coercive diplomacy.

Given the strategic situation in the early sixties, Kahn's convictions are not wholly unrealistic. Once some of the RAND people were in power, however, they discovered that there was no missile gap and that the United States actually enjoyed tremendous strategic superiority. It became particularly evident in the Cuban missile crisis; but would superiority last forever? Was it not conceivable that one day the Soviets might achieve symmetry in capabilities? Whether coercive bargaining functions under such circumstances is much less certain. It might then become a sure guide to Armageddon. Rationality is only on Kahn's side as long as superiority is assumed.

Kahn's argumentation contains other problems as well. Coercive bargaining depends on a counterforce capability, on knocking out the opponent's means of retaliation rather than his cities. Counterforce is tantamount to a first-strike capability, to a capacity of disarming an opponent (assumed to possess vulnerable weapons) in a surprise attack. Counterforce has more than deterrent value – it is also useful for blackmail or compellence. Such a posture is potentially offensive and produces crisis instability because an opponent who is aware of his own vulnerability will be tempted to launch a preemptive strike in a tense situation. Coercive bargaining can produce the very effect it tries to prevent and become self-defeating.

Furthermore, if coercive diplomacy is to be practiced across a wide spectrum of conflict it requires an enormous array of arms. In its initial years, the Kennedy Administration did not hesitate to procure different kinds of new weapons systems, and between 1960 and 1962 Secretary of Defense McNamara actually backed the war-fighting doctrine. The enthusiasm waned, however, when McNamara realized that the policy of maximalism (as it was also called) opened the doors wide for demands by the different armed services. It therefore was mainly for budgetary reasons that war-fighting was thereafter given a lower priority. But it goes to show that war-fighting fans the armaments race.

How can the arms race be stopped, how can crisis stability be regained? Or, in terms of Kahn's own list of objectives: how can objectives 4 and 5 be attained without jeopardizing the rest? There is only one solution: abandon the pure theory of war-fighting and borrow a page from the opposite doctrine, from finite deterrence and assured destruction. When the central weapons systems of both opponents have the capacity to survive a surprise attack (when they are invulnerable) no side possesses a first-strike capability, and both are then less nervous. Furthermore, when these invulnerable forces have the capacity to retaliate and to assure destruction (counter-city) there is a reduced need for more weapons and the arms race can be stopped. Finite deterrence works with a finite number of weapons.

Assured destruction is premised on a tacit agreement, an agreement not to be offensive, not to fan the arms race. In the words of Gentz such an agreement represents true self-interest and is compatible with balance or parity. The logic of war-fighting, however, represents narrow self-interest and does not lead to balance, it entails superiority, hegemony and hierarchy.

Evidently, Kahn's conception of deterrence is incompatible with balance of power theory; it cannot be built into Waltz's neo-realist theory. Although Waltz is not totally explicit on this point, one gains the impression that he relies on mutual assured destruction (MAD) as a central concept. This explains at least in part "the strong pressures" that make the two great powers conservative.

MAD makes powers conservative because it emphasizes unwillingness to use force more than willingness to do so. The message is that both states are willing to use force if necessary but will do so only as a measure of last resort. This strategy raises the nuclear threshold and helps to gain time, two important factors in crisis management.

MAD has the additional advantage of reversing the image of war. Instead of assuming, as Kahn does, that even nuclear war is normal and rational, the implication is that nuclear war is basically abnormal and irrational. Nuclear war as an instrument of conflict management is reevaluated, associated with a different cost–benefit calculation. Nuclear war is classified as a qualitatively different type of war. The lives of nations become incompatible with the use of nuclear weapons.

A step in the direction of assured destruction is also an admission that control of nuclear escalation is problematical. Concepts like extended deterrence, graduated response and first use are accorded a more critical assessment. Crisis management is not as easy as is often assumed, and threats have a more complex structure than is generally admitted. Especially the problems of communication and perception in threat situations have been underestimated. Assurance may be a valuable ingredient in successful crisis management.[83]

Kahn's maximalism, and in particular Type III Deterrrence, was tested in Vietnam – and found wanting. President Johnson, under the influence of a number of RAND-trained advisors, pursued an escalatory policy of intrawar threats, but the North Vietnamese were not impressed. Only after seven years of war, and the most massive bombing of Hanoi, did the North Vietnamese agree to a peace. It turned out to be a mere truce. Coercive bargaining had not worked at the subnuclear level – but would it work at the nuclear level?

In conclusion, a word about the Neo-Clausewitzians. The term became fashionable at the time Kahn was writing his books, and the concept covered all theoreticians who endorse war-fighting theory. Some of them strongly emphasize their affinity with the old master. Kahn, as shown, wants to convey the idea that he is writing a modern version of *On War*, and Aron did a voluminous study of Clausewitz.[84]

However popular the association with Clausewitz at that time, it does not imply the existence of a single coherent school of thought. Aron leans more toward balance whereas Kahn is a proponent of superiority. For the Neo-Clausewitzians, as for their idol, nuclear war is a continuation of all kinds of politics, of hegemonic politics or "grand policy" and of balance of power politics or "petty policy." Both Clausewitz and his modern disciples lived through an age of great changes in warfare – and they did not quite know yet where they stood.

GRAY: GEOPOLITICS

The term "geopolitics" is popular among some realists but, like Henry Kissinger, they tend to use it loosely and with no specific relation to geography. Yet, there is a more rigorous meaning, one that goes back to the writings of Sir Halford Mackinder, a British geographer, who published his major work on the topic around the turn of the century.[85] During World War II a Dutch American, Nicholas Spykman, elaborated on Mackinder's ideas and made them more widely known in the United States. Colin S. Gray in *The Geopolitics of Super Power*[86] carries on the tradition of Mackinder and Spykman by demonstrating the relevance of geopolitics to the Soviet-American rivalry during the Cold War. As late as 1988 he argued that American military and political strategy could be placed on a more solid footing and become what he calls Grand Strategy.

Given the end of the Cold War, one is tempted to see Gray's theory as an anachronism, as a product of particular circumstances that no longer prevail. In part this is true. Gray does indeed establish a close link between geopolitics and ideology, and to that extent the theory is dated. If we look beyond this fact, however, the theory continues to be of interest. There are still great land powers in Eurasia, and these may possibly continue to be rivals of great sea powers that control the oceans. If that should again be the case, geopolitics remains of interest.

When looking at the oceans and continents of our planet, Mackinder saw the Eurasian landmass (or what he also calls the World Island) on the one hand, and the enormous oceans on the other. Eurasia has a core, the Heartland, traditionally occupied by one power, by the dominant continental state. The Heartland is surrounded by a string of countries that Mackinder calls the Inner Crescent and Spykman the Rimland. Europe, North Africa, the Middle East, South Asia, Indochina and the continental Far East are part of the Rimland. The "islands" surrounding Eurasia form the Outer Crescent or what others have also called the Periphery. It includes the Western Hemisphere, Greenland, the British Isles, most of Africa, the outer parts of Southeast Asia, Australia, New Zealand and Japan.

Mackinder attached a military and a political significance to these terms. The state dominating the Heartland pursues a strategy of land power, the state dominating the Outer Crescent a strategy of sea power. Politically the continental power is authoritarian in nature, the oceanic power democratic and liberal. The struggle between the two arises over control of the Rimland. In order to feel secure, the Heartland power has to have indirect control over these areas, and the oceanic power, in order to protect its communications and sea lanes, must be assured that the Rimland is not in hostile hands.

The struggle between the continental and the insular power centers on control of the Rimlands. Because land power cannot engage sea power directly, the two must be translated into the currency of the other, a process raising complex strategic and tactical issues in the Rimland. In a general way, however, the oceanic power must endeavor to balance the continental power.

Geopolitics is in part related to balance of power theory and the American policy of containment and has a historic dimension because once the British gave up their role of balancing land power by sea power the Americans had to take it over. The British confronted various hegemons on the continent, the Hapsburgs, the French, the Russians, and the Germans. The United States has so far dealt with the latter two. During the Cold War the World Island was dominated by the Soviet Union.

According to Mackinder, the strength of the continental position depends heavily on the control of Eastern Europe. Much of the struggle between continental powers has been over that area because the power that controls Eastern Europe can hope to control the world. The logic is the following:

> Who rules East Europe commands the Heartland; who rules the Heartland commands the World Island; who rules the World Island commands the world.[87]

The Soviet Union, because it occupied Eastern Europe after the end of the World War II, was a danger to the security of Eurasia and the entire world. Colin Gray is firmly wedded to this idea. He is a strict interpreter of Mackinder and of the theory of geopolitics.

Gray perceives great continuity in international politics. The adjective he uses regularly is "enduring": there is an enduring confrontation between land and sea power, an enduring struggle between authoritarian and democratic ways of life, an enduring need to pursue *Realpolitik*. Nothing has changed the nature of world affairs, not the advent of nuclear weapons nor the conversion of Russia to Bolshevism. Gray is very explicit on both points:

> It is not widely appreciated that the shape of the post-World War II international security order was the product of geopolitics, not of nuclear weapons ... The most important change brought by nuclear weapons is that nuclear-armed states in political conflict are far more cautious in their national security dealings than are nonnuclear-armed states, or than great powers were prior to 1945.[88]

> It must be emphasized that the principal American adversary is the Soviet state and its power, not the arcane nonsense of Marxist or socialist ideology ... It is important to note that the ideological antipathy between the superpowers provides strictly redundant fuel for their rivalry. That rivalry is locked in place by the exclusivity of their strength.[89]

If anything influences the shape of Cold War politics it is the demise of the multipolar Eurocentric system and the emergence of a global bipolar system. The new order has not altered the laws of geopolitics; only the context becomes more dramatic. The stark conflict between expanding authoritarian land power and defensive democratic sea power is clearer than ever. At heart, however, the "game of high politics," as Gray likes to say, is the same as always.[90]

Having described the nature of the game, Gray goes on to show that the two superpowers are not equally adept at playing it. Different geography breeds different strategic cultures. The Soviet Union is a continental state with a permanent security problem, the United States is an insular country accustomed to security and freedom. The two nations cannot change their strategic culture because "physical geography largely governs economic geography, which determines social geography, which in its turn is a major influence on the evolution of political forms."[91] The practitioner of strategy must be aware of the different strategic cultures and has to include them in his calculations.

Gray shows that Soviet strategic culture has roots in Russian history, in Byzantine tradition, in Czarist autocracy and in the conspiratorial dogma of Lenin. It is a bureaucratic form of despotism dominated by an élite, by the all-powerful Communist Party. And, like its predecessors, this élite seeks security by dominating Eurasia, thereby threatening the security of the dominant sea power:

> If the Soviet Union were effectively in security command of Eurasia, it would enjoy locally unrestricted access to the open ocean and could draw upon the industrial, scientific, and agricultural resources of Western Europe, or at least deny those resources to the United States. Given such a hegemony, the Soviet Union would be far better placed than today either to press steadily against a much contracted U.S. perimeter or, if need be, to wage war against the United States.[92]

Gray does not believe that the Soviet Union is in a position to run a world empire but he expects it to try: "The logic of the course of Soviet empire will likely require that the Soviet leaders attempt to achieve the impossible dream: the total security implicit in the vision of a truly universal Great Russian Empire."[93] The attempt is based on a two-step grand design: first isolating the United States and then defeating it slowly "by political means or – if feasible – rapidly by military force."[94]

The military option may be forced upon the Soviets by developments at home. Gray is convinced that the Soviet leaders "would attempt external military adventure before they would accept the necessity of domestic change so fundamental as to place in question the authority and capacity to rule of the CPSU."[95]

In the American strategic culture there is no impulse to expand and to conquer. Having been founded as an idealistic experiment in Christian and liberal communal living, the United States enjoyed "free security" for over a century by virtue of its isolation and by protection through the British Navy. In these exceptional circumstances it developed a conception of free and limited government in a fundamentally peaceful world.

Once the United States discovered that not all countries regarded peace as normal and that its security was endangered it developed an ambivalent strategic culture vacillating between the extremes of isolation and intervention. In the Cold War, this Janus-like tension has been largely overcome and "steadiness of course in U.S. national security policy at the highest level with respect to essentials has been the norm."[96] At lower levels, however, and particularly at the level of day-to-day security management and congressional politics, great ambivalence still exists.

What disturbs Gray particularly are extremist tendencies such as Right-isolationism and Left-isolationism, or Right-unilateralism and Left-unilateralism: "These four somewhat imprecisely detectable tendencies agree at least on one proposition: that the United States should cease to depend upon allies in a multilateral framework in its pursuit of the national interest."[97] Or, in geopolitical terms, these groups do not see the need to organize the Rimland against the Soviet Union. They are particularly unaware of how important NATO is to the United States.

Gray discusses the problems of NATO in detail and admits many difficulties. Ultimately, however, he is sanguine about the future of the alliance. Too many interests dictated by political geography are shared by Western Europe and the United States, and containment is on solid ground. Yet, there is one potentially divisive issue – the nuclear question. Gray shows how NATO governments

> have chosen to adopt a theory of supposedly controlled escalation – termed flexible response – rather than a doctrine of defense by denial, apparently believing that their publics would repudiate them if they prepared for war rather than for galloping holocaust as their approach to deterrence.[98]

Flexible response and first use have been proclaimed as official NATO policy because European governments are unwilling to spend the money on a credible conventional capability, on "defense by denial," but the nuclear strategy also lacks credibility, hence "galloping holocaust."

Flexible response is not credible because "U.S. strategic forces as extended deterrent have been substantially neutralized by the Soviet acquisition of a strategic-nuclear force posture that should function, in all strategic logic, as an effective counter-deterrent."[99] In other words, the United States cannot credibly threaten first use of nuclear weapons in Europe because the Soviet Union would, for a long stretch along the path of nuclear escalation, retain a constant capability to retaliate. It is the result of parity, of letting the Soviets catch up in nuclear weapons, and the prospect is bleak: "The Western Alliance could not prevail in a short conventional war, could not prevail in a protracted conventional war, and could not prevail in a short nuclear war."[100] The only remedy is for the United States to regain strategic superiority.

For this reason Gray is dissatisfied with the containment as practiced in the eighties and demands a more credible version – what he calls dynamic containment. It is not basically different from existing containment but takes more cognizance of the dictates of geopolitics and constitutes a true Grand Design. The design provides the basic outlines for strategy, determines ends and means, but in concrete matters, at the level of tactics, it is flexible and can constantly be adapted to changing needs – hence dynamic containment.

Needless to say, Gray disapproves of any disengagement from Europe and from the Rimland in general. He reviews various plans that had been presented for devolution and for a withdrawal to Fortress America, and finds them wanting. He endorses the opposite strategy, the rolling back of Soviet influence. He does not endorse a return to the type of rollback favored by James Burnham and John Foster Dulles in the fifties because those schemes, by challenging the Heartland position of the Soviet Union, were not mindful enough of the realities of geopolitics.[101] But Gray does approve of rolling back the Soviet Empire in its more far-flung positions, in areas of the Inner and Outer Crescent. He embraces the Reagan Doctrine as a useful instrument of his Grand Design but wishes it were stripped of some of its ideological overtones.

When summing up his Grand Design Gray sets clear priorities:

> Rank-ordering is geostrategically inescapable if the United States is prepared to pay more than lip service to rigorous strategic thinking. In descending order of importance, the United States must attend to its strategic forces, maritime forces, and ground and tactical air forces.[102]

Given the geopolitical position of the United States, the country is not directly threatened by either land or sea forces. The sole real threat is nuclear, hence the primary importance of the strategic forces. But, as explained, Gray wants these forces to regain their compellent value. American strategic forces, in his estimation, have a negative, not a positive value. In their negative role they constitute a counterdeterrent, in their positive role they have compellent strength.[103] And, once more, Gray warns that

> in the absence of a clear measure of U.S. strategic superiority, the positive, compellent duties of strategic forces ought to be regarded as an atavistic example of wishful thinking, even if they are a regrettable strategic necessity.[104]

Next in importance are the maritime forces. Given the geopolitical constraints, these, too, must be superior to those of the Soviet Union: "Maritime preponderance is an absolute prerequisite if the United States is to assert its landpower overseas."[105] The United States, having to rely for its security on unimpeded contact with its allies on the Rimland, cannot tolerate another naval power as its equal. Only in the remaining categories of forces can America do without superiority.

These are Gray's recommendations for a steady and successful American strategy in the Cold War. Let me now turn to an analysis of his ideas. What, to begin with, is his conception of war and of peace? Gray never says explicitly that war is normal and rational, but what he does say clearly is that Americans are naïve to assume that peace is normal and natural. The following passage, a summary of his description of American insular strategic culture, speaks for itself:

> First, the United States, as an insular power that developed very substantially in isolation from the quarrels of balance-of-power Europe, continues to harbor the belief that peace is the normal and universally desired condition of mankind...
>
> A second characteristic of U.S. culture is an optimism about progress in human affairs...
>
> Third, the American people are prone to personalize international relations... American society prefers to believe that all, or virtually all, problems – domestic and international – are susceptible to solution or major alleviation through direct person-to-person treatment.
>
> Fourth, it has long been the American way to believe that persons of good will, attentive to the needs of their societies, can always reach agreement if they try hard enough. A willingness to compromise is the essence of the process of negotiation so widely familiar to Americans...
>
> The fifth characteristic of the American people as a political entity...is to hoist order and stability as values to be promoted and defended internationally.[106]

Peace, justice, optimism, faith in man and in his ability to reason and bargain – these are all idealist values. In exposing them as dangerous Gray shows that he adheres to opposite values, to a realist worldview. However, is his realism hiearchic or anarchic in nature, does he want the United States to aim for balance or for superiority? Gray makes many references to balance of power politics and often states that it is compatible with geopolitics.[107] Yet a closer look at his use of the term suggests that for him balance of power politics is a very imprecise term. He regularly equates it with *Realpolitik* or any kind of conflictual politics:

> Whether one elects to explain the long-range character of superpower competition strictly in terms of *Realpolitik*, or of ideology, or of some sophisticated-seeming blend of the two, a basic appreciation that the character of the relationship essentially is one of conflict will remain the same (and valid). The explanations that lean most heavily upon geopolitics and the traditional *Realpolitik* of balance-of-power assumptions can point to sources of Soviet policy inspiration that are at least as enduring as are explanations that define Soviet policy chiefly in ideological terms.[108]

The association of balance of power politics with *Realpolitik* is quite revealing. In German the term can stand for the foreign policy of Metternich, Bismarck, William II, or Hitler; it can refer to equilibrium or hegemony. It is as ambiguous a term as power politics is in English and lacks academic rigor. In German one could easily argue that Gentz, Clausewitz and Bernhardi are all theoreticians of *Realpolitik*. Gray, by constantly using the term gives the impression of scholarly precision but, in fact, he clarifies nothing. To find out where he really stands different evidence is necessary.

Gray's theory is premised on the assumption of perpetual conflict between a dominant Eurasian land power and an equally dominant oceanic sea power. Two hegemonic states (or coalitions of states) emerge, and the question is whether these states are hegemonic within their respective spheres or whether they are also hegemonic relative to each other. In principle, the two powers could arrive at some sort of balance while maintaining hegemony within their spheres. But will they, given the logic of complete enmity? The Soviet Union, the way Gray describes it, is certainly not aiming at equality with the United States but seeks superiority and world domination. What are then the options for the United States?

Balance was part of the Nixon–Kissinger policy of détente, at least in as much as that administration sought parity in some areas of the strategic arsenal. But Gray is adamantly opposed to détente and makes it the object of much ridicule. Instead, he emphatically endorses the doctrine of nuclear war-fighting, of compellence and of naval predominance. These strategies emphasize superiority at the cost of balance, and I am therefore inclined to classify him as a hierarchic realist. Gray wants the United States to be Number One, he offers a geopolitical justification for the role of a World Policeman. If there is a convergence of interest between the two superpowers it is because the United States imposes it upon the Soviet Union.

Although he does not say so explicitly, Gray assumes that the two superpowers operate in a state of war in which the law of the strongest prevails. And the United States, if only it adopted Gray's Grand Design, is bound to be the stronger. Geopolitics, the logic that determines all, is on the side of the oceanic power. The oceanic world enjoys strategic and economic resources that the continental world lacks. The oceans allow for greater flexibility, for a more efficient conduct of war. And, like Herman Kahn, Gray quietly assumes that the United States can outproduce and outgun the Soviet Union. In this respect, Gray is very much in the Mackinder tradition of English imperialism.

Gray's image of the state system also resembles that of Kahn. The international order is hierarchical, containing dominant and subordinate states. The dominant power has the responsibility of running the system, of defining the rules of the game and of enforcing the law. The management of the system is monistic. The leading state is forced into this position because the other nations are incapable of playing the role, fulfilling the function, and assuming the responsibility. They are either too weak, or too irrational. They claim full sovereignty, independence, and equality but are unable to live up to these expectations. The true universal interest cannot be the sum of all national interests separately expressed. Only the dominant power is capable of defining and enforcing a true universal interest; actually, its national interest is identical with the universal interest.

Gray's conception of the state is quite explicit. America is an idealistic state, and he wished it were less so. The country is naïve in matters of war and peace, and only the very top of the political–military élite understand the true meaning of international politics, the implications of the primacy of foreign policy. At that level there is constancy, at the lower level there are unfortunate vacillations between extreme interventionism and extreme isolationism, both on the left and on the right of the political spectrum. Like Waltz and Kahn, Gray sees America as a nation with a soft core and a hard shell, a state with a democratic lifestyle on the inside and a militaristic lifestyle on the outside.

His image of the Soviet Union is different, of course. Its tradition is authoritarian, on the inside and on the outside. And, given the nature of geography, change is impossible. Living at the center of Eurasia and having no natural and safe frontiers, the Soviets have a profound security problem which they can only manage by authoritarian means. The Communist Party dominating the country will rather start a war than permit domestic change.

The argument raises a question about causality. Gray argues that geography creates an authoritarian Eurasian state with an imperialistic strategic culture that in turn produces war. As the term "geopolitics" suggests, geography is of a higher order than politics and determines it; the root cause of war is geography. In other words, the Soviet Union (or its successor states) cannot possibly become nonauthoritarian and peaceful. Nonauthoritarian developments are transitional at best.

The Soviet Union has disintegrated more quickly than anyone would have thought possible. Bolshevism is gone but it is not yet certain whether democracy will follow. On Russia, in particular, the jury is still out. However, if the Heartland is ever inhabited by a nonexpansionist state the theory of geopolitics is disproven. It then becomes evident that the cause of Soviet expansion rested more in politics than in geography. Gray's theory would then reveal its second-image character: authoritarian (or communist) states are assumed to be inherently aggressive, to initiate a struggle for survival and to produce a state of war. Perhaps this is the real foundation of Gray's theory. It matches his Hobbesian perspective and, as with Waltz, it reveals his tacit reductionism. It would mean that his theory ultimately rests on a contextual definition of states that is never fully explicated.

ROSECRANCE: FREE TRADE

Richard Rosecrance's *"The Rise of the Trading State"*[109] has been inspired by the Japanese experience. In the first half of this century, Japan rose as a political–military state – and failed. In the second half of the century, it rose as a trading state – and succeeded spectacularly. More than any other nation in the world, Japan symbolizes the failure of the political–military strategy and the success of the trading strategy.

The book has also been inspired by other developments. While Japan rose as a trading state, America declined, relatively speaking, as a superpower, as a political–military state. Furthermore, liberalism and free market economics have been rediscovered in the last decade: in Great Britain (Thatcher Revolution), in France (Mitterrand's turnabout), in the United States (deregulation). Finally, but this happened after Rosecrance wrote his book, communism collapsed in Eastern Europe, and with it the political–military strategy of the Soviet Union.

Last, but not least, Rosecrance's approach can be seen as part of the trend toward international political economy in our field. Like Gilpin, he uses the language of microeconomics and rational choice but, unlike Gilpin, Rosecrance is much less the economist, and his book is anything but a serious study in economics. Only in a general way does Rosecrance develop an economic argument; the bulk of the book uses traditional international relations language. The study is somewhat unsystematic and repetitive, but it is nonetheless interesting, mainly for its forthright treatment of a classical theme – peace through free trade.[110] It is a theory that fits neatly into the anarchic idealist worldview.

Rosecrance begins with a word about method. He deplores that most theories of international relations are one-sided, relying on one factor to explain complex realities. In fact, many theories are monocausal and deterministic:

> Most theories of international politics have offered one model of the subject: a single set of mandates according to which nations continue to behave today as they did in the past. These monistic approaches have helped to explain individual facets of international relations, but they have not succeeded in making comprehensible the full variety of international experience.[111]

Rosecrance suggests a dualistic approach free of determinism. Such an approach starts from the traditional state-centered perspective but assumes that states have a real choice. They are free agents and can choose between the logic of the trading state and that of the political–military (or territorial) state. States have a choice because history is not predetermined, because there is no one (monistic) trend.

There will always be a security problem tied to the conception of the territorial state, and there will always be an economic problem linked to the conception of the non-territorial state. It is not a question of either/or but of probabilities, of probable trends. Rosecrance is unwilling to say that the rise of the trading state is inevitable but merely that, beginning with 1945, circumstances "seem" to favor such a development. Conversely, circumstances "seem" to favor the relative decline of the territorial state. Many of Rosecrance's central statements are couched in probabilistic terms:

> It is not the American model that Japan will ultimately follow. Rather, it is the Japanese model that America "may" ultimately follow.[112]

> In an independent world states will be "more likely" to follow trading strategies, but they will "not certainly" do so.[113]

A resurgence of Westphalian territorial conceptions along such lines cannot be entirely ruled out. But it does not "appear likely."[114]

Given these probabilistic statements, the real question is why, since 1945, states have been more likely to opt for nonterritorial trading strategies. Rosecrance's answer is couched in the language of rational choice: "That depends upon the cost and benefit of waging war on the one hand and of engaging in trade on the other."[115] There was a time in the history of nations when the cost–benefit calculation tended to favor national advancement through territorial expansion, but these days are gone. Since 1945 the cost–benefit calculation tends to favor the trading strategy:

> It was not until after 1945 that large-scale territorial expansion began to evolve as too costly, too dangerous and too uncertain as a general strategy of national advancement. As that lesson gradually dawned, a trading strategy and the development of the international trading system could begin to substitute peacefully for the military–political and territorial system.[116]

Why is 1945 such an important turning point? What are the new factors tilting the cost–benefit calculation in favor of the trading state? Rosecrance does not address the question in a systematic way, but the following four factors appear to be of special importance: (1) the revolution in military technology, (2) a change in domestic politics, (3) rising international interdependence, and (4) a proliferation of new and small states.

The revolution in military technology has made war extremely destructive and very costly. Nuclear weapons, by general consent, seem to be most useful when not used at all, when employed as a deterrent. They are certainly impractical for the purpose of territorial conquest. Since 1945, there has been a "continuing stalemate in the military–political world."[117] Large-scale territorial expansion is not a realistic alternative any more.

War has also become very costly. Even in peacetime, the major nations spend a hefty portion of their national product on armaments, and it is quite uncertain whether these weapons will ever be used. The only outcome that is not uncertain is "that the peacetime stockpiling of military hardware will become more expensive, rising at least 3 to 5 percent above inflation per year."[118] In short, before 1945 the military–political world was efficient – today it has ceased to be so. The opportunity costs of the territorial system have been raised to such an extent that the trading strategy is becoming an attractive alternative.

There is also a change in domestic politics. In the past, wars brought national cohesion and strengthened domestic support for a regime. This has changed: "In the twentieth century some wars have led to greater domestic opposition and discontent."[119] As wars have become more difficult and more costly to win, domestic support has declined;[120] patriotism and nationalism have become fluctuating assets that tend to diminish with the length and indecisiveness of war.[121] Changes in domestic politics have also made it more difficult for a conqueror to occupy and govern territories. As nations develop, become more educated and accessible to information, it is increasingly difficult to occupy and rule them as in ancient times.[122]

Rising interdependence is another factor. When nations were largely out of contact, when they were politically sovereign and economically self-sufficient, the cost–benefit calculation of territorial conquest appeared favorable. But as "interdependence grew with large populations, with industrialization, and with need for resources, the military–political world faced greater difficulties."[123]

While it is true that interdependence has not increased equally for all states, it plays a progressively important role in the cost–benefit calculation of all countries. World War II and decolonization had the effect of creating a large number of small countries incapable of becoming economically self-sufficient. For them, interdependence is a question of survival: "The basic effect of World War II was to create a much higher world interdependence as the average size of countries declined."[124]

The fourth and last factor is the proliferation of the number of states. Rosecrance argues that from the Middle Ages on, there has been an amalgamation of states: some states have become territorially very large while others have been absorbed. At the beginning of this century, only a handful of imperial states dominated the international system and decided questions of world peace and world war.

World War II changed that. On the one hand, two superpowers emerged dominating much of the international system; on the other, scores of new nations were added for whose survival interdependence became an absolute necessity: "It seems safe to say that an international system composed of more than 160 states cannot continue to exist unless trade remains the primary vocation of most of its members."[125] The sheer number combined with the impossibility of autarky "raises peaceful possibilities that were neglected during the late nineteenth century and the 1930s."[126] Some of these new states may still be tempted by the territorial option and by sequestering themselves from the trading system "but there are overwhelming advantages to be gained from participating in it."[127]

Rosecrance's overall argument can be summed up as follows: the end of the Second World War represents a decisive turning point in the history of nations and the development of the international system. Before, the cost–benefit calculation of nations opting for war was favorable at times, thereafter it has become increasingly unfavorable. Four disincentives have been built into the system: nuclear war-making technology, democratization of nations, growing interdependence and proliferation of small states. Nations may still occasionally opt for war, but there is a growing probability that the trading strategy is gaining the upper hand.

As Rosecrance says, his theory is dualistic and contains probabilistic statements about future trends. There is, on the one hand, a traditional world characterized by political–military rationality, a world in which national improvement through territorial expansion and conquest makes sense. On the other hand there is a modern world where national improvement through international trade is rational. One is a world of war, the other a world of peace. Recent events have strengthened the development of the modern and peaceful world.

The military–political world is made up of territorial states that are politically sovereign and independent, and whose economy is largely self-sufficient. For Rosecrance these states are homogeneous because they share the same objectives and perform the same systemic functions: "They all seek the same territorial objectives and each, at least among the major powers, strives to be the leading power in the system."[128] War is endemic,[129] and because no major power is willing to accept hegemony there is a permanent struggle to maintain a certain equilibrium.[130] Rosecrance's political–military world corresponds with the main features of the anarchic realist worldview and with balance of power theory.

The political–military world is unable to promote national improvement because it is trapped in a vicious circle. The territorial principle tied to autarky creates a system of power maximization and self-help, a system that promotes zero-sum reasoning and suboptimal solutions. Suboptimal solutions in turn create a need for aggression and conquest – the circle closes and national impoverishment grows. Rosecrance wants to break out of the circularity. As he states in his preface, "the main thesis of this book is that a new 'trading world' of international relations offers the possibility of escaping from such a vicious circle."[131]

The trading world offers hope because it represents the opposite of the political–military world, because it removes the causes leading to power competition:

> In general terms, the competition for power emerges in social relations wherever needs are provided for independently and without reciprocity and where resources are limited. If needs do not have to be met independently, a reciprocal division of labor may give rise to stable cooperation.[132]

The trading world ends the independent provision of needs, it terminates self-help. The trading model stands for reciprocity, interdependence, and the division of labor. States operating in such a system are heterogeneous because they fulfill different functions and play differentiated roles. National improvement becomes possible – and so does peace. When trading freely, nations manage to coexist peacefully. Rosecrance's conception of a trading world coincides with the anarchic idealist worldview.

Although Rosecrance tries to avoid determinism and instead adheres to a dualist approach, he is quite certain that circumstances since World War II favor the rise of the trading state and with it the theory of "peace through free trade." Nations that ignore this fact will fail. Gone are the days when nations could hope to improve their wealth by empire, conquest and war. Like Adam Smith, Rosecrance is convinced that the logic of liberal economics is more powerful than the logic of mercantilist economics. And, like Hobson and Angell, Rosecrance is convinced that liberal economics go hand in hand with a decentralized and peaceful international system. There is no need for any kind of hierarchy, not for hegemony, not for integration, not even for regimes.

Realists like Gilpin argue that British hegemony was the backbone of liberal trade in the nineteenth century and advance what is called a "hegemonic stability" theorem. Rosecrance is doubtful. He shows that within the overall European balance of power Britain played the role of an equal, that militarily it was in no way superior to any one of the major continental powers.[133] Of course, Great Britain was the leading economic power and a lender of last resort:

> The interdependent world economy may occasionally function well when a single nation can act as market and lender of last resort, but it appears that it can also operate when no single economy performs those two functions.[134]

Liberal world trade can succeed without a hegemon – and there is also no need for world government or for international regimes.[135] Rosecrance admits that regimes like the GATT do at times constrain national behavior "and tolerably manage to police compliance in a variety of international realms... [But] there is no regime which governs the military or armaments behavior of the United States or the Soviet Union."[136] If disarmament succeeds without the establishment of formal regimes, why should the same not be true for international trade?

Rosecrance's conception of the international system begins to emerge. It is a robust, spontaneous and self-steering order. It needs no central management and control because the parts are self-disciplined and are capable of self-control. In a peaceful anarchic system all parts contribute to its management – it is subsystem-dominant. There is no serious security problem. The steering mechanism emphasizes diplomacy, dialog and bargaining. There is no need for monistic or oligopolistic leadership and coercion. Among trading states a spontaneous convergence of interest is possible.

The system has a public and a private sphere, a national and a subnational sphere. For a free-trade liberal like Rosecrance the truly vital activities are located in the subnational sphere, are carried on by private individuals, companies and associations. They produce wealth and well-being, they are the real cause of national improvement. They are the truly vital parts that make up the whole, they represent the ultimate ends in terms of which the means must be defined. They are the foundation of logic and of rationality. Public and national actors play a subordinate role, they constitute at best the framework which allows private actors to perform more efficiently; they are a means to promote private ends.

Actors have clear-cut objectives – maximization of their respective utility. The most efficient means is the market mechanism, peaceful give-and-take or bargaining. Nonpeaceful means are inefficient, irrational, and unnatural. Since the end of World War II, war as an instrument of conflict management has become increasingly expensive, self-defeating, and counterproductive. This applies particularly to nuclear war. As Kant said 200 years ago, weapons have finally become so destructive that they are useless.

Rosecrance has faith in the spread of education and science, in the working of participatory politics and democracy. Democracy favors dialog and bargaining over manipulation and coercion, it is a modern form of government suitable for modern peoples' needs. Democracy is inherently peaceful, and the primacy of domestic policy assures the peaceful coexistence of states. Rosecrance's definition of nations is entirely contextual – they are liberal entities within an anarchic liberal world-system.

Most of these arguments derive from classic liberalism and can also be found in the theories of Kant, Hobson and Wilson. Kant refers to Republicanism, which for him means constitutional government and the separation of powers.[137] Hobson and Wilson share this conception of democracy but place more emphasis on social justice than Rosecrance and Kant do. Within the wide spectrum of liberalism they stand somewhat more to the left.

Rosecrance's emphasis on learning is very pronounced. All nations, large and small, rich and poor, are capable of learning – even the Soviet Union. As one generation follows the next, that country, too, is a potential candidate for joining the ranks of trading states. Rosecrance expressed such ideas in 1986, at a time when the abandonment of the Soviet political–military strategy was not yet evident and *glasnost* and *perestroika* had hardly been announced.

The contrast to Colin Gray could hardly be greater. As far as the Soviet Union is concerned Gray cannot conceive of social learning because Soviet political and strategic culture is determined by geography. The security problem created by the huge Eurasian landmass militates against social learning. Robert Gilpin, too, is skeptical whether any nation will learn. In his estimation nations are likely to adhere to the old rationality even when confronted with nuclear weapons.

Within the realist worldview great powers are more important than small powers. Rosecrance reverses the logic and praises the virtues of smallness. Small states have small internal markets, a low degree of self-sufficiency, and consequently are more likely to convert to the trading strategy. Small states feel the forces of interdependence more strongly than large ones and are less likely to follow the political–military logic. Rosecrance must be thinking of Singapore, Taiwan, South Korea, and Hong Kong.

Bigness has drawbacks. Great powers have huge internal markets, a higher degree of self-sufficiency and are tempted to overvalue the territorial strategy. In addition, their most spectacular asset, nuclear weapons, is becoming expensive and useless. These weapons have produced a political–military stalemate because their use is irrational. Economically they entail an inefficient allocation of scarce resources. Of course, Kahn, Gray, and Gilpin would disagree. Kahn believes that the use of nuclear weapons is rational, and Gray and Gilpin argue that the most powerful nation of the world guarantees order and stability, without which free trade is impossible.

The bedrock of Rosecrance's theory is his optimistic image of man. Not all of mankind is at present attuned to the trading logic, but there is great potential. Given the proper setting, men are energetic, productive and rational. When speaking about the nineteenth century, Rosecrance says that "the trading system depended on setting free the productive and trading energies of peoples and merchants who, without guidance and direction from the administrative capital of the state, would find markets for their goods overseas."[138] This reminds one of Wilson. He, too, strove to liberate private initiative and to "set people free."

Of course, this is a capitalist conception of freedom: a Marxist does not believe that it will lead to peace and harmony. On the contrary, the private ownership of the means of production entails exploitation, the division of society into two opposing classes, revolution and war. For a Marxist the rise of the trading state is certainly not identical with the advent of rationality, well-being, and peace.

Rosecrance's book is not an explicitly anti-Marxist tract, but it could well be. The rise of the trading state symbolizes the decline of the political–military state but it also entails the demise of the socialist state. The book was written before the changes in the the Soviet Union became evident and, from a liberal standpoint, contains a fairly accurate prediction and analysis of what happened. As Joseph S. Nye, Jr. remarks in his review of Rosecrance's book, the study represents a revival of liberal theories and, within that general category, a revival of classical commercial liberalism.[139] The parallels to Adam Smith, Jeremy Bentham, and Richard Cobden are obvious.

Adam Smith in his *Wealth of Nations* strongly criticizes mercantilism and imperialism, the political–military strategy of the day. He makes the practices responsible for the prevailing misery. Bentham and Cobden are also staunchly anti-imperialist but more radical than Smith. They see a direct link between free-market liberalism and the promotion of peace. Unlike Smith, they are convinced that war disappears once free trade holds sway.[140]

Norman Angell sees a particularly strong link between free trade and peace. He calls war in the early twentieth century a "great illusion" and even an "impossibility." Rosecrance's theory is not so deterministic, he is less of a utopian. Based on his dualist method he is merely willing to say that the link between free trade and the abolition of war is one of increasing probability. His image of man is not quite as optimistic as that of Angell and consequently he considers his own logic as somewhat less compelling. Rosecrance would never argue that war is an impossibility; he actually states several times that wars can still occur. He is quite definite, however, that in the longer run the forces of modernity and of interdependence will tend to favor the trading logic, and truly rational actors see this today rather than tomorrow.

At times Rosecrance takes a neutral stand regarding the impact of the forces underlying interdependence, of science, technology, economics, and communication. They could, he says, "be a force for either peace or war."[141] Such statements are in tune with his dualist approach, with his attempt to show that man still has a choice between the two logics. Basically, however, Rosecrance shares Angell's conviction that the nature of these forces favors peace over war. Only in the short run is his conception of these "forces" less compelling. At heart, both theorists believe that a transformation of international politics is possible.

KEOHANE: REGIMES

After Hegemony is an appropriate title for Robert Keohane's book.[142] Like so many other theorists in the seventies and eighties, he deals with the question of "lost hegemony," and the title indicates that Keohane wonders what comes after. Will there be, as Gilpin suggests, destabilization, war, and a new hegemony, or, as Rosecrance proposes, a stable world order based on free trade? Keohane leans more to the optimistic side; he argues that the post-hegemonic period is more likely to be characterized by cooperation than by conflict, and he demonstrates that regimes will make a valuable contribution.[143]

Keohane begins with a critical analysis of hegemonic stability theory.[144] He shows that the theory is premised on two arguments: one, that order in world politics is created by a single dominant power and the formation of regimes depends on hegemony; two, that the maintenance of order and of regimes requires continued hegemony.[145] With the first argument Keohane disagrees in part, with the second he disagrees entirely. Hegemony can facilitate the formation of regimes but once they are established hegemony becomes unnecessary because post-hegemonic cooperation is possible without it.[146]

Keohane rejects traditional realism, but does not intend to embrace idealism either. His aim is to develop an intermediate position, to draw idealist conclusions from realist premises. He intends to defeat the realists with their own weapons, and the instrument is rational choice. Keohane argues that cooperation can be promoted by egoism and self-interest:

> I assume, with the Realists, that actors are rational egoists. I propose to show, on the basis of their own assumptions, that the characteristic pessimism of Realism does not necessarily follow. I seek to demonstrate that Realist assumptions about world politics are consistent with the formation of institutionalized arrangements, containing rules and principles, which promote cooperation.[147]

Keohane's intention is clear: he rejects pessimistic realism and wants to demonstrate that there is optimism hidden in realism. Keohane's optimism is not derived from an idealist position because he rejects traditional idealism as much as he does traditional realism. Keohane makes a very definite effort to distance himself from both traditional camps.

Keohane disagrees with Waltz's contention that world politics resembles a state of war.[148] If it did, regimes would be more like temporary alliances because "institutionalized patterns of cooperation on the basis of shared purposes [like regimes] should not exist except as part of a larger struggle for power."[149] Furthermore, he rejects Gilpin's unidirectional view of the relation between wealth and power because "reflection on wealth and power as state objectives soon yields the conclusion that they are complementary."[150]

Keohane keeps his distance from the idealists as well. He disagrees with traditional institutionalists like Mitrany (the theorist of functional integration), who argue that "shared economic interests create a demand for international institutions and rules."[151] The assumption that shared interests create a "demand" rests on an optimistic assumption about the role of ideals "or about the ability of statesmen to learn what the theorist considers the 'right lessons'."[152]

Keohane develops his own position. At first he defines basic terms: interdependence, cooperation, harmony, and regime. Interdependence should not be mistaken for cooperation or harmony. Interdependence can have cooperative or conflicting consequences, harmonious or disharmonious implications. It "can transmit bad influences as well as good ones: unemployment or inflation can be exported as well as growth and prosperity."[153]

Cooperation and harmony are not identical either. When interdependence is harmonic, when the international economy is self-steering, as some liberals assume it is, there is no need for cooperation:

> Cooperation takes place only in situations in which actors perceive that their policies are actually or potentially in conflict, not where there is harmony. Cooperation should not be viewed as the absence of conflict, but rather as a reaction to conflict or potential conflict.[154]

Cooperation is a formal intergovernmental activity, a process of policy coordination, and it can produce regimes.[155] The concept of "regime" was first introduced by John Ruggie in 1975[156] and later amended at a conference chaired by Stephen Krasner.[157] Since then regimes are generally defined as "sets of implicit or explicit principles, norms, rules and decision-making procedures around which actors' expectations converge in a given area of international relations."[158] Keohane adds that principles, norms, rules and decision-making procedures contain injunctions about behavior: "They prescribe certain actions and proscribe others. They imply obligations, even though these obligations are not enforceable through a hierarchical legal system."[159]

He then investigates how regimes survive in the post-hegemonic period. As already mentioned, he contends that regimes continue to prosper for purely self-interested and egoistic reasons. It is what rational choice literature teaches and what microeconomic theory has known for some time. The lesson must now be applied to the study of international politics.

Keohane demonstrates these arguments with reference to the Prisoners' Dilemma. The two prisoners, although having compatible interests (both want to leave prison), cannot attain their goal for lack of information, communication, and trust. Their individually (or egoistically) rational calculations lead to a suboptimal solution – both remain in jail.[160] The dilemma teaches a sobering lesson: even among actors (or states) with identical interests, optimal or positive-sum solutions may be impossible. The analogy with international relations is evident. States may be interdependent and have an interest to set up or to maintain regimes, but a lack of information, communication or trust can prevent a favorable outcome.

Keohane shows that the Prisoners' Dilemma is part of Mancur Olson's logic of collective action. Olson distinguishes between private goods whose consumption is limited (by private property rights) to the party producing them, and public (or collective) goods that can be consumed by all. Cigarettes are private goods, clean water or fresh air are examples of collective goods. Although everyone enjoying the consumption of public goods is supposed to contribute to their production, experience shows that this is often not so:

> As in Prisoners' Dilemma, the dominant strategy for an egoistic individualist is to defect, by not contributing to the production of the good. Generalizing this calculation yields the conclusion that the collective good will not be produced, or will be underproduced, despite the fact that its value to the group is greater than its cost.[161]

The situation seems bleak – both the Prisoners' Dilemma and the logic of collective action show that rational choice calculations based on egoistic individualism can lead to suboptimal outcomes not conducive to the establishment of regimes. But there is a solution. Experiments with the Prisoners' Dilemma have demonstrated that if it is repeatedly played as a game cooperative strategies emerge. Furthermore, Mancur Olson shows that if consumption of public goods is limited to a small number of individuals who monitor each other's behavior defection is less likely.[162]

These two factors, iteration of plays and small group dynamics, lead to optimal solutions and regimes; there is no need for hegemony:

> Intensive interaction among a few players helps to substitute for, or to supplement, the actions of a hegemon. As a hegemon's power erodes, a gradual shift may take place from hegemonic to post-hegemonic cooperation. Increasingly, incentives to cooperate will depend not only on the hegemon's responses but on those of other sizeable states.[163]

Put in more concrete language, regimes like the GATT and the IMF have continued to function because there is a gradual shift toward post-hegemonic cooperation where a few sizeable actors like Japan and the European Community help to substitute and supplement the actions of the former hegemon. Between America, Japan, and the EC the Prisoners' Dilemma fails to arise because small-group dynamics are at work. It is the application of Mancur Olson's logic at the international level.

Keohane also refers to the microeconomic concept of market failure. Economists use the idea to demonstrate the importance of information for the successful functioning of markets.[164] Keohane suggests that the same is true of regimes – they should be seen as information-producing systems that reduce transaction costs. He goes on to strengthen his case by discussing an inversion of the Coase theorem and by drawing conclusions about the importance of property rights, legal liability, and the limitation of uncertainty.[165] All these insights demonstrate "why the erosion of American hegemony during the 1970s was not accompanied by an immediate collapse of cooperation, as the crude theory of hegemonic stability would have predicted."[166]

This concludes Keohane's argumentation against hegemonic stability theory. It rests on three insights: the positive effects of game iteration, the favorable monitoring effects of small-group dynamics, and the cost-reducing results of information production. The rest of Keohane's book adds nothing of importance to the central argument. In a separate chapter he relaxes some of the assumptions about strict rationality and refines the argument.[167] He looks at the practice of regimes and finds many of the theoretically derived statements confirmed.[168] For the student interested in learning more about the history and the functioning of regimes, these chapters are useful.

How valid is Keohane's theory? As I pointed out earlier, Keohane tries to show that there is a third way between realism and idealism, "that realist assumptions about world politics are consistent with the formation of institutionalized arrangements, containing rules and principles, which promote cooperation."[169] Keohane proposes to explain the functioning of regimes without reference either to harmony or hegemony; he suggests a route that combines realism and idealism, that begins with realist assumptions and ends with idealist conclusions. Is such a route possible?

James Buchanan, a prominent exponent of rational choice (or public choice) theory, also premises his theory on realist assumptions and infers idealist consequences. He assumes a Hobbesian state of war, then postulates a constitutional contract based on universal consent, and from there deduces individualistically rational behavior and market economics.[170] One wonders how the conversion process operates, how a state of unrestrained war is transformed into a state of restrained and humane competition. What is it that converts aggressive warriors into peaceful merchants, that alters human nature and rationality?

The conversion is possible because some parameters are tacitly relaxed. By permitting iteration the Prisoners' Dilemma is converted into a Prisoners' Game! When the prisoners have only one chance their situation resembles a true dilemma. In such a setting there is no opportunity to monitor the opponent's behavior and to supply needed information, to develop small-group dynamics. However, when the dilemma is "played" several times it begins to resemble a game of strategy or a market situation. Games can be played repeatedly, and in a market situation the give-and-take and bargaining are endless because the rules permit this. Small wonder that nations that play by the rules of games also play by the rules of regimes!

What are these rules, what governs repetition? No doubt certain harmonies are assumed, certain mutually accepted rights are respected, but Keohane does not say which. By permitting repetition he relaxes a basic parameter of the Prisoners' Dilemma without explicating its nature. In effect, he quietly converts a veritable dilemma into a mere game.[171] The new rules permit Keohane's prisoners to develop tit-for-tat strategies, thereby creating room for learning. In the process they alter their mutual perceptions and images, and the favorable learning experience is as much the result of benign assumptions as of iteration, monitoring, information supply, and small-group dynamics. Inputs determine outputs; idealism in – idealism out. We are confronted with the kind of circularity typical of endogenous theorizing. Keohane's definition of nations as "game players" is tacitly contextual. If the definition were explicit, if his generalizations were fully revealed, we could easily deduce the nature of regime dynamics.

There are a number of indications that Keohane is unaware of his idealism. Take, for example, his discussion of equality. He emphasizes strongly that his own definition of cooperation and of regimes has no relation whatsoever "to the mythological world of relations among equals in power."[172] But is the "equality myth" not an integral part of the rules that permit the repetition of games, and of the definition of nations as "game players?" If actors were not granted equal rights to exist, trade, play, inform, and negotiate there would be no markets, games, and regimes.

Keohane's unawareness of his own liberal assumptions also shows in his treatment of such terms as "public interest" and "general will." The following quotation is taken from the concluding passages on rational choice:

> This chapter has used theories of rational choice and of the functions performed by institutions to help us understand the creation, maintenance, and evolution of international regimes. My analysis has assumed that governments calculate their interests minutely on every issue facing them. It has not relied at all on assumptions about the "public interest" or the General Will; no idealism whatsoever is posited.[173]

Keohane, once again, is unaware that regimes, games and markets by definition contain a public interest, a public good or a general will. If they did not, if truly egoistic and selfish interests prevailed, markets, games and regimes would deteriorate into a state of war. Keohane fails to realize that there is narrow and enlightened self-interest. He operates quietly with an enlightened definition of self-interest. Once that definition is spelled out rational choice loses its attraction for the justification of regime theory, at least for those idealists who want to fight the realists with their own weapons. It simply does not work.

Keohane's tacit idealism shows clearly toward the end of the book where, at one point, he criticizes the realist conception of the state. He disapproves of a state that "keeps its options open and its decision-making processes closed." A policy of "keeping others guessing" may bring tactical gains but undermines a state's ability "to make beneficial agreements in the future."[174] Woodrow Wilson would have agreed. He, too, thought that closed decision-making processes (or secret diplomacy) were prejudicial to international cooperation, and he advocated the fullest possible flow of information (or open diplomacy) for his regime, the League of Nations. But Wilson knew that information alone would not change a government's mind. Information, like interdependence, can be a two-edged sword, working for war or for peace. For him information, if it is to promote cooperation, must go hand in hand with democratic government and enlightened public opinion, with a positive image of man and of the state.

If Keohane were aware of his own values he would realize how much he has in common with Wilson. Both have an equally skeptical perception of anarchy. Wilson and Keohane argue that in a decentralized order even fully rational actors cannot cooperate optimally – coordination is necessary. Neither believes in spontaneous order and cooperation, neither adheres to the extreme harmony position. Both argue that conscious efforts must be undertaken to reduce barriers, to exit from the Prisoners' Dilemma and to overcome anarchy. Regimes represent such efforts, and so did the League of Nations. Both Keohane and Wilson fit uncomfortably into the anarchic idealist worldview because they reject the notion of automatic order in anarchy and would like to move beyond it, into a somewhat less anarchic and more hierarchical world. Both formulate a transformation theory of international relations.

Let me end this critique with a reference to Keohane's philosophy of science. He is aware that isolated behavior, or what he calls "atomistic instances of cooperation," cannot constitute the foundation for his theory of regimes. Theories are tied to meaning, to relating parts to wholes:

> It makes little sense to describe naturalistically what goes on at a Balinese cock-fight unless one understands the meaning of the event for Balinese

culture. There is not a world culture in the fullest sense, but even in world politics, human beings spin webs of significance...Any act of cooperation or apparent cooperation needs to be understood within the context of related actions, and of prevailing expectations and shared beliefs, before its meaning can be properly understood. Fragments of political behavior become comprehensible when viewed as part of a larger mosaic.[175]

This conception of science has much in common with my own outlined earlier. Theories are more than laws and "naturalistic descriptions" because they are premised on "webs of significance" and permit "understanding." Cooperation (and regimes, one might add) can be understood only with reference to "shared beliefs" and "meaning," or else they resemble "fragmented" behavior not part of any whole.

Keohane obviously adheres to an interrelational conception of science and prefers endogenous over exogenous knowledge. Yet he rejects such attributes of interrelational knowledge as projections, subjectivity, values, logic, holism, rule-orientation, and contextual definitions. If he embraced these attributes he would have to deal explicitly with the inherent logic of regime theory and to discuss the substance of those "principles, norms, rules, and decision-making procedures around which actors' expectations converge." As it is, Keohane deals with the definition only formally; it remains a shell without content. Of course, if he went into the substance he would reveal his idealism. Why not? Is it no longer fashionable to be a professed liberal?

OSGOOD: TENSION REDUCTION

Rosecrance and Keohane use the language of political economy to develop theories grounded in an anarchic idealist worldview. Charles E. Osgood is also part of the idealist camp but he is different in a number of ways. His approach is that of a political psychologist and his theory has a hierarchic bent. And, most noticeably, Osgood is highly explicit about basic assumptions, about method and values.

Osgood published his well-known study *An Alternative to War or Surrender* in 1962, at the height of the Cold War.[176] In it he outlined a strategy leading out of the Cold War dilemma. According to Osgood the predicament consisted, on the one hand, in the pursuit of a hard line ending in escalation and war and, on the other, in the pursuit of a soft line resulting in peace by surrender. He suggested a middle course avoiding both the martial and the pacifist trap. Osgood recommended unilateral steps to reduce tension or, more precisely, the graduated and reciprocated initiation of tension reduction (GRIT).

For many years Osgood's unilateralism was regarded as hopelessly idealistic and unworkable. GRIT was included in a number of readers on international relations, but more out of intellectual curiosity than from a sincere belief that this approach would work.[177] But times are changing. In the post-Cold War era the unilateral initiation of tension reduction became a common feature of international politics. For a while, Mikhail Gorbachev was using this instrument with particular skill to demonstrate his New Thinking; he initiated a process of deescalation that resembled a reversal of the arms race – a regular "peace spiral." Of course, unilateral initiatives are no substitute for negotiations; there was still a need for formal talks and agreements, for the INF treaty, for the START negotiations, and for the CSCE process. Nevertheless, unilateralism worked and Osgood's theory is of renewed interest today.

Osgood's study is important for yet another reason. It represents one of the more lucid and forthright applications of psychology to the study of war and peace. Today, political psychology is an established branch of political science; unfortunately its growth has been accompanied by massive fragmentation.[178]

A few years ago, Stanley Hoffmann, as President of the International Society of Political Psychology, spoke about the problem and made an effort to group the various political psychologists. He distinguished between traditionalists and radicals. What separates the two schools is "a split about what is possible, which is tied to a different reading of reality." Traditionalists "do not believe that the essence of world politics is susceptible to drastic and early change barring disaster. In their eyes, easy, quick transcendence, a sudden mutation, is not at all possible."[179] The radicals, on the other hand, are those who believe that world politics is susceptible to drastic change, easy transcendence, sudden mutation. Charles Osgood belongs to the second group. He develops a transformation theory of international relations that moves the world from conflictual anarchy toward peaceful hierarchy.

As hinted at, the alternative to war and to surrender suggested by Osgood amounts to a reversal of the arms race, to a process of deescalation. An arms race is a graduated and reciprocated, unilaterally initiated, internation action which increases tension. Osgood's model is the reverse: a unilaterally initiated, graduated and reciprocated process of tension reduction:

> It is perhaps best viewed as a kind of international (rather than interpersonal) communicating and learning situation, where the communication

is more by deeds than by words and where what is learned – hopefully and gradually – is increased mutual understanding and trust.[180]

Beside reducing tension and increasing understanding, such a process, according to Osgood, has additional advantages: it enables the United States to take the initiative in foreign policy, it launches a new kind of international behavior appropriate to the nuclear age, and finally, it gradually creates an atmosphere of mutual trust in which negotiations on critical political and military issues will have a better chance of succeeding. Unilateralism is not a direct road to peace but a first step in that direction and does not stand in the way of bilateral and multilateral negotiations. Unilateralism breaks the ice, so to speak.

How does it work? Osgood gives the example of two men facing each other on a long, precariously balanced seesaw. As either of the two takes a step outward, the other is forced quickly to compensate with an equal step. Moving outward, however, ends in mutual suicide since the seesaw is not endless. Moving inward brings the two men more security but demands that they reverse the process. How can it be done? This is Osgood's recommendation:

> let us suppose that, during a quiet period in their strife, it occurs to one of these men that perhaps the other is really just as frightened as he himself is. If this were so, he would also welcome some way of escaping from this intolerable situation. So this man decides to gamble a little on his new insight. Loudly he calls out, "I am taking a small step *toward* you when I count to ten!". The other man, rather than risk having the precious balance upset, also takes a small, tentative step *forward* at the count of ten. Whereupon the first announces another larger step forward, and they both take it as the count is made.[181]

Osgood is aware that in the real world the process is more complex and subject to various conditions. All told, he lists fifteen different conditions, of which I am mentioning only the more important ones.

The first two relate to armaments. Osgood does not propose alterations in the military balance at the outset of the process. Unilateral initiatives "must not cripple our capacity to meet aggression." Osgood avoids the pacifist road, he rejects the idea that weapons as such are evil and cause war. His scenario begins with the maintenance of strong national defense, nuclear and conventional.

Most of the conditions Osgood mentions have to do with the nature of the initiatives: they must be graduated in risk according to the degree of reciprocation, diversified and innovative in character, unpredictable as to sphere, locus and time of execution, they must exhibit sincere intent to reduce and control tensions, they must be announced publicly and have to include an explicit invitation to reciprocate.

The first phase of the process changes the relations between the contestants but does not alter the structure of the international system. Osgood therefore proposes a second phase in which the system as such is transformed. Unilateral initiatives must aim at transferring sovereignty from national to international auspices, reducing imbalances between have and have-not nations and seek to strengthen democratic ways of life.[182]

So much for the model in its simplest outlines. Osgood is well-aware that a number of its most central components rest on assumptions about the nature of the contestants, about Americans and Soviets, about people in general and about his own methodology or, more precisely, about his own "reading of reality." To his credit, Osgood discusses all of these questions self-consciously. There are no hidden assumptions in his study.

Osgood believes that the present is characterized by a great cultural lag: there is a wide gap between man's technical and his political civilization. If man wants to survive in the face of modern technological developments he must alter his political institutions. This happens in stages of learning.

At a low stage, man unconsciously projects his own norms on to others, is incapable of recognizing the relativity of his own images and adheres to a rigid pattern of cognitive consistency that prevents true learning. When faced with a problem that clashes with his own norms, he will either deny the existence of the problem (and hope that it will go away) or force his norm on to the problem "in a fit of emotion." That, as Osgood says, is the "Neanderthal's way."[183] Developed man reacts differently: he realizes the relativity of his norms and becomes capable of true learning.

Applied to the Cold War, it means that Soviets and Americans must abandon their rigid intent to maintain cognitive consistency and begin to question their own norms. If they did they would discover that some of the differences are purely perceptual because there exist a number of similarities. Osgood frankly admits that his theory

> assumes that the Soviet people and their leaders are more like us than like the bogey men our psycho-logic creates, and that therefore we can do business with them. It assumes that their prime motive, like ours, is security, not world domination, and that they are as eager as we are to avoid full-scale nuclear conflict. It assumes that the men in the Kremlin are susceptible to the pressures of public opinion, both from within and from without, since such pressures are an index of the success or failure of their system.[184]

Overcoming perceptual consistency leads the two peoples to discover their true nature, their real self: the prime motive of both is security, not domination or war; both want to do business, to engage in a dialog, to bargain, to persuade and to learn; both are sensitive to the opinion of others because they want to appear reasonable and rational.

The Americans are further along the way of political and psychological development than the Soviets, further removed from the Neanderthal mentality. American initiative is therefore necessary to get the international learning process started. The Soviets cannot by themselves realize the relativity of their own norms. They still adhere to a false image of their identity and sovereignty. If this misconception can be exposed for what it is then the Cold War can be overcome.

Osgood also wants to transform the international system. The present decentralized system is dysfunctional and inefficient because it is out of step with scientific, technological, and economic developments. He is convinced that progress in "communications, transportation, weaponry, and all other forms of group interaction have made some form of world government not only feasible but absolutely essential for survival in the nuclear age."[185] In matters of security nations are still attempting to attain both international security and national autonomy, but today this proves to be impossible. States must realize, as did the thirteen American colonies after the War of Independence, that limiting their autonomy provides benefits.

Again, unilateralism shows the way. The United States must initiate such a development, and it can do so by strengthening the United Nations. A first step would be to upgrade the World Court, an organ of the United Nations. America should, for instance, repeal the Connolly Amendment which limits American willingness to submit to rulings of that body. The whole world would gain "by firmly establishing the precedent of a powerful nation subjecting itself to the rule of international law, and thereby making it more difficult for other nations to evade the same legal procedure."[186]

Other branches of the United Nations would be strengthened if America took the lead in transferring new tasks to various bodies, matters pertaining to outer space or to the exploration of the bottom of the seas. Such moves would give "full rein to the creativeness of our scientists while at the same time gradually reducing the unstabilizing impacts of their breakthroughs upon international relations."[187] It would be an important step toward bringing the technological and political development of mankind into line.

Osgood's theory has a hierarchic component. He believes that the problems facing man can be overcome only with the establishment of a more centralized and hierarchical international system. The whole must be in line with the needs of the parts, it must be able to accommodate functions that are vital for the survival of mankind. A supranational body would define collective ends and select appropriate means. Osgood has a Wilsonian penchant but goes beyond mere collective security. Some of his ideas, as will be shown, parallel those of Richard Falk. Osgood's image of hierarchy is favorable.

Correspondingly, his image of anarchy is negative. The present international system is primitive, both organizationally and psychologically. Organizationally it cannot handle the problems of interdependence, and psychologically it is an expression of the Neanderthal mentality, of rigid cognitive consistency as it exists at the lowest stage of mental development. At such an archaic level peace and well-being are impossible.

Osgood's image of the nation-state is skeptical, too. In contrast to such idealists as Kant, Hobson, Angell and Rosecrance he feels that good government and a liberal economy alone will not make for peace. Osgood is convinced that, in part at least, the nation-state is obsolescent: states must abandon some of their sovereignty. His image of the United States is less negative, however. Although that country is also forced to give up sovereignty, it is perceived as being capable of initiating first steps toward world government. The United States seems to be the least settled with the Neanderthal mentality and the most likely to lead the rest of the world in the right direction. This reminds one of Kant and of Wilson who also argued that enlightened great powers were central to the transformation of world politics.

Osgood's image of man and of society is generally positive. The average man, whether American or Soviet, is ready for peace. Soviets and Americans have different cultural norms but once they realize the relativity of their norms it becomes apparent that similarities are greater than differences. There is a hidden potential for adjusting cognitive patterns, a potential that can be activated by the proper strategies. If the potential were lacking, or if there existed a potential for conflict, the "learner" on the see-saw would interpret the "teacher's" words differently. He would then assume that the call for cooperation is a ruse meant to distract his mind, to destabilize the situation and to win. The logical strategy is then to attack, to conflict, and not to cooperate.

In Osgood's theory Soviets and Americans discover that there are no serious security problems between them, that their differences are relatively superficial. Their conflicts are simple misunderstandings capable of resolution by dialog and by reasoning. Peace and harmony are the normal conditions between the two nations, war and disharmony are abnormal and unnatural. People have the potential for improvement.

The proper learning strategies have to be implemented by enlightened statesmen with the will and the courage to be insistent, to repeat the same tactics over and over again. With patience and intelligence zero-sum reasoning can be overcome, narrow and selfish interests can be converted into public and converging interests. Like in Wilson's theory, enlightened personalities can be found. And, like in Keohane's interpretation of the Prisoners' Dilemma, iteration brings favorable results.

Osgood's image of the forces of modernity is not as uniformly favorable as that of Angell and Rosecrance. To be sure, science, technology and economics promote progress and well-being but they must also be controlled and governed. Nuclear technology is a good example. Given the proper institutional context it can benefit man, but given the present international system it is bound to hurt him. One is reminded of Chernobyl. Had the International Atomic Energy Organization possessed some control over the reactor it might never have burnt out.

In contrast to Keohane, Osgood's convictions and values are here for everyone to see. He avoids the language of rational choice and, therefore, has no illusions about achieving cooperation based on narrow self-interest, about learning based on simple iteration. As Osgood says explicitly, his learning process "*assumes* that the Soviet people and their leaders are more *like us* than like the bogey men our psycho-logic creates" [emphasis added].[188] For Osgood harmony and equality are not a "myth." They are the foundations of his definition of rationality and of logic.

In Stanley Hoffmann's eyes Osgood is a radical political psychologist because "drastic and quick change, easy transcendence and sudden mutation" are seen as possible. And, as Hoffmann also says, the roots of this philosophy are in a "different reading of reality." This is no doubt true. Osgood "reads" the substance of international relations differently from Hoffmann, the two have an entirely different "reading" of man, of the state, of the state system, and even of the theory itself. In Osgood's worldview men and states have a choice, they can opt for one logic or the other; and ultimately the idealist logic is compelling.

At the time Osgood formulated his theory, idealism was not the dominant strand in the theory of international relations and the circumstances prevailing during the Cold War did not favor GRIT. One wonders, as some reviewers have done, whether the Soviets would have valued reciprocity[189] and whether the mutual problems were based on superficial misunderstandings and unrealistic fears.[190] It cannot be denied, however, that at least Gorbachev and Yeltsin have shown an ability to take a good look at the Soviet self-image, to realize the relativity of their own norms, to overcome rigid cognitive consistency and to learn.

FALK: CENTRAL GUIDANCE

Richard A. Falk is a scholar of public and international law and the incarnation of what Keohane calls "institutionalists." In the eyes of many he is also a thoroughly utopian liberal with a missionary zeal to transform the international system and to propagate world government. He is seen to be in the tradition of Grenville Clark and Louis B. Sohn who, in the late fifties, published a study on how to convert the United Nations into a world government.[191] That proposal is narrowly legal and remindful of the kind of formalism that dominated theorizing about world government too often in the past.

Falk's study is much more broadly based. It is part of a comprehensive project launched in the mid-sixties. Entitled WOMP (World Order Models Project), the effort represented an American initiative but included scholars from all over the world. Projects were elaborated by an African, a Latin American, a European, and an American member.[192] No two plans are alike because it was the intention of the initiators to activate a diverse group of scholars and to grant each a wide range of freedom.

To provide the project with a common denominator several points were agreed upon. All authors share a deep apprehension about the present state of world affairs; they agree that for a large portion of mankind the existing international system is incapable of assuring the most common basic needs. They also agree on a definition of these needs, or values, as they prefer to call them: minimization of large-scale collective violence (V1), maximization of social and economic well-being (V2), realization of fundamental human rights and of conditions of political justice (V3), and maintenance and rehabilitation of ecological quality (V4). To promote these values, the authors agree to draft relevant utopias and to outline the necessary steps to implement them.

It is beyond the scope of this study to look at all the plans. I confine myself to a discussion of the model proposed by Richard Falk, the American member. Falk is an eminent scholar of international law teaching at Princeton University, and he approaches the task in an academically challenging and most comprehensive manner. He outlines over twenty different models before settling for his preferred one – Central Guidance. In the presentation that follows I shall start with a brief summary of Falk's most important models and then proceed to a more detailed presentation of Central Guidance. Needless to say, this is a full-blown transformation theory that rests squarely on a hierarchical idealist worldview.

Falk begins with a description of the existing world order and demonstrates that it is a complex system consisting of a multitude of different actors of various sizes and characters. Most important are the governmental actors who monopolize all the military power and also claim the right to control the nongovernmental actors. Among the nongovernmental actors Falk distinguishes global actors, global specialized actors, regional actors, regional specialized actors, and transnational actors (corporations). Although nominally the governmental actors deal with each other on the basis of equality and independence, the reality is very different:

> The inequality of governments in all relevant dimensions leads to relationships of dominance and dependence in external affairs, and to a wide range of domestic governing strategies. This inequality also creates opportunities for intervention by the more powerful governments in the affairs of weak states, thereby eroding the realities of national independence and sovereign equality which are formally attained with statehood.[193]

Figure 3.1 is a rough approximation of the present world order system. It portrays the inequality of the nation-states and also depicts the existence of some nongovernmental actors.

Before outlining the many possible future world models, Falk looks into the past. The world system as it existed around 1890 embraced no global governmental actor and only a very few global specialized actors. Instead there were several colonial clusters. A gap already existed between great and small powers but the many small and weak states were still missing.

Looking into the future, Falk distinguishes ten possible world models and various submodels. All told, he arrives at 24 different international systems. The following is a list of the ten most important ones:

1. Enhanced State System
2. World Government System (4 subsystems)
3. Regionalist System (3 subsystems)
4. Functionalist System (3 subsystems)
5. World Empire System (2 subsystems)
6. Concert System (3 subsystems)
7. Condominium System
8. Small-State System (2 subsystems)
9. Anarchistic System (4 subsystems)
10. Central Guidance System

To get the feeling of Falk's argumentation and to understand why he favors Central Guidance, it is important to take a closer look at the Regionalist and the Functionalist Models. The two are important building blocks for Central Guidance.

Figure 3.1 Existing World Order System

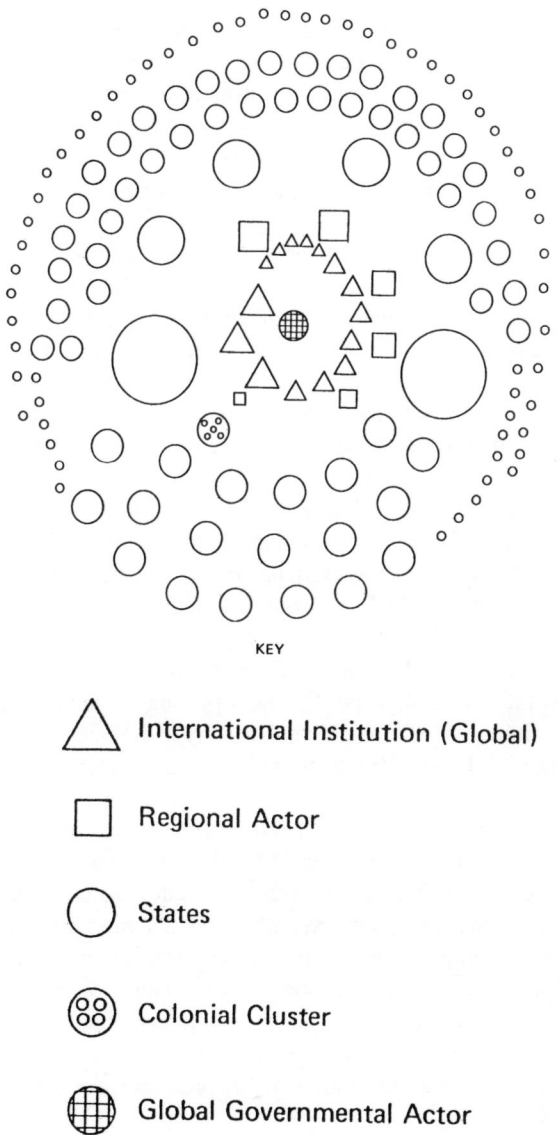

KEY

△ International Institution (Global)

☐ Regional Actor

◯ States

⊛ Colonial Cluster

⊕ Global Governmental Actor

Source: Falk, *A Study*, p. 163. Reproduced with permission of the author and publishers.

Falk welcomes regionalism in general but values regional integration in particular. When true integration occurs, statism (as he calls it) is diminished because political loyalties and identities are transferred from the states to new supranational entities. If more world regions moved toward integration the result would be favorable because this "preserves diversity and pluralism within the world system as a whole, and allows political identity to take shape around a 'we' that is understood in contrast with the 'they' who live beyond regional boundaries."[194] But regionalism alone is no substitute for Central Guidance, it is at best one of the building blocks for a future world order.[195]

Falk outlines three possible types of regional world order models: Type A, which emphasizes the expansion, although uneven, of regional actors; Type B, in which the growth of regional actors is complemented by the absolute and relative decline in state capabilities and competence; and Type C, where there is a growth and proliferation of regional actors, political and functional, accompanied by a drastic reduction of the importance of states.[196] The last of the three models is most directly linked to Central Guidance.

Functionalism is another building block. As shown, it can be tied to regionalism, but it can also be an independent phenomenon when it develops at the global level, as the existence of many specialized world organizations demonstrates. Falk welcomes functionalism at all levels and conceives of three different outcomes: Type A, an even development at the regional and at the global levels; Type B, an uneven build-up favoring global institutions; and Type C, the opposite development, favoring regional institutions. Falk favors a balanced type of development.

Unlike David Mitrany, Falk does not believe that functionalism alone is a valuable road to peace: "There is no present basis for believing that functional logic, as embodied in specialized institutions, can by itself transform the world order system by the year 2000."[197] Functional organizations cannot make such a contribution because they are dominated by national governments and by statism. However, Falk is sure that functionalist institutions will increase in number, grow in size and expand in function, and he believes that they will make a substantial contribution to the quality (but not to the structure) of world order. Like regional integration, functional cooperation is one of the building blocks of a more centralized world order.

Falk then turns to a description of his preferred world order model – Central Guidance:

> This particular model is the most viable one for a global movement committed to a program of drastic reform by the end of the century, without

recourse to violence and without the sort of systemic shock that might be administered by global warfare, pandemic, widespread famine, or major ecological collapse.[198]

Central Guidance rests on a number of assumptions about the development of the major actors, the states in general and of regional and functional international organizations:

> Our basic assumptions are that the preference model will result from a major build-up of functional agencies at the regional and world level, a steady growth in regional general-purpose actors, an accelerating rate of growth in the organs of the global general-purpose actor, and stagnancy followed by a shrinkage of state actors, especially the largest ones.[199]

The trend is depicted in Figure 3.2 overleaf.

By the turn of the century, such specialized international organizations as the IMF, GATT or IATA are expected to grow significantly, closely followed by similar specialized regional organizations. With a certain delay the importance of private transnational corporations (such as multinationals) increases measurably, and the influence of the United Nations or its successor organization grows as well. The nation-states, however, gradually lose power. After the first decade of the next century, the nation-states are the least important of all the international actors.

Central Guidance is a conscious rejection of world government. The system is not primarily characterized by centralization but by a wide dispersion of power among a variety of actors. The projected growth curves for international actors show that even though the general-purpose world actor overtakes the state actors in the next century, the various regional and global functional actors have more weight. The institutions responsible for central guidance are correspondingly weak.

Still, the mechanism for central coordination represents an important extension of the United Nations, and Falk hopes that it will be an entirely new organization. To emphasize the difference Falk labels it World Polity Association.[200] He chooses the name consciously to convey discontinuity. As the organizational chart of the new international organization shows, it bears little resemblance to the United Nations Organization.

The principal policy-making body of the World Polity Association is the World Assembly. It carries prime responsibility for the promotion of the basic values outlined earlier – world peace (V1), economic well-being (V2), human rights (V3), and ecological equilibrium (V4). The World Assembly consists of three chambers, an Assembly of Governments, an Assembly of Peoples, and an Assembly of Organizations and Associations.

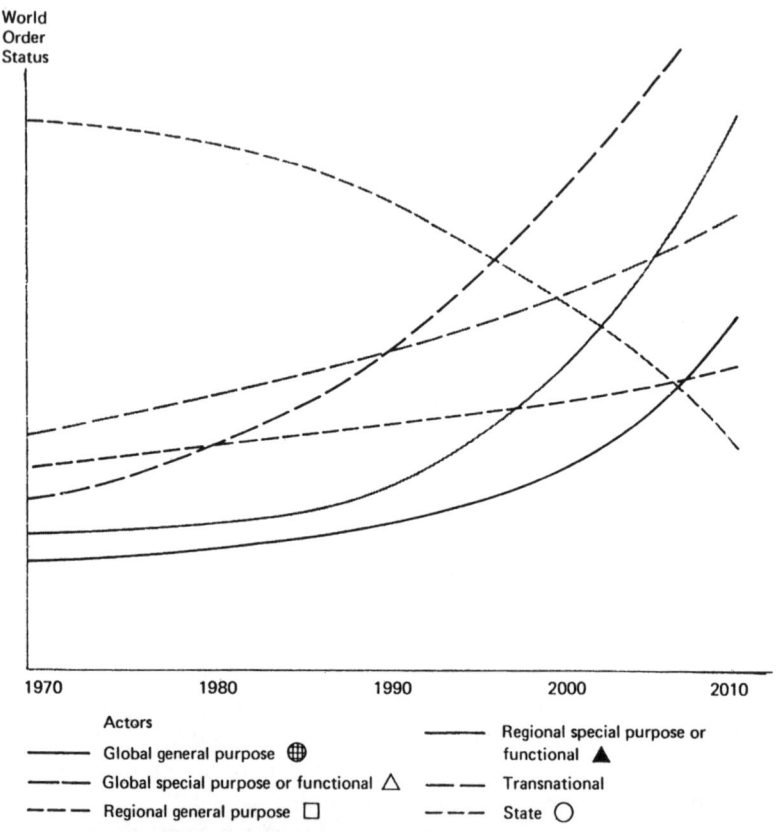

Figure 3.2 Projected Growth Curves for Actors in the World Order System

Source: Falk, *A Study*, p. 226. Reproduced with permission.

Each has 200 votes (although not necessarily 200 members), and binding decisions require a four-fifths majority in each of the three chambers. Recommendations, as distinct from decisions, demand only a two-thirds vote in each of the chambers. An appeal against decisions of the World Assembly to the World Court is possible for review by any ten representatives of any of the three chambers. There is also an elaborate process of accommodation remindful of the American system of checks and balances.[201]

The executive organ of the World Polity Association is a Council of Principals. It is in continuous session and has four major functions:

Figure 3.3 World Polity Association

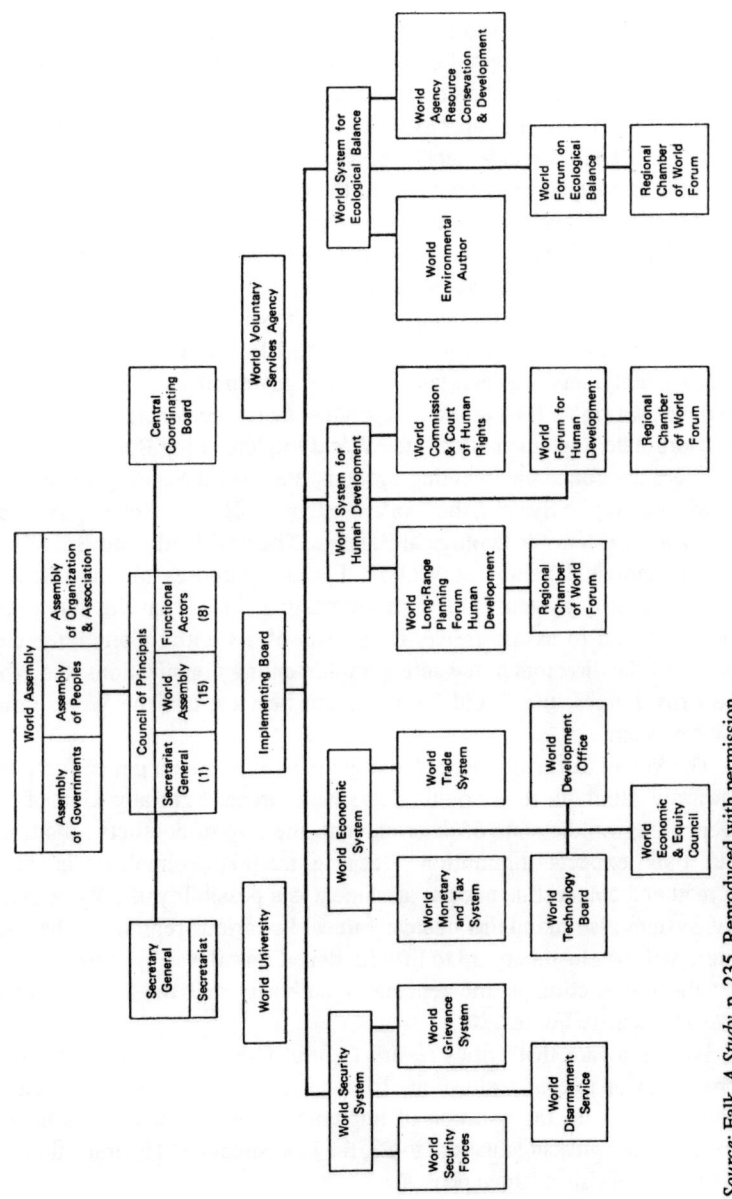

Source: Falk, *A Study*, p. 235. Reproduced with permission.

(1) proposing action to implement World Assembly decisions; (2) taking action in the event of the World Assembly being unable to reach a decision; (3) taking action in the event of one or more of the three chambers proclaiming by majority vote the existence of a state of "world emergency;" and (4) acting when power has been delegated by the World Assembly.[202] The Council is composed of a Secretary General and seven representatives from each of the three chambers; the head of each specialized agency participates in a nonvoting capacity when the Council deals with issues related to its field. The Secretary General votes only to break ties.[203]

There is a supervisory body called the Central Coordinating Board with the function of overseeing the implementation of directives issued by the executive and of providing information feedback. This monitoring function is crucial because bureaucracies at the universal level tend to be more cumbersome than those at the national level. It is also important because the actual implementing agencies of the World Polity Association are more independent than the ministries of national governments – they are systems in their own right. They are so independent that a special organ is necessary to coordinate implementation – the World Implementing Board.

There are four implementing systems: the World Security System, the World Economic System, the World System for Human Development, and the World System for Ecological Balance. They evidently correspond with the fundamental values of WOMP. For the purposes of this study the World Security System is the most interesting since it has the duty to prevent war and to assure peace. It consists of a Central Committee composed of the directors of the actual implementing organizations: the World Security Forces, the World Disarmament Service, and the World Grievance System.

The World Security Forces are organized more like a police force than an army although they could, if the need arose, fight any kind of war. Depending on the state of disarmament, the size of conflicts might vary, but Falk expects diminution. Because nuclear technology is widely spread and clandestine nuclear armament is a possibility, the World Security System also maintains nuclear forces. In various regions of the world there will be clusters of up to fifty hardened missiles subject to activation by the dual action of the repository authority and the Director of the World Security Forces.[204]

Falk is aware that critics regard Central Guidance as another utopian project incapable of realization. To counter such criticism he devotes an entire chapter to the question of implementation, of moving, as he says, from S1, the present situation, to S2, the goal situation. The transition from S1 to S2 consists of three phases:

- 1970s: Political Consciousness linked to the Domestic Imperative;
- 1980s: Political Mobilization tied to the Transnational Imperative;
- 1990s: Political Transformation combined with the Global Imperative.[205]

The main objective of the first decade, of the Era of Consciousness, is to bring about "a world order consensus, beginning with issues of diagnosis, proceeding toward the affirmation of WOMP values, and implementing some early transnational steps."[206] In this phase, it is vital to heighten, within each nation, the consciousness for the four basic values and to achieve a consensus leading to first transnational actions. Such actions take place when nongovernmental organizations (NGOs) like Amnesty International, Greenpeace, Oxfam, or Peacewatch become active across national borders.

During the following decade, in the Era of Mobilization, a large number of pressure groups for world order values becomes active around the globe and begins to raise demands that national governments can no longer meet. The inadequacy of the present international system is sharply revealed and the need for change becomes obvious. This prepares the terrain for the third and final phase, for the Era of Transformation, where drastic institutional alterations occur at the global level. Falk sums up the entire transition process with the following words:

> We are most optimistic about a sequence of changes that could bring about over time a dramatic and coherent set of results: first, value change via education; second, the growth of a world order reform movement via organizational activism; third, the institutional implementation of a new global consciousness via institutional innovation.[207]

Falk has great faith in education and private activism, in what he also calls the "populist process."[208] He speaks of "independent educational efforts" that can be "significant," of "powerful learning experiences" that will create "strong dispositions in favor of nonviolence, equity, and ecological equilibrium."[209] Falk is convinced that "education and related strategies of persuasion can help to mobilize or even 'create' social forces committed to world order change."[210] There is a highly optimistic image of man at the core of the transition process. The same image, of course, penetrates the entire theory.

Given Falk's favorable conception of man, his image of élites is more skeptical. He distinguishes between progressive and beleaguered segments of the élite. The latter are part of the public sector and coincide with statism, the former belong to the private sector and live in the "open spaces" that the state allows to exist. The process of transition is initiated by the progressive elements: "The early initiatives will have to be pioneered by progressive individuals and groups acting within 'the open spaces' tolerated by beleaguered S1 elites."²¹¹ As a typical idealist, Falk has more confidence in subnational than in national actors, in corporations, professional associations, church organizations, labor unions and liberation groups.²¹²

Woodrow Wilson has a similar conception of man and of élites. He, too, thinks highly of the common man and distinguishes between two types of élite: there are politicians representing their private interests and those representing the true public interest. The former he associates with pressure groups, with undemocratic forms of government, and with war. The latter are identified with enlightened leadership, with democratic government, and with peace.

But an important difference exists between Falk and Wilson. Wilson regards American leadership as particularly enlightened, whereas Falk sees a potential for enlightened leadership in all countries – he is more truly cosmopolitan. Actually, Falk is quite critical of American leadership. He devotes an entire chapter to "America's Stake in Global Reform" and concludes that "the United States' relationship to global reform is complicated and confusing."²¹³ America is an ambivalent culture, capable of the best and of the worst. America is a beacon light of freedom and a killer of civilians in Vietnam. His judgment is remindful of Niebuhr.²¹⁴

Falk's skeptical view of politicians, of bureaucrats, and of the military stems from his critical image of the state. No other theorist reviewed here has such a thoroughly negative conception of the state, not even Osgood. States as they exist today are incapable of promoting the four WOMP values and are dominated by the beleaguered portion of the élite. To improve their performance their sovereign independence must be restricted and transcended.

Falk's critical conception of the state is the reason for his rejection of the first of his ten models, the Enhanced State System. It envisages an evolutionary process of incremental and pragmatic steps. The model relies heavily on existing nation-states and is an expression of the spirit of beleaguered élites.²¹⁵ It represents "business as usual" and "induces a pacified mind-set that is a great convenience for vested interests."²¹⁶

As is to be expected, Falk has a highly negative image of anarchy and of the existing international system. It is the product of statism and is deficient in every respect:

> On balance, the logic of Westphalia now seems unable to protect the most vital needs of most of humanity. It no longer provides sufficient security against attack, nor permits reasonable progress in attaining social and economic justice; it cannot protect the environment from

deterioration, or satisfactorily allocate and conserve the scarce minerals and resources that will be taken from the oceans.[217]

The Westphalia system is irrational at its core: it is torn between equality in theory and inequality in reality.[218] In theory, states are meant to be equal but in fact they are highly unequal, and the consequence is not equilibrium, as is often claimed, but disequilibrium and war. The statist system constitutes the major cause of war. Falk takes deterrence as an example. Mutual deterrence is supposed to increase the prospects of peace but in fact fans the arms race ending not in stable balance but in an unstable and degenerating process and in war. It follows that

> the first and central priority of the movement for a preferred world is to make progress toward *diminishing the role of the war system in international life* and toward *dismantling the national security apparatus in the major states of the world.*[219]

Falk's negative image of anarchy is obvious. Given the imperfect nature of states, order in anarchy is impossible. Sovereign and independent states cannot coexist peacefully in a self-help system and hope to cope with the problems of mankind. The sum total of their various national interests does not add up to a true universal interest, to a public good serving all of mankind. If that end is to be attained different means are necessary. There is a need for transcending anarchy. The whole cannot be identified with the parts, it must be more than the parts.

Falk is a liberal idealist like Angell, Rosecrance, and Keohane, but his assessment of the existing international situation is much more dramatic. The problems mankind faces today are tremendous. In the near future, various crises will break out: nuclear war, tyranny, large-scale famine, economic and environmental collapse. These problems are compelling and they force men to act quickly and to set up a hierarchical world order. Interdependence alone does not suffice, neither does free trade nor the promotion of regimes. The international system is not as robust as Angell, Rosecrance or Keohane tend to assume.

Falk overestimates the compelling nature of the process. According to his timetable we should find ourselves today in the Era of Transformation where various global calamities force mankind to implement the World Polity Association. There are indeed a number of global calamities, and there are also some efforts to strengthen international organizations, but there is no World Polity Association. Falk's vision is excessively impatient. Like Norman Angell, Richard Falk may be right in his prediction – but premature. The two embrace overly compelling theories, which gives their schemes a utopian twist.

In Falk's theory hierarchy has a positive value. Central Guidance is beneficial because it compensates for the deficient nature of the parts. It represents a whole in which the parts play subordinate roles, a system in which the myriad activities of mankind become functional. "Centrally guided" institutions, when run by progressive members of the élite, define the true ends of mankind and select the means intelligently. Cost–benefit calculations become rational and guarantee efficiency. The suboptimal outcomes typical of the Prisoners' Dilemma come to an end because there is a transition from zero-sum to nonzero-sum reasoning. War is abolished because it is unnatural and abnormal.

The "centrally guided" institutions stand above the parts, they have a will of their own and represent an independent variable. The international system now begins to think, to reason and to act, it can make or break the peace and constitute the efficient cause of war. In an anarchic system only the parts have this ability, in a hierarchic system the whole has it as well. The system now has power.

Falk is aware that power can be misused, that it can become an end in itself. He therefore shies away from excessive centralization and hierarchy. It explains why Falk refuses to speak of world government:

> Governmental presences can be and often are oppressive, ineffectual, wasteful, diversionary. It is essential to retain a skeptical view of world government as a world order solution, while at the same time proposing designs that maximize its positive features.[220]

The positive features are contained in Central Guidance. Power in this system is divided horizontally among the various institutions of the World Polity Association, but it is also divided vertically by creating something akin to world federalism. In the final analysis, the overall incidence of government in the world is reduced. There is a relatively weak World Polity Association and there are relatively weak states: "The weaker the governmental presence becomes on a national level, the smaller the governmental presence that will be needed on a global level."[221]

Like Osgood, Falk does not hide his convictions and values. He is entirely explicit about the new system and its functions, about wholes and parts, ends and means, causes and effects. From clearly contextual definitions and generalizations he deduces his own specific logic of world politics. Falk is an endogenous theorist who defines a new game and spells out the rules.

4 Worldviews: A Summary

So far, entire theories have stood in the foreground while their components remained in the background. Now, as a summary, the order is reversed – the components are moved up front while the theories themselves remain in the back. The focus is on conceptions (or images) of man, of society, of government, of technology and science, of economics, of law, etc. In one combination or another, these are contained in all theories.

Once again, the purpose is to show the contours of our field and to demonstrate that the similarities among theoretical efforts are greater than the differences, that the works of so many scholars in international relations are less isolated than commonly assumed. To facilitate understanding and integration the names of relevant authors are mentioned in parentheses. This includes the fifteen theorists discussed earlier but also such well-known names as Locke, Hobbes, Smith, Hegel, Marx, Lenin, and so on.

ANARCHIC IDEALIST THEORIES[1]

Anarchic idealist theories tend to rest on an optimistic image of man; man is perceived to be predominantly reasonable, informed, nonviolent, and in control of his passions (Angell, Paine).[2] But man is not perfect. On the contrary, these theories often begin with an image of imperfect man (Kant), of human beings with faults and weaknesses, partially irrational, uninformed, uneducated, passionate or sinful but who can be perfected because they are capable of learning (Angell, Falk). Idealists have an optimistic expectation of the potential of man, of his ability to become more reasonable under favorable circumstances (Wilson). Problems, whether social, economic or political, are relatively superficial and are mostly misunderstandings which can be eliminated with intelligence and goodwill (Angell). The typical process of conflict resolution comprises dialog and reasoning (Osgood).

Man is the true foundation of social reality, he is prior to any collectivity, including the state. Man existed before there were states, he has established them simply for the promotion of his own interests and well-being (Locke).[3] Man is also more important than collectivities – they are a means to serve his ends and not ends in themselves. Never is man a means to serve collective ends. Man is an end in himself, he is a given, a natural phenomenon that needs no justification. This is a self-evident and irreducible truth (Jefferson).[4] Evidently, this is an individualistic philosophy of man.[5]

The favorable image of man is closely tied to such principles as autonomy, self-discipline, voluntariness, and equality. They constitute fundamental values and are identified with Humanism, Liberalism and the Age of Enlightenment. They are perceived to be the only rational values and are intimately related to the concept of freedom (Falk, Locke). They constitute the foundation of human rights, they represent assets which cannot be taken from man without violating his personality and identity. The assets are material and immaterial, they embrace the right to own property and the right to preserve his integrity (Jefferson). Because each man possesses such rights they are at once the most precious private and public good.

Not all men are exactly alike; there are differences in culture and religion but the similarities among human beings are greater than the differences (Wilson, Osgood). This entails a cosmopolitan and humanistic conception of man and excludes a nationalistic, ethnic or racial one (Hobson). Man identifies with all kinds of groups and has multiple identities but at heart he is himself, his individual identity is dominant.

As indicated, reasoning is the favorite process of conflict resolution but related to it are such skills as bargaining and negotiating – the instruments typical of economic man and of the market-place (Rosecrance). Men are intelligent enough to trade with each other in any way they desire and to pursue their own self-interest, to calculate cost and benefit, to make rational choices and to compete (Keohane, Smith).[6] Competition is unproblematic because cooperation and harmony among men are greater than conflict and disharmony, which guarantees that competition does not end in violence. Coercion and violence are not the normal instruments of conflict management (Angell).

Competition is more like a game or a sport, a contest where certain rules prevail; human behavior is norm-oriented. The rules represent a public good guaranteeing each player his survival and his integrity – no one plays for "all." The contest has no affinity with zero-sum reasoning where one player wins all and the other loses all; it is more like a nonzero-sum reasoning where both are bound to win and where the contest remains a true game.[7] The outcome of the game, therefore, permits absolute gains and not merely relative ones (Keohane, Rosecrance).

Idealist competition is also different from the Prisoners' Dilemma. In that scenario insufficient communication, cooperation or trust leads rational calculators of self-interest to suboptimal solutions, and the result is that both inmates stay in jail. This cannot happen to idealist competitors because their definition of rationality is based on enough cooperation to reach an optimal solution. Idealists argue that the Prisoners' Dilemma can be overcome (Keohane, Osgood, Falk).

Worldviews: A Summary

Most idealists have a dualistic image of man. At heart man is reasonable but there is a margin of unreason in all of us. That is why man cannot live without government (Kant, Locke). There is an occasional maverick in any society who is not fully self-disciplined and does not respect the integrity and the rights of others. There are also practical problems that exceed individual capacities. A state that can provide protection and assistance is useful, but in view of man's basically benevolent nature a strong and authoritarian state is undesirable because it hampers the potential for human development (Hobson, Wilson).

This reveals the idealist image of the state. There is room for a "soft" state, one that is strong enough to protect and assist but not powerful enough to endanger basic values (Falk, Locke). A "hard" state is the cause of many social ills, including war. For a powerful state coercion may become normal and natural, the rule and not the exception. To guard against misuse, state power must be restricted, divided, and limited (Kant). And man has to have a say in the determination of the public good. The state is founded upon the consent of the governed. Sovereignty rests ultimately with the people although portions of it are transferred to the government on the basis of a social contract.

The ideal state finds its justification in individualistic values, and it has to serve human needs. The public interest must reflect the individual interest, the public good must be premised on the private good or else it loses its legitimacy. Expressed in terms of natural law, state power must be premised on inviolable and inalienable human rights (Locke).

The state is a means to promote man's goals and never an end in itself. If man is part of a whole, of the state, then it is only because the whole serves the parts and not vice versa. State sovereignty and independence are not ends in themselves; they are in constant need of justification and deserve a fair degree of skepticism. In extreme situations a citizen therefore has the right of resistance (Locke). The state, to use modern language, is a dependent, not an independent variable. Idealist theories of international relations cannot be state-centered.

Not surprisingly, idealist thinkers have much faith in subnational or private actors, in clubs, associations, companies or parties; they have faith in societal pluralism (Angell, Rosecrance, Falk). Such groups, like individuals, are assumed to be largely self-steering, independent, and autonomous, and supposed to function with a minimum of governmental interference. They contribute more to the pursuit of happiness than state actors. The state has a supporting role at best; private man is more important in this model than public man (Rosecrance). For private and subnational actors to perform at optimal levels, an open and transparent society is necessary.

The relations between states are dominated by the same principles: they also rest on values such as independence, self-determination, self-discipline, voluntariness, and equality – liberally conceived (Kant, Hobson). The anarchic idealist model is incompatible with one-sided dependence, dominance, involuntariness, and inequality, with colonialism, imperialism, and mercantilism (Bentham, Hobson, Wilson).[8] They have to be abolished so that all states may partake in the progress of history and attain a higher degree of well-being.

Barriers between states must be removed: persons, capital, services, and goods need to circulate freely (Kant). An unhampered exchange of ideas and commodities helps to cement democratic and liberal principles worldwide. Idealists are against protectionism and against discrimination. Psychological barriers such as stereotypes, prejudices, and misconceptions are reduced, whereas trust and understanding are promoted (Angell, Hobson). Differences among nations subside, similarities emerge. With fewer misconceptions among states, international conflict can be managed by the carrot rather than by the stick, by reassurance rather than by threats (Rosecrance).

This cosmopolitan perspective is tied to a liberal conception of sovereignty and independence, and consequently it is compatible with a favorable assessment of interdependence; idealists believe that commercial, technological, scientific, and cultural ties promote peace (Angell, Rosecrance, Falk). The "forces of modernity," such as science, technology, and economics, are benign in nature and operate to the benefit of mankind (Spencer).[9] Idealists know of the importance of these bonds for the improvement of humanity and are conscious of their vulnerability. Idealists warn that interference with interdependence (through war) has disastrous consequences. They see no incompatibility between political independence and functional interdependence but argue for the separation of the two. In particular, they advocate the separation of politics and economics (Rosecrance).

Interdependence is particularly conducive to strengthening peace when promoted by individuals, by private associations, by companies or transnational corporations. As in domestic politics, private actors are more conducive to peace and well-being than public ones. Interdependence establishes bridges between domestic and international politics, it "domesticates" international politics and leads to what some call post-international politics (Rosenau).[10] If the primacy of domestic policy prevailed in international affairs, wars would no longer occur. Domestic politics are democratic, and international politics should be the same. When those who suffer most from war take part in the decision-making process, wars no longer break out (Kant). The primacy of domestic policy also entails an emphasis of human rights over states' rights in international affairs, an emphasis of individual rights over collective rights (Falk).

Among democratic and liberal states security is not a central concern. There is only a limited need for armed forces between nations, just as there is only a limited need for police forces within nations (Kant, Angell, Rosecrance). From a domestic viewpoint, a powerful military establishment and a "garrison state" are a threat to democracy and to the rule of law (Falk). Idealists believe in limiting the influence of the military upon politics and in limiting defense budgets. They are particularly opposed to large standing armies (Kant) and tend to approve of arms control and disarmament, or any step that in their mind initiates processes of deescalation and peace.

Given a world with great potential for harmony, the idealist assumes that war is rare, abnormal, unnatural, irrational, and unethical. It is irrational because it entails a negative cost–benefit calculation: war doesn't pay (Kant, Hobson, Angell, Rosecrance). War is certainly not the rational and neutral instrument or process suggested by realists. Quite the opposite – war is a crass violation of the basic rights of individuals and nations, of such principles as independence, self-determination, voluntariness, and equality.

War is unnatural, abnormal, and unethical because it conflicts with the true nature of man. If man could help it, if governments did not corrupt his nature and if he had a say in the unleashing of war, it would never occur. The history of mankind could be less tragic. It is unnecessary to conceive of war as a regular and uncontrollable occurrence, a plague that everyone at times has to endure (Rapoport).[11]

Idealists may approve of wars for self-defense, but generally they are reluctant to fight wars; and when they are forced to, they do not engage in "business as usual." Their wars are fought with exceptional goals in mind and turn into crusades to establish freedom and justice for all mankind. Because they want to abolish war altogether and build a perpetual peace they are likely to assume that they are fighting the "last war" (Wilson, Doyle).[12]

The idealist argument can be carried to an extreme. This happens when the potential in man for perfection is assumed to be so great that no state is necessary. Problems arising between men can be handled informally and without government; the result is peaceful anarchy or a state of affairs where the whole, society, is identical with the parts. Actually, the parts are the whole (Godwin, Sharp).[13]

Radical anarchists see the causes of war exclusively in government and call for "political disarmament"; radical pacifists consider weapons to be the true cause of war and call for "military disarmament." Together, anarchists and pacifists postulate a world free of weapons and free of nations

(Godwin, Sharp). But when nations and wars cease to exist there is no possibility of studying the relations and conflicts between them – hence our discipline has no foundation. This occurs in the communist utopia, for instance, where war and the state both wither away (Marx).[14]

Most anarchic idealist theories of international relations avoid such extremes: they are anarchic only at the international level. Government is needed among people but not among states because these are not assumed to have a dualistic nature – they are ultimately self-disciplined and rational. This reveals the anarchic idealist image of the state system. The assumption is that self-help is unproblematical and that there is no need for collective security, supranational integration or world government (Kant, Hobson, Rosecrance). Such structures represent a menace to basic values, to independence, self-determination, voluntariness, and equality; they even contain the germ of war. Higher authorities enforcing discipline are unnatural and unnecessary. They are also irrational and inefficient because their actions entail a negative cost–benefit calculation (Röpke).[15]

There is no need for a higher level of organization concerned with the general, collective or universal interest because such an interest is the automatic and spontaneous sum of all particular (national and subnational) interests (Angell). Or, expressed in terms of systems, the international system is the sum of its subsystems, it is subsystem-dominant. The whole consists of many parts, but these are not subordinate to the whole. On the contrary, the parts are the whole, they are identical with it. The result is an informal or tacit world community.

The resulting system is decentralized: the authoritative allocation of values is based on the principle of self-help and the management is universalist because all actors participate in the making and executing of decisions. Problems are solved through coordination and not through sub- and superordination; interventionism of any kind is rejected. Diplomatic conferences are an expression of universalist management. At such gatherings each state has one vote, and decisions must be unanimous. Or, put differently, each state has the power of veto. In short, the processes of conflict management are entirely voluntaristic.

Subsystem dominance also characterizes the international economy. The international market mechanism is seen to be self-steering and robust (Röpke, Rosecrance). In the absence of a security problem states and economic actors are not concerned with relative gains but can take absolute gains for granted. There is also no need for economic policy coordination and for regimes because the interests of producers and consumers can be accommodated without international organizations. The separation of politics and economics is possible (Smith, Röpke). That is why such theories do not see the need for an international "political" economy, let alone for international economic sanctions.

Theories built on spontaneity and self-help offer no basis for enforceable law. To be sure, there is a law of nations but it, too, is purely voluntaristic because the system has a built-in respect for the rule of law (Kant, Röpke). Such law has more in common with universally recognized ethical standards than with law that can be applied authoritatively. Anarchic idealism holds that such law is sufficient to manage international relations. It is often referred to as natural law because it is derived from an enlightened definition of the nature of man and of the state. It is intimately tied to the values mentioned earlier, to independence, self-determination, voluntariness, and equality.

This reveals an inconsistency inherent in many anarchic idealist theories. Why should enforceable law be necessary within states but not among them? Why do voluntaristic processes and informal structures suffice at one level of social life but not at another? Here is where hierarchic idealism becomes relevant because it avoids that inconsistency.

HIERARCHIC IDEALIST THEORIES

Hierarchic idealist theories are also founded on the conviction that peace is probable and normal but, in contrast to anarchic idealist theories, they do not assume that peace is probable in a decentralized setting based on self-help. Different processes and structures are necessary. The sovereign independence of states has to be limited and a hierarchical order has to be established so that peace, if necessary, can be enforced.

Hierarchic and anarchic theories share the same image of man; the state image, however, is somewhat different. States are assumed to be liberal and democratic but they are not perceived to be uniformly rational and to coexist peacefully at all times. Even liberal and democratic states may occasionally be unreasonable and lack complete self-discipline. The dual nature of states creates a security problem. As at the domestic level, self-help is not a sufficient foundation for peace, justice, and well-being. Order in anarchy is impossible at whatever level of society. In such circumstances anarchy constitutes a permissive cause of war (Wilson, Osgood).

Hierarchic idealism is tied to a negative image of anarchy. An anarchic system is primitive, underdeveloped, and inefficient. It is incapable of fulfilling the most basic functions, such as promoting order, justice, well-being, and peace (Falk). An anarchic system cannot satisfy these needs because the sum of the interests of its parts (the states) is not identical with the interest of the whole. The result is that all suffer, the parts and the whole. The system produces inequality, dependence, involuntariness and inefficiency of such proportions that at times it is in danger of disintegration.

A superior form of organization is needed to overcome these deficiencies, an organization capable of defining a common interest transcending the mere sum of particular interests, an organization capable of providing not only private but also public goods, not merely relative gains but also absolute gains. It must be a truly higher interest, one that stands above the states' interests and that can, if the need arises, be enforced against the will of the states. There must be an organization conforming to the needs of mankind, one that elevates the true interests of man to the level of a universal human interest (Wilson, Falk).

Hierarchic idealists, too, welcome interdependence and perceive it as a force binding nations together, but political independence stands in the way of taking full advantage of these functional forces. Also, these forces are not uniformly benevolent and need a measure of control. There is a need to institutionalize and coordinate governmental action at the international level and it may even be necessary to install a measure of central management at the cost of national sovereignty (Osgood, Falk). Regimes, international organizations and supranational authorities can help states and other transnational actors overcome the communication problem inherent in the Prisoners' Dilemma. They can also be helpful in setting up international rules and regulations that facilitate rational cost–benefit calculations and promote nonzero-sum reasoning (Keohane).

Intervention is necessary because the international economic system is not seen to be completely self-steering; it is not as robust as some would like it to be. Basically, the "forces" of science, technology, communication, and commerce are benign and bind nations together, yet a highly interdependent world economy is too complex and vulnerable a network to function without some central steering. Interests among economic actors cannot be maximized without the presence of political institutions that prevent market failure. These organizations can provide the necessary information and create negotiating platforms for optimal policy coordination (Keohane). Hierarchic idealism seeds the need for international "political" economy because the separation of politics and economics is considered to be impossible (Keynes, Cooper).[16] It also approves of economic sanctions to preserve international peace and stability (Wilson).

Hierarchic idealism is premised on a positive image of international hierarchy. When higher authorities enjoy autonomy they can develop a will and an intelligence of their own permitting them to allocate values more efficiently than decentralized authorities; they are capable of defining proper ends and selecting adequate means, of calculating costs and benefits rationally (Falk, Osgood).

When the parts are properly integrated the whole profits. But integration must be voluntary; it has to rest on the free will of the parts. These are only willing to play a subordinate role and to obey as long as the higher authority is promoting their fundamental rights, as long as its power is legitimate. The hierarchical order and the authoritative processes of allocating values must grow out of a social contract, a covenant. When the contract is violated it loses its *raison d'être* (Wilson).

The management of the international system conforms to the standards of constitutional government. It rests on the will of the people and the consent of the governed, its power is divided and there are institutionalized checks and balances (Wilson, Falk). The decision-making processes are majoritarian. Depending on its constitution, the authority is equipped with various instruments of power. It can possess classical sovereignty, that is, the monopoly of physical violence, but it can also share that power with the states. The higher authority may build up its own armed forces as those of the member states are reduced. In this case there is a process of disarmament at the lower level coupled with a process of rearmament at the higher level (U.N. Charter).

Hierarchic idealist theories, however, are incompatible with complete disarmament because they are committed to the rule of law and to the enforcement of international law. There is no voluntaristic conception of law in such theories, no belief that a set of ethical rules can be implemented with self-help. The use of violence is, however, only legitimate when it serves the promotion of universal rights; it is illegitimate the moment it becomes an end in itself (Wilson, Falk).

ANARCHIC REALIST THEORIES

Anarchic realist theories rest on the assumption that the coexistence of sovereign and independent nation-states is possible, but that it is not peaceful because in a self-help system war is a likely and normal phenomenon that cannot be eliminated. Where decentralized structures prevail violent processes of conflict management are natural. Order in anarchy is possible but it is never a peaceful order.

The image of man at the heart of such theories is negative (Hobbes, Machiavelli).[17] Human beings are perceived to have a problematic nature: they are uninformed, passionate, undisciplined, and even violent. Men lack the intelligence to perform rational cost–benefit calculations, are incapable of discerning their own best interests, and even if they do, they lack the willpower to act in accordance with those interests. Men are weak, and it is natural for them to live in a permanent state of conflict because their motives are conflictual rather than cooperative (Bernhardi). Conflict is normal among human beings. To assume otherwise is to underestimate the need for order and security in society (Niebuhr).[18]

Human problems are deeply rooted in the subconscious, and, given the impenetrable nature of the human psyche, there is no easy way to get at the root of these problems and to cure them. Human problems are not as superficial as idealists assume, they are more than misunderstandings that can be eliminated by rational dialog and persuasion (Carr, Morgenthau).[19] If problems have a tough core then tough processes are necessary to solve them: instead of appealing to reason there is need for manipulation, psychological or physical manipulation. The use of force (or the threat of force) is one of the most effective means of manipulation. Man is imperfect, and there is no potential for improvement. Man is incapable of learning, of lessening his high degree of imperfection.

This view of man is tied to a specific image of the state. Because man cannot find fulfillment and salvation within himself he must find it outside himself – in the collectivity, in the state (Hobbes, Hegel).[20] The state compensates for the deficiencies of man: where man is passionate, the state is rational; where man is weak, the state is strong (Burke, Treitschke).[21] And because man lacks true personality, the state is personified – it possesses reason and will, there is a *raison d'état* and a *volonté d'état*. States have intelligence and a will to survive; they are rational actors, entailing a state-centered perception of world politics (Waltz). Yet states are not uniformly rational. States have a dualistic nature: there is a certain potential for unreason in each state. States may at times lose their will to exist or they may endanger the existence of other states by pursuing a "revisionist" policy. On the whole, however, they are "satisfied" and prefer mutual coexistence to any other situation (Gentz, Kahn).

Representatives of the state, statesmen, define the contents of *raison d'état* and *volonté d'état*, and they lead and guide the rest of society through the dangerous waters of politics (Gentz, Bernhardi, Gray). Society is stratified and hierarchical, embracing various social layers and classes. The statesmen at the top are aided by well-trained servants of the state, by generals and diplomats, by specialists in warfare and diplomacy. They in turn are supported by hierarchically organized institutions like the armed forces and the diplomatic service. At the bottom of society are the state's subjects or masses. The skeptical image of man mentioned earlier applies to the common people but not to those who guide them –

Worldviews: A Summary

the leaders are capable of learning and of perfection. The distribution of perfectability is asymmetrical – some men are capable of improvement, most are not. It is an inegalitarian and élitist image of mankind (Kennan, Kissinger).[22]

The state needs an élite because it must survive in a hostile environment, at home and abroad. At home it confronts the irrational masses of citizens, abroad a host of hostile powers (Treitschke). The supreme goal is to survive in this two-sided state of war, and, to succeed, the state is highly centralized and hierarchical (Bernhardi). It is a tight collectivity in which individuals are means serving a higher end, subordinate parts of a whole with well-defined functions and roles. The values are not individualistic, they do not emphasize independence, self-determination, self-discipline, voluntariness, and equality. Within this type of state the emphasis is on dependence, subordination, involuntariness, and inequality (Gentz).

Externally the state has to be strong because it confronts others of a similar kind. The result is a serious international security problem. To survive, a state requires well-equipped armed forces and a foreign policy with a pronounced emphasis on national security (Gray, Kahn). Foreign policy need not be in the hands of the military but it should be conducted by statesmen with an understanding of the logic of conflictual anarchy (Waltz, Gray, Machiavelli).

Statesmen are not expected actively to seek conflict but they must regard war as a rational instrument and have to be willing to use it when necessary (Clausewitz). At times, war can be avoided because the mere threat of war (deterrence) will suffice, but it is important to prepare for the worst case. To that end it is vital to be in possession of a broad range of military instruments to handle any situation and to control any crisis (Kahn). Insufficient armament and particularly disarmament leads to a power vacuum and to unstable situations inviting aggression and causing war (Gray). Stability in the international system is more likely when all states are sufficiently secure and armed (Waltz).

To be ready for the worst, such a state needs more than military protection; it must also be protected economically. The state promotes a measure of autarky to promote national industries ready to supply the country in times of war (Montchrétien, List).[23] Depending on the geographical location of a country, it may be important to have a merchant navy and to guarantee self-sufficiency in agriculture. Politics and economics go hand in hand and cannot be separated. Economics is one of the important foundations of power but state power is also an important foundation of economics (Gilpin). Terms like "Nationalökonomie," "international political economy" or "economic security" are evidence of the fusion (Krasner).[24]

Despite such considerations states do engage in international economic exchange. However, the international economic order is perceived to be fragile because states have to worry constantly about the relative gains accruing from international exchange, gains that directly affect their relative position of strength (Krasner, Grieco).[25] Also, cooperation among states is only temporary. States basically cooperate for security reasons, in order to counterbalance a hegemon, but such cooperation is short-lived and today's friend can become tomorrow's enemy (Waltz). As a result, international trade and interdependence are not valued too highly. The impact of the "forces of modernity," of science, technology, communication, and commerce is ambivalent: they can strengthen or weaken a country (Waltz). Interdependence cuts both ways – it can tie nations together but it can also lead to rivalries and constitute a cause of war. History knows of many wars over trade and raw materials (Krasner).

In order to be ready for the worst it is also necessary to employ psychological processes of control. It is vital to protect the minds of people from foreign propaganda and to shield the acts of government from foreign spies. Censorship, secrecy, and deception are normal instruments of national defense (Machiavelli). And, since any state may become a potential enemy, espionage is necessary. In a liberal state "gentlemen do not read each other's mail" but in a conservative state such rules have little meaning. The country has to be in a constant state of vigilance and alertness. And, in order to be prepared for the worst, intelligence organizations must provide the state with the necessary information to act intelligently (Gray).

There is no room for the separation of powers, for checks and balances or for the guarantee of basic freedoms (Gentz). In case of war all forces of a nation have to unite in pursuit of defense (Treitschke). Domestic politics are not allowed to obstruct foreign politics, or, put differently, the primacy of domestic policy must give way to the primacy of foreign policy (Gray). It is the dire logic of the international self-help system that must determine foreign policy and not the logic of domestic considerations. There is no room for a foreign policy based on human rights because in this model the interests and values of the collectivity have a higher priority than those of the individual. States' rights are dominant, not human rights (Bernhardi, Kissinger, Gray).

The nature of the state system is determined by the unwillingness of all states to accept a higher authority. Since states tend to be authoritarian in nature such an authority would mean domination and imperialism. It is therefore in the best self-interest of a state to prevent hegemony of any kind and to prefer a decentralized order. On this issue there is consensus, on this point the various national interests converge (Gentz, Waltz).

The aim of all foreign policy is to guarantee the survival of the state, to assure stability, order, and security (Morgenthau). The most stable and secure order is one in which the major states are roughly equal in power. If the balance is threatened the most obvious process to rectify it is to form alliances with other states against a potential challenger. It is a world of no permanent friendships or enmities but of constantly changing alliances dictated by no other sentiment (such as religion, ideology, or dynastic bonds) than the "reason of state." Such cooperation is natural and rational because it is assumed that each state has the will and the power to aim for its own survival (Gentz, Waltz).

When war breaks out, the contest is never apocalyptic, it is not a question of fighting the first or the last war in history. War is an entirely normal and neutral process of conflict regulation (Clausewitz, Gilpin). It is more like a game or a sport with definite rules. The rules are written down in the law of war and of neutrality, a body of international rules and regulations defining initiation, conduct, termination, and abstention. They have the effect of limiting war, of defining its intensity, extension, and duration. The enforcement of such international law is purely voluntaristic and based on the principle of self-help.

Rules that limit violence have the effect of checking passion, of constraining irrationality. It is rational to make war, but it is also rational to contain it. Anarchic realist theories assume a modest degree of cooperation and consensus – states do not operate in a total Hobbesian state of war (Gentz, Bull).[26] There is no absolute zero-sum reasoning where one loses all while the other wins all. The logic of the contest guarantees one public good – the survival of all states. Anarchic realist theories are always state-centered but never war-centered (Waltz).

As in any anarchical system, the whole is merely the sum of its parts. Expressed in terms of interest, the interest of the parts is tantamount to the interest of the whole. There is no general interest ruling over the parts, no higher-order interest. The national interest is the only relevant one because it is identical with that of the anarchic system. The national interest is the only guide for state action, but that does not mean that it can stand for any policy a state wishes to pursue. It is not in the national interest for a state to lose its will for existence, to forgo the forming of counteralliances or to pursue an ideological foreign policy. A foreign policy based on national interest implies playing by the rules of the anarchic realism (Gentz, Morgenthau).

Power is all-important but it is a means rather than an end. The object of anarchic realism is not to maximize power; on the contrary, the object is to prevent the maximization of power by any one state. Ideally power must be distributed evenly but that is hardly ever the case. In reality there are great and small powers, and for the system to function well it is primarily the great powers that have to abide by the rules (Gentz). They are in a position to challenge the system, but great powers are also in a position to preserve it. Minor powers play minor roles, and important powers play important roles. It is a power élite that makes the system work, that makes the anarchic realist model function. The system is not as egalitarian as it appears at first. The management of the system is oligarchic (Bull).

HIERARCHIC REALIST THEORIES

Hierarchic realist theories are also founded on the conviction that war is probable and normal but, in contrast to anarchic realist theories, it is not assumed that war is compatible with the coexistence of a multiplicity of independent and sovereign states. War is central to this logic; it is an expression of the law of the strongest and goes hand in hand with hierarchical order.

Hierarchic and anarchic realist theories share the same conception of man. Man has an imperfect nature and needs a strong state to compensate for its deficiencies. But the image of the state is somewhat different. While it is true that the primacy of foreign policy imposes on all states the need to be strong, not all can live up to this standard – some are stronger than others (Gray, Kahn, Gilpin). The logic is very simple – in an unrestrained Hobbesian state of war the "fittest" emerges as the hegemon. This state is physically, mentally, and morally superior, it is qualitatively different. It is the only veritable state in the system, it is "the" state. It alone possesses full sovereignty and independence, and it alone is entirely rational. There is an asymmetrical distribution of state attributes: the hegemon is uniformly rational, the rest exhibit various degrees of lesser rationality. The position of the lesser states is also characterized by varying degrees of dependence and inequality. This entails a different conception of processes and of structure (Hegel, Bernhardi).

The state of war determines the internal nature of the leading state – it is a hard state inside and out, a veritable "garrison state." The primacy of foreign policy imposes on the hegemon internal structures dictated by the logic of war. Conversely, the structure of the state system is a reflection of the internal structure of the hegemonic state. The hegemonic state and the system have identical structures – hierarchical stratification is the rule everywhere (Wallerstein).[27]

The lesser states are appendages of the hegemonic state, they are copies of the hegemonic state. Put differently, the dominant state exports and imposes its social, economic, cultural, and political order (Lenin, Leroy-Beaulieu).[28] Furthermore, the dominant state controls the dependent states by establishing close ties between the ruling classes of both; it creates veritable "bridgeheads" in the lesser states (Galtung, Senghaas).[29]

Such theories rest on a negative image of anarchy. Given the great differences among states and the imperfect nature of most, constant war can be expected. As in the Hobbesian state of war, the life of states is solitary, poor, nasty, brutish, and possibly short. Order, justice, and well-being are impossible because the national interests of the parts do not amount to a general interest serving the whole. Zero-sum reasoning prevails. One state wins all while the others lose all – their sovereignty, independence, and equality. The lesser states succumb either because they realize the hopelessness of their situation or because they are conquered in war. One state is bound to emerge victorious. Hierarchic realism is war-centered, not state-centered, and power is an end as well as a means (Bernhardi).

Dominant actors rise and fall, the dynamics of international politics are cyclical. At the beginning and end of each cycle there is a major war from which a new hegemon emerges. During major wars the structure of the international system is defined anew, power is redistributed. The hierarchic realist worldview is not state-centered but war-centered (Bernhardi, Gilpin).

In imperialist theory war is also a normal and rational process of conflict management but it is not neutral. Because war is an expression of the law of the strongest there is a tendency to see it not as a means but as an end and to have a positive value. Some hierarchic realist theories end with the glorification of war (Treitschke, Bernhardi). Wars unleashed by the hegemon are good, wars unleashed by the lesser states are evil. Given this polarization there is no third position; once war breaks out there is no possibility for a country to remain indifferent. Neutrality has no place in such theory (Bernhardi).

There is a positive image of hierarchy. The leading state disciplines those that are undisciplined, it brings order, justice, and well-being to those that cannot provide it themselves, it produces public goods for those that cannot do it on their own (Gilpin, Disraeli).[30] The system resembles an organic whole within which the parts perform a variety of roles and duties. The hegemon defines the functions and, if necessary, enforces them against the will of the parts; he acts upon superior knowledge and on behalf of a higher interest. The hegemon has the right to allocate values authoritatively as he sees fit, he has a right to intervene. The center commands, the periphery obeys – the management of the system is monistic (Bernhardi).

Rationality is dictated by the same logic. Hierarchy stipulates the criteria by which costs and benefits are weighed, by which ends and means are brought into line. It is rational to maximize power in terms of hegemonial interests; it would be irrational, however, to maximize power in terms of equilibrium. In contrast to the anarchic realist model, the criteria here are not derived from the notion of balance. Hegemonic rationality may state its logic in terms of stability, but it cannot equate stability with balance. From a hegemonic point of view equilibrium is inherently unstable and transitory (Bernhardi, Gilpin).

Power in the international system is concentrated, and the decision-making processes are closed. With weak and irrational states the hegemon cannot communicate openly, sit at a negotiating table and bargain. These states are incapable of reasoning, hence persuasion does not work. In an imperialistic world there is no room for classical diplomacy and conventional international law (Leroy-Beaulieu).

International law is hegemonic or imperial law, it is a mere extension of the hegemon's domestic law and its content is what the hegemon determines it to be. It is an instrument for implementing its will and for justifying the use of war. The hegemon has a right to spread and enforce the law throughout the system (Bernhardi). Hegemonic rule guarantees law and order, and it has a civilizing effect upon the lesser members of the system. The hegemon has a mission to fulfill. Depending on the degree of maturity of the lesser states, the leading state will establish dependencies and protectorates. It will rule some states directly and others indirectly (Leroy-Beaulieu).

The international economy is also run by the hegemon (Gilpin). It is an imperial economy because it serves primarily the purpose of producing goods and services that cement the hierarchical world order. There is no free world market and no freedom of the seas. Mercantile instead of private companies dominate the scene, and they are run with the blessing of the hegemon. Imperial monopolies are common, and their main function is to fill the treasury of the hegemonic state. Economic warfare is legitimate and frequent. Politics and economics are one: imperial politics promotes wealth, and wealth promotes imperial politics. The foundation for trade is laid by the state, which is why "trade follows the flag" and relative gains, favorable to the hegemon, are assured (Disraeli, Leory-Beaulieu). The lesser states profit economically from the world order which the hegemon guarantees, but in order to prevent excessive "free-riding" they are expected to make a contribution, to pay for some of the cost of maintaining large armies and navies (Bernhardi).

In contrast to anarchic realist theories, where the fortunes of war produce perpetual vacillations but no real change, hierarchic realist theories can incorporate a highly dynamic conception of change, of progress in history. The "laws of history," the "laws of biology" or the "law of uneven growth" may benefit a particular state in a given period of time, determine its rise and, later on, also its fall. Such a cyclical conception of hegemony is quite compatible with hierarchical theory (Gilpin, Bernhardi).

Conclusions

The previous chapter summarizes the four worldviews and constitutes a conclusion of the main findings of this study. The few remarks that follow are not intended, therefore, to elaborate on the content of worldviews. It is necessary, however, to add a few concluding words about their formal nature.

As mentioned at the outset, the purpose of this study is not to develop new theory but to gain an overview over existing theory. Worldviews add no new substance to the theory of international relations but they add perspective. There are so many different theories, there is such a multitude of concepts, variables, factors, paradigms, models, and approaches in our field that the student of international relations can easily become confused and discouraged. Perspective, therefore, is useful.

Because the substance and the method of theory are inseparable this study aims at perspective in both areas. What scholars do is related to how they do it; the method of science is tied to its substance. This is particularly true of the social sciences, where, as I have argued, it is difficult to obtain consensus on definitions and to isolate terms from their context. Many of the central social science concepts are contested, and deconstruction, therefore, cannot neatly be separated from reconstruction.

The consequence is obvious: when important terms remain contested knowledge cannot be truly cumulative. It is difficult to conceive of a well-structured building when the structure of the building-blocks is contested and when the building process itself is subject to disagreement. Under such circumstances scholarship tends to be repetitive as much as cumulative and there is a penchant for idiosyncratic definitions and theories. As a result dispersion and repetition are just as probable as integration and cumulation.

All is not lost, however. The fact that social science is more repetitive and less cumulative than natural science does not imply that social science knowledge is impossible. Repetition itself is a basis for theory because it combines elements of established knowledge with elements that are new. Each generation of humans confronts a social reality that is partly old and partly new. Social science reflects this reality; it, too, is never wholly new and never wholly old. It is an error to believe that contemporary theories are total innovations, but it is equally wrong to assume that modern knowledge is no more than updated wisdom of former times. Contemporary theories tend to be combinations of both. The fact that there is some repetition and constancy in the social realm makes the formulation of social knowledge possible. Only total chaos would prevent it.

This is as true of international relations as it is of other fields in the social sciences. Among nations, too, there is constancy and change. Nation-states have dominated the scene for centuries but their character and status have undergone changes. Most of the 200 nations existing today claim to be sovereign and independent, a claim that in some cases has been maintained over hundreds of years. At the same time sovereignty and independence are undergoing change; in the last decade of the twentieth century sovereignty and independence are no longer what they once were. There is change, but there is also continuation; there is innovation, but there is also repetition.

Worldviews represent an effort to grasp the most constant features among nations – war and peace, anarchy and hierarchy. The lives of nations vary but most of them have to deal with the dualities of peace and war, anarchy and hierarchy. The first duality relates to the dynamism among nations, to processes, while the second relates to order and structure. The matrix, therefore, contains two basic dimensions.

The matrix helps in the classification of such important concepts as nation, sovereignty, independence, dependence, interdependence, hegemony, imperialism, equilibrium, liberalism, conservatism, security, national interest and so on. And, as has been demonstrated, as ordering devices worldviews are superior to the billiard-ball, the cobweb, and the layer-cake paradigms.

Of course, actual theories are more demanding than concepts and worldviews. Full theories contain statements about particular types of war and peace at particular times, about specific kinds of anarchy and hierarchy at specific moments in history. Theories establish relations between diverse factors: some theories rest on correlations and probabilities, others are based on interrelations and on logical deductions. Theories, therefore, explain phenomena with greater precision than do worldviews.

Given the contested nature of our basic terms theories can add to dispersion. Worldviews counteract this danger because they force a theorist to relate his terms and variables to the fundamental problems among nations. Worldviews limit conceptual dispersion and promote conceptual cumulation.

Worldviews also reveal a theorist's judgement about norms and values, they indicate what a scholar regards as the rule and as the exception in the relations among nations. Some theorists consider peaceful relations to constitute the rule and warlike relations the exception, while others contend that war constitutes the rule and peace the exception. The same applies to anarchy and hierarchy. Some theorists regard anarchic coexistence as the rule and hierarchic supra- and subordination as the exception; others regard the opposite as normal and natural. Judgements about rules, about what is normal, natural, and rational take any theorist to the core of science because they are directly related to methodology, to the cognitive task of detecting order in chaos.

Since cognition is selective, theories of international relations rest on partial perceptions of man, of the state, and of the state system. Theorists have images of these phenomena, and images relate to values. The judgement that some form of behaviour is normal, natural, and rational is a judgement of value. Worldviews, therefore, force a theorist to reveal his values.

Worldviews also draw a distinction between theories that are transformational or nontransformational. It is rather common for scholars to adhere to one worldview in the analytic part of their theory while opting for a different worldview when it comes to making prescriptions. The distinction is important when one attempts to get an overview of the many theories in our field.

Of course, some theories are primarily analytic in character while others tend to be heavily prescriptive, yet it is equally true that to some degree theories contain both components. At close scrunity theories with a predominantly analytic component make tacit assumptions about prescription, and vice versa. It is an illusion to believe that theories can either be exclusively contemplative or action-oriented. Worldviews help us to reveal such deficiencies and remind us that knowledge in the social sciences has as practical a function as knowledge in the natural sciences. This is particularly true of our field which deals with some of the basic issues of human survival.

Finally, worldviews permit us to deal with both classic and contemporary theories. The divide between the two is by no means as deep as is commonly assumed. Because social science theory is as much repetitive as it is cumulative, former generations have already thought about the central phenomena of international relations and are considered classics exactly because they have done so with clarity and precision. Dealing with established authors adds to the effort of gaining perspective.

Notes

Introduction

1. For a similar use of the term "worldview" see David Sanders, *Losing an Empire, Finding a Role, British Foreign Policy since 1945*, Macmillan, London 1990, pp. 11–12, 257–8.
2. Kenneth N. Waltz, *Man, the State and War*, Columbia University Press, New York 1954.
3. Raymond Aron, *Peace and War, A Theory of International Relations*, Doubleday, Garden City, NJ 1966.
4. Kenneth N. Waltz, *Theory of International Politics*, Random House, New York 1979.
5. Friedrich von Gentz, *Fragments Upon the Balance of Power in Europe*, M. Peliter, London 1806.
6. Friedrich von Bernhardi, *Germany and the Next War*, Longmans, Green and Co., New York 1914.
7. Carl von Clausewitz, *On War*, Princeton University Press, Princeton, NJ 1976.
8. J. A. Hobson, *Imperialism: A Study*, University of Michigan Press, Ann Arbor, Mich. 1972.
9. Norman Angell, *The Great Illusion*, G. P. Putnam's Sons, New York 1911.
10. Immanuel Kant, *Perpetual Peace*, George Allen & Unwin, London 1917.
11. Ray Stannard Baker and William E. Dodd, *The Public Papers of Woodrow Wilson*, Harper & Brothers, New York 1926 (3 vols).
12. Waltz, *Theory* (see note 4).
13. Herman Kahn, *Thinking About the Unthinkable*, Horizon Press, New York 1962.
14. Colin S. Gray, *The Geopolitics of Super Power*, University Press of Kentucky, Lexington, KY 1988.
15. Robert Gilpin, *War and Change in World Politics*, Cambridge University Press, Cambridge, MA 1981.
16. Richard Rosecrance, *The Rise of the Trading State, Commerce and Conquest in the Modern World*, Basic Books, New York 1986.
17. Robert O. Keohane, *After Hegemony: Cooperation and Discord in the World Political Economy*, Princeton University Press, Princeton, NJ 1984.
18. Charles E. Osgood, *An Alternative to War and Surrender*, University of Illinois Press, Urbana, IL 1962.
19. Richard A. Falk, *A Study of Future Worlds*, Free Press, New York 1975.
20. Charles R. Beitz, *Political Theory and International Relations*, Princeton University Press, Princeton, NJ 1979; James N. Rosenau, *Turbulence in World Politics, A Theory of Change and Continuity*, Princeton University Press, Princeton, NJ 1990; Hedley Bull, *The Anarchical Society, A Study of Order in World Politics*, Macmillan, London 1977; Hans J. Morgenthau, *Politics Among Nations, The Struggle for Power and Peace*, Alfred A. Knopf, New York 1960; Samuel P. Huntington, *The Soldier and the State: The Theory and Politics of Civil–*

Military Relations, Harvard University Press, Cambridge, MA 1957; Richard Ned Lebow, *Between Peace and War, The Nature of International Crisis*, Johns Hopkins University Press, Baltimore, MD 1981; John Mueller, *Retreat from Doomsday, The Obsolescence of Major War*, Basic Books, New York 1989.

1 Worldviews and Theories

1. Martin Hollis and Steve Smith, *Explaining and Understanding International Relations*, Clarendon Press, Oxford 1990, p. 38; M. Banks, "The Evolution of International Relations Theory," in M. Banks (ed.), *Conflict in World Society*, Wheatsheaf, Brighton 1984, pp. 3–21; M. Smith, R. Little and M. Shackleton (eds.), *Perspectives on World Politics*, Croom Helm, London 1981, pp. 11–22.
2. Stephen D. Krasner, "State Power and the Structure of International Trade," *World Politics*, vol. 28, no. 3, April 1976, pp. 317–47; Joseph M. Grieco, *Cooperation among Nations, Europe, America, and Non-Tariff Barriers to Trade*, Cornell University Press, Ithaca, NY 1990.
3. Richard N. Cooper, *The Economics of Interdependence, Economic Policy in the Atlantic Community*, McGraw-Hill, New York 1968.
4. Immanuel M. Wallerstein, *The Modern World-System*, Academic Press, New York 1974; Dieter Senghaas, *Weltwirtschaftsordnung und Entwicklungspolitik; Plädoyer für Dissoziation*, Suhrkamp, Frankfurt a/Main 1977; Johan Galtung, "A structural theory of imperialism," *Journal of Peace Research*, vol. 8, no. 1 pp. 81–117.
5. Kenneth N. Waltz, *Theory of International Politics*, Random House, New York 1979, p. 25.
6. Keith L. Nelson and Spencer C. Olin, Jr., *Why War? Ideology, Theory, and History*, University of California Press, Berkeley, CA 1979. p. 4. See also David Sanders, *Losing an Empire, Finding a Role, British Foreign Policy since 1945*, Macmillan, London 1990, p. 11. Sanders distinguishes three categories that closely resemble the three paradigms and the categories of Nelson and Olin; he speaks of the Structural–Realist, the World Society and the Marxist perspective.
7. Johann Baptist Müller, *Konservatismus und Aussenpolitik*, Duncker & Humblot, Berlin 1988. This is one of the rare studies on the conservative tradition in foreign policy where a clear distinction is drawn between two different schools, between conservatives that identify with imperialism and conservatives that support the balance of power.
8. Another somewhat similar attempt at categorizing theories of international relations was apparently undertaken by Martin Wight, the well-known English scholar. It is reported that he distinguished between realism, rationalism and revolutionism or what he also called the Machiavellian, Grotian and Kantian paradigm. See Brian Porter, "Patterns of Thought and Practice: Martin Wight's 'International Theory'," in Michael Donelan (ed.), *The Reason of States: A Study in International Political Theory*, George Allen & Unwin, London 1978; also Hedley Bull, "Martin Wight and the theory of international relations," in Gabriele Wight and Brian Porter (eds.), *International Theory, The Three Traditions*, Leicester University Press, London 1985.

9. Kenneth N. Waltz, *Man, the State and War*, Columbia University Press, New York 1954.
10. J. David Singer, "The Level-of-Analysis Problem in International Relations," in G. John Ikenberry (ed.), *American Foreign Policy, Theoretical Essays*, Scott, Foresman, Boston, MA 1989, pp. 67–80.
11. Waltz, *Man, the State and War*, p. 160.
12. Ibid., p. 14.
13. Müller, *Konservatismus und Aussenpolitik* (see note 7).
14. Gordon A. Craig and Alexander L. George, *Force and Statecraft, Diplomatic Problems of Our Time*, Oxford University Press, New York 1983, pp. 3–153; Ludwig Dehio, *The Precarious Balance; Four Centuries of the European Balance of Power*, Knopf, New York 1962.
15. Waltz, *Theory*, pp. 81–8.
16. William Godwin, *Enquiry Concerning Political Justice*, Pelican Books, Baltimore, MD 1976.
17. Thomas Hobbes, *Leviathan*, Washington Square Press, New York 1969.
18. Waltz, *Theory*, pp. 81–8.
19. The term "law of the strongest" is taken from the German "Gesetz des Stärkeren." It is intimately tied to the Darwinist notion of the "survival of the fittest" and is a useful concept expressing unambiguously the idea of superior power.
20. Thomas S. Kuhn, *The Structure of Scientific Revolutions*, University of Chicago Press, Chicago, IL 1962.
21. J. Bronowski, *Science and Human Values*, Harper & Row, New York 1965, pp. 19, 20, 27.
22. J. Bronowski, *The Common Sense of Science*, Random House, New York 1954.
23. Michael Polanyi, *Personal Knowledge, Towards a Post-Critical Philosophy*, Harper & Row, New York 1964, pp. 49–65.
24. David Easton, *A Framework for Political Analysis*, Prentice-Hall, Englewood Cliffs, NJ 1965, p. 7.
25. David Easton, "The Current Meaning of 'Behavioralism'," in James C. Charlesworth (ed.), *Contemporary Political Analysis*, The Free Press, New York 1967, p. 12.
26. Raymond Aron, *Peace and War: A Theory of International Relations*, Doubleday, Garden City, NJ 1966, pp. 1–18.
27. I find the distinction between explanation and understanding useful in order to draw a clear linguistic line between correlational and interrelational theories. Unfortunately, some scholars use the terms in a confusing manner. Two British authors are a case in point: Martin Hollis and Steve Smith, *Explaining and Understanding International Relations*, Clarendon Press, Oxford 1991. The title of the study is promising but the content is disappointing. Hollis and Smith argue that realists explain while idealists understand. This is hardly convincing because neither realists nor idealists rely on correlational–exogenous modes of theory. Explanation is typical of behavioral scholars, endogenous understanding of idealist *and* realists. Hedley Bull, Raymond Aron, Reinhold Niebuhr, Stanley Hoffmann, all self-proclaimed realists, would certainly agree with this categorization. It is true, of course, that some realists adopt a pseudo-exogenous position by assuming that their theories are free of assumptions about man and his inner motives and purposes. As I will demon-

strate later on, Kenneth Waltz himself commits this error. In an attempt to avoid "reductionism" he presents a "pure" and fully "systemic" (or structural) theory. However, in doing so he violates his own conception of science. Like all traditionalists, Waltz presents a theory based on endogenous understanding rather than exogenous explanation. For a detailed discussion of "understanding" in the social sciences see Fred R. Dallmayr and Thomas A. McCarthy (eds.), *Understanding and Social Inquiry*, University of Notre Dame Press, Notre Dame, Ind. 1977.

28. Hedley Bull, "International Theory: The Case for a Classical Approach," in Klaus Knorr and James N. Rosenau (eds.), *Contending Approaches to International Politics*, Princeton University Press, Princeton, NJ 1969, pp. 26–8.
29. Waltz, *Theory*, p. 4.
30. J. David Singer and Michael D. Wallace (eds.), *To Augur Well, Early Warning Indicators in World Politics*, Sage Publications, Beverley Hills, CA 1979. See also Waltz, *Theory*, p. 3.
31. Morton A. Kaplan, *System and Process in International Politics*, John Wiley & Sons, New York 1957, p. 4.
32. Ibid., p. 4.
33. Bull, "*International Theory*," pp. 28–30.
34. I have so far avoided the word "concept" and used "term" instead. But "concept" is a useful word because it is broader than "term" and can be seen to embrace both de- and reconstruction. This broad usage of the word (which is then identical with the traditionalist notion of theory) is contained in a number of introductory texts to international relations. See, for instance, Charles O. Lerche, Jr., and Abdul A. Said, *Concepts of International Politics*, Prentice-Hall, Englewood Cliffs, NJ 1963.
35. Bronowski, *Common Sense*, p. 129.
36. Waltz, *Theory*, pp. 5, 8; Bronowski, *Science and Human Values*, pp. 11–16; Bronowski, *Common Sense*, p. 131.
37. The "law of demand and supply," for instance, is deduced from a generalized and contextual definition of man, of the famous "*homo economicus.*" Waltz fails to see this interrelational foundation of law; in his view laws have their foundation in correlational statements only. See Waltz, *Theory*, pp. 1–3. For a discussion of rational laws see Anatol Rapoport, "Various Meanings of 'Theory'," in James N. Rosenau (ed.), *International Politics and Foreign Policy, A Reader in Research and Theory*, Free Press, New York 1961, pp. 44–52.
38. Deduction can be mathematical if the basic concepts are uncontested. Since that is rarely the case in international relations mathematical models are difficult to apply to our field. For an excellent discussion of logical deduction see Carl G. Hempel and Paul Oppenheim, "The Covering Law Analysis of Scientific Explanation," in Leonard I. Krimerman (ed.), *The Nature and Scope of Social Science, A Critical Anthology*, Appleton-Century-Crofts, New York 1969, pp. 54–68.
39. Karl R. Popper, *The Poverty of Historicism*, Harper & Row, New York 1957, pp. 41–83; Bronowski, *Common Sense*, pp. 58–67.
40. Waltz, *Theory*, p. 8. For an interesting discussion of the ends–means logic see also Vernon Van Dyke, *Political Science: A Philosophical Analysis*, Stanford University Press, Stanford, CA 1960, pp. 10–13.

41. Van Dyke, *Political Science* pp. 29–33. Van Dyke is quite explicit about the teleological nature of functional explanations. For another interesting discussion of functional analysis see William Flanagan and Edwin Fogelman, "Functional Analysis," in Charlesworth, *Contemporary Political Analysis*, pp. 72–85.
42. Waltz uses the term "interconnection" instead of "interrelation." See Waltz, *Theory*, p. 9.
43. Bronowski, *Science and Human Values*, pp. 51–8.
44. Waltz shows that any true theory is control-oriented. See Waltz, *Theory*, p. 6.
45. Robert O. Keohane, *International Institutions and State Power*, Westview Press, Boulder, CO 1989, pp. 158–79; also in *International Studies Quarterly*, vol. 32, no. 4, December 1988, p. 380.
46. It is also tantamount to what Rapoport calls a "cataclysmic" conception of war. For a more detailed discussion see Anatol Rapoport, Introduction to *Carl von Clausewitz, On War*, Penguin Books, London 1968, pp. 11–80.
47. John J. Mearsheimer, "Back to the Future, Instability in Europe After the Cold War," *International Security*, vol. 15, no. 1, Summer 1990, pp. 9–10.

2 Classical Theories

1. Friedrich von Gentz, *Fragments upon the Balance of Power in Europe*, M. Peliter, London 1806. For the original version see Friedrich von Gentz, *Fragmente aus der neuesten Geschichte des politischen Gleichgewichts in Europa*, St Petersburg, 1806.
2. A. H. L. Heeren, *History of the Political System of Europe and its Colonies*, S. Butler & Son, Boston, MA 1829; also A. H. L. Heeren, *Handbuch der Geschichte des europäischen Staatensystems und seiner Colonien*, J. F. Römer, Göttingen 1809.
3. For publications on von Gentz and on the general historical context see Golo Mann, *Secretary of Europe: The Life of Friedrich Gentz, Enemy of Napoleon*, Archon Books, Hamden, Conn. 1970; Paul R. Sweet, *Friedrich von Gentz, Defender of the Old Order*, Greenwood Press, Westport, Conn. 1970; Harold Nicolson, *The Congress of Vienna, A Study in Allied Unity: 1812–1822*, Viking Press, New York 1967; Henry A. Kissinger, *A World Restored, The Politics of Conservatism in a Revolutionary Age*, Grosset & Dunlap, New York 1964.
4. Heeren, *History*, p. 11.
5. Gentz, *Fragments*, pp. 6–7.
6. Ibid., pp. 7–8.
7. Ibid., pp. 13–14.
8. Ibid., pp. 4, 55.
9. Ibid., p. xxiv.
10. Ibid., pp. 54–9.
11. This era is also referred to as "Concert Europe." For an interesting contemporary discussion of concerts see Charles A. Kupchan and Clifford A. Kupchan, "Concerts, Collective Security, and the Future of Europe," *International Security*, vol. 16, no. 1, Summer 1991, pp. 114–61; for a more historical treatment see Henry A. Kissinger, *A World Restored*, (see note 3).

12. Minimal consensus is central for the working of both a balance of power and a concert; neither can do without it. For a discussion of this point see Kupchan and Kupchan, "Concerts."
13. Emer de Vattel, *Le droit des gens ou Principes de la loi naturelle*, J. C. B. Mohr, Tübingen 1959.
14. I am thinking here mainly of Hans J. Morgenthau, the best-known theorist of "power politics." Morgenthau does at times make reference to ends and means, wholes and parts, but these remarks are isolated and never developed systematically. See Hans J. Morgenthau, *Politics Among Nations*, Alfred A. Knopf, New York 1967, pp. 3–94.
15. Anatol Rapoport (ed.), *Clausewitz 'On War,'* Pelican Books, Baltimore, MD, 1968, pp 69–71.
16. Bernard Brodie, "The Continuing Relevance of *On War*," in *Clausewitz, On War*, p. 58.
17. Michael Howard and Peter Paret (eds.), *Carl von Clausewitz, On War*, Princeton, University Press, Princeton NJ 1976.
18. Brodie, "Continuing Relevance," pp. 641–50.
19. *Clausewitz, On War*, p. 75.
20. Ibid., p. 77.
21. Ibid., p. 77.
22. Ibid., p. 77.
23. Ibid., p. 79.
24. Ibid., p. 80.
25. Ibid., p. 84.
26. Ibid., p. 85.
27. Ibid., p. 86.
28. Ibid., p. 87.
29. Ibid., p. 87.
30. Ibid., p. 88.
31. Ibid., p. 88.
32. Michael Howard, "The Influence of Clausewitz," in *Clausewitz, On War*, pp. 30–6.
33. *Clausewitz, On War*, pp. 75–6.
34. Brodie, "Continuing Relevance," p. 645.
35. Hans Delbrück, *Geschichte der Kriegskunst*, Georg Stilke, Berlin 1920. Delbrück is virtually the only German interpreter without a simplistic perspective. For a general treatment of the various Clausewitz interpretations see Jürg Martin Gabriel, *Clausewitz Revisited: A Study of his Writings and of the Debate over their Relevance for Deterrence Theory*, The American University, Washington, DC 1971 (unpublished); also Raymond Aron, *Clausewitz, den Krieg denken*, Propyläen, Frankfurt a/Main 1980.
36. For a discussion of Clausewitz's "dialectic" see Jürg Martin Gabriel, *Clausewitz Revisited*, pp. 86–96; also Raymond Aron, *Clausewitz*, pp. 321–31.
37. Friedrich von Bernhardi, *Germany and the Next War*, Longmans, Green and Co., New York 1914. For a British translation see Friedrich von Bernhardi, *Germany and the Next War*, Edward Arnold, London 1914.
38. Heinrich von Treitschke, *Politics*, Harcourt, Brace & World, New York 1963; H. W. C. Davis, *The Political Thought of Heinrich von Treitschke*, Charles Scribner's Sons, New York 1915.

39. Bernhardi, *Germany*, p. 16.
40. Ibid., p. 18.
41. Ibid., p. 18.
42. Ibid., p. 19.
43. Ibid., p. 20.
44. Ibid., p. 20.
45. Ibid., p. 21.
46. Ibid., p. 22.
47. Ibid., p. 24.
48. Ibid., p. 25.
49. Ibid., p. 26.
50. Ibid., pp. 27–8.
51. Ibid., p. 25.
52. Ibid., p. 25.
53. Ibid., p. 26.
54. Ibid., pp. 27–8.
55. Ibid., p. 29.
56. Ibid., p. 30.
57. Ibid., p. 32.
58. Ibid., p. 38.
59. Ibid., p. 38.
60. Ibid., pp. 43, 45.
61. Ibid., p. 71.
62. Ibid., p. 79.
63. Ibid., p. 81.
64. Ibid., p. 84.
65. Ibid., p. 99.
66. Ibid., p. 106.
67. Ibid., pp. 108–9.
68. Ibid., pp. 109–10.
69. Ibid., p. 110.
70. Social Darwinism can also combine with idealist notions of international relations. See, for instance, Herbert Spencer, *The Principles of Sociology*, D. Appleton & Co., New York 1897; Herbert Spencer, *Illustrations of Universal Progress*, D. Appleton & Co., New York 1889; William Graham Sumner, *War and Other Essays*, Yale University Press, New Haven, Conn. 1919.
71. Immanuel Kant, *Perpetual Peace*, George Allen & Unwin, London 1917; introduction by M. Campbell Smith, p. 33.
72. M. C. Jacob (ed.), *Peace Projects of the Eighteenth Century*, Garland Publishers, New York 1974.
73. Howard Williams, *Kant's Political Philosophy*, Basil Blackwell, Oxford 1983, p. 37.
74. Ibid., pp. 36–9.
75. Kant, *Perpetual Peace*, p. 62.
76. Ibid., p. 107.
77. Ibid., p. 107.
78. Ibid., p. 108.
79. Ibid., p. 109.
80. Ibid., p. 110.

81. Ibid., p. 110.
82. Ibid., p. 110.
83. Ibid., p. 111.
84. Ibid., p. 111.
85. Ibid., p. 112.
86. Ibid., p. 112.
87. Ibid., p. 113.
88. Ibid., p. 113.
89. Ibid., p. 114.
90. Ibid., p. 114.
91. Ibid., p. 114.
92. Ibid., p. 115.
93. Ibid., p. 120.
94. Ibid., p. 121.
95. Ibid., p. 125.
96. Ibid., p. 125.
97. Ibid., p. 125.
98. Ibid., pp. 126–7.
99. Ibid., pp. 122–3.
100. Williams, *Kant*, pp. 12–18.
101. Kant, *Perpetual Peace*, p. 123.
102. Ibid., p. 128.
103. Ibid., p. 129; see also Williams, *Kant*, pp. 253–60.
104. Ibid., p. 136.
105. Ibid., p. 134.
106. Ibid., pp. 134–5.
107. Ibid., p. 59; also Williams, *Kant*, p. 257.
108. Ibid., p. 137.
109. Ibid., p. 138.
110. Ibid., p. 139.
111. Williams, *Kant*, p. 260.
112. Kant, *Perpetual Peace*, pp. 139–40.
113. Ibid., p. 141.
114. Adam Smith and Jeremy Bentham are also outspoken in their anti-mercantilism. See for instance Jeremy Bentham, "Emancipate Your Colonies! An Appeal to the National Convention of France in January 1793," Effingham Wilson, London 1838; Adam Smith, *An Inquiry into the Nature and Causes of the Wealth of Nations*, Clarendon Press, Oxford 1976 (Book IV deals with mercantilism).
115. Schumpeter also argues this case. He contends that in theory purely capitalist societies are peaceful but that in reality no such state exists. All existing liberal societies contain (atavistic) remnants of former times. See Joseph A. Schumpeter, *Imperialism and Social Classes*, Augustus M. Kelley, New York 1951, pp. 83–99.
116. Edmund Burke, *Reflections on the Revolution in France*, edited with an introduction by Conor Cruise O'Brien, Penguin Books, Baltimore, MD 1969.
117. Michael Doyle, "Liberalism and World Politics," *APSR Review*, vol. 80, no. 4, December 1986, pp. 1151–69; Michael Doyle, "Kant, Liberal Legacies, and Foreign Affairs," *Philosophy and Public Affairs*, vol. 12, no. 3, Summer 1983, pp. 205–35.

118. Kant, *Perpetual Peace*, pp. 117–18.
119. For an excellent and highly readable account of Kant's overall philosophy see Williams, *Kant*, pp. 1–51, 244–71.
120. J. A. Hobson, *Imperialism: A Study*, University of Michigan Press, Ann Arbor, Mich. 1972.
121. V. I. Lenin, *Imperialism: The Highest Stage of Capitalism*, International Publishers, New York 1959.
122. Hobson, *Imperialism*, p. xiv (introduction by P. Siegelman); see also Harrison M. Wright, *The "New Imperialism": Analysis of Late Nineteenth-Century Expansion*, D. C. Heath and Company, Boston, MA 1961.
123. Kenneth N. Waltz, *Theory of International Politics*, Random House, New York 1979, pp. 18–37.
124. Hobson, *Imperialism*, pp. 11–12.
125. Ibid., pp. 39–40.
126. Ibid., pp. 53–4.
127. Ibid., p. 81.
128. Ibid., p. 82.
129. Ibid., p. 85.
130. Ibid., p. 86.
131. Ibid., p. 86.
132. Ibid., p. 90.
133. Ibid., p. 91.
134. Ibid., p. 138.
135. Ibid., p. 145.
136. Ibid., p. 145.
137. Ibid., pp. 153–95.
138. Ibid., pp. 196–222.
139. Ibid., pp. 223–84.
140. Ibid., pp. 285–355.
141. Ibid., p. 363.
142. Ibid., p. 364.
143. Ibid., p. 364.
144. V. I. Lenin, *Imperialism,* (see note 121); Johan Galtung, "Eine strukturelle Theorie des Imperialismus," in Dieter Senghaas, *Imperialismus und strukturelle Gewalt: Analysen über abhängige Reproduktion*, Suhrkamp, Frankfurt a/Main 1978, pp. 29–104; Dieter Senghaas, *Weltwirtschaftsordnung und Entwicklungspolitik: Plädoyer für Dissoziation*, Suhrkamp, Frankfurt a/Main 1977; Immanuel M. Wallerstein, *The Modern World System*, Academic Press, New York 1974.
145. Hobson, *Imperialism*, p. 363.
146. J. D. B. Miller, *Norman Angell and the Futility of War*, Macmillan, London 1986, pp. 1–15.
147. Norman Angell, *The Great Illusion*, G. P. Putnam's Sons, New York 1911.
148. Norman Angell, *Die Falsche Rechnung*, Vita Verlag, Berlin 1913.
149. Angell, *Great Illusion*, pp. 3–14.
150. Ibid., pp. 31–4.
151. Ibid., p. 36.
152. Ibid., p. 52.
153. Ibid. pp. 54–5.

154. Ibid., pp. 55–6.
155. Ibid., p. 88.
156. Ibid., p. 160.
157. Ibid., p. 180.
158. Ibid., p. 178.
159. Ibid., p. 189.
160. Ibid., p. 213.
161. Ibid., p. 245.
162. Ibid., p. 257.
163. Ibid., p. 318.
164. Miller, *Angell*, p. 10.
165. John J. Herz, "Rise and Demise of the Territorial State," *World Politics*, vol. 9, no. 4, July 1957, pp. 473–93; John Mueller, *Retreat from Doomsday, The Obsolescence of Major War*, Basic Books, New York 1989.
166. It was up to another Englishman to formulate a theory of integration and of supranationality: David Mitrany, *A Working Peace System*, Quadrangle Books, Chicago, IL 1966.
167. Robert O. Keohane and Joseph S. Nye, *Power and Interdependence*, Harper-Collins, New York 1989.
168. Norman Angell, *America and the New World-State: A Plan for American Leadership in International Organization*, G. P. Putnam's Sons, New York 1915.
169. Edward Hallett Carr, *The Twenty Years' Crisis, 1919–1939*, Harper & Row, New York 1964, pp. 12, 25–6, 39, 43, 115.
170. John Maynard Keynes, *The Economic Consequences of the Peace*, Macmillan, London 1971 (originally published in 1919). See also Norman Angell, *The Peace Treaty and the Economic Chaos of Europe*, Swarthmore Press, London 1919.
171. Although interdependence and integration are important realities in Europe, there is an astonishing lack of theory to accompany them. There was an outpouring of integration theory in the United States in the sixties, but European scholars particularly have largely avoided the topic, and recent attempts are again undertaken by Americans; see Philippe C. Schmitter, "The European Community as an Emergent and Novel Form of Political Domination" (draft), Stanford University, April 1990.
172. For a useful bibliography of recent literature on collective security see Charles A. Kupchan and Clifford A. Kupchan, "Concerts, Collective Security, and the Future of Europe," *International Security*, vol. 16, no. 1, Summer 1991, pp. 118–19.
173. Theodore P. Greene (ed.), *Wilson at Versailles*, D. C. Heath & Co., Boston, Mass. 1957; Ivo J. Lederer (ed.), *The Versailles Settlement, Was it Foredoomed to Failure?*, D. C. Heath, Boston, MA 1960.
174. Arthur S. Link, *Woodrow Wilson: Revolution, War, and Peace*, H. Davidson, Arlington Heights, IL 1979, pp. 1–5.
175. Ray Stannard Baker and William E. Dodd, *The Public Papers of Woodrow Wilson, College and State*, vol. II, Harper & Brothers, New York 1926, pp. 121–2.
176. Ibid., p. 128.
177. Ibid., p. 189.

178. Ibid., p. 135.
179. Ibid., p. 52.
180. Ibid., p. 212.
181. Ibid., p. 196.
182. Ibid., p. 213. Wilson gave various speeches in which he "lectured" special interest groups about "public virtues"; see ibid., pp. 217–21.
183. Ibid., pp. 213–14.
184. For a more detailed discussion of Wilson's conception of international politics see Robert E. Osgood, *Ideals and Self-Interest in America's Foreign Relations*, University of Chicago Press, Chicago, Ill. 1953; Arthur S. Link, *Woodrow Wilson* (see note 174); Charles Seymour, *Woodrow Wilson and the World War*, Yale University Press, New Haven, Conn. 1921; Charles Seymour, *American Diplomacy during the World War*, Johns Hopkins University Press, Baltimore, MD 1934.
185. Baker and Dodd, *College and State*, p. 381.
186. Ray Stannard Baker and William E. Dodd, *The Public Papers of Woodrow Wilson, War and Peace*, vol. I, Harper & Brothers, New York 1926, p. 12.
187. Arnold Wolfers and Lawrence W. Martin (eds.), *The Anglo-American Tradition in Foreign Affairs*, Yale University Press, New Haven, Conn. 1956, p. 273.
188. Ray Stannard Baker and William E. Dodd, *The Public Papers of Woodrow Wilson, The New Democracy*, vol. I, Harper & Brothers, New York 1926, p. 410.
189. Baker and Dodd, *War and Peace*, p. 159.
190. Ibid., p. 159.
191. Baker and Dodd, *The New Democracy*, pp. 379–81.
192. Baker and Dodd, *War and Peace*, pp. 159, 161.
193. Ibid., p. 12.
194. Ibid., p. 14.
195. Ibid., p. 258.
196. Ibid., p. 397.
197. Ibid., p. 398.
198. Baker and Dodd, *The New Democracy*, p. 307.
199. Ibid., p. 304.
200. Ibid., p. 413.
201. Link, *Wilson*, p. 5.
202. Baker and Dodd, *The New Democracy*, p. 186.

3 Contemporary Theories

1. Hans J. Morgenthau, *Politics Among Nations*, Alfred A. Knopf, New York 1966; Stanley Hoffmann, *The State of War*, Frederick A. Praeger, New York 1965; Stanley Hoffmann, *Janus and Minerva, Essays in the Theory and Practice of International Politics*, Westview Press, Boulder, CO 1987. Of the two, Morgenthau pretends to be the more systematic and scientific, but his most am-bitious attempt to bring some discipline into realism fails: see Hans J. Morgenthau, *Scientific Man Versus Power Politics*, University of Chicago

Press, Chicago, Ill. 1946. Hedley Bull, a British–Australian theorist, develops a somewhat more systematic theory of realism in his *The Anarchical Society: A Study of Order in World Politics*, Macmillan, London 1977, pp. 101–26. For an excellent general discussion of realism see Michael Joseph Smith, *Realist Thought from Weber to Kissinger*, Louisiana State University, Baton Rouge, LA 1986.
2. Kenneth N. Waltz, *Theory of International Politics*, Random House, New York 1979, p. 251. For a more concise version see Kenneth N. Waltz, "Balance of Power," in J. Salmon, J. O'Leary and R. Shultz (eds.), *Power, Principles and Interests*, Ginn Press, New York 1986.
3. John Gerard Ruggie, "Continuity and Transformation in the World Polity: Toward a Neorealist Synthesis," *World Politics*, vol. XXXV, no. 2, January 1983, p. 272.
4. Waltz, *Theory*, p. 9.
5. Ibid., p. 11.
6. Ibid., pp. 18–19.
7. Kenneth N. Waltz, *Man, the State and War*, Columbia University Press, New York 1954, pp. 159–238.
8. Ibid., pp. 16–158.
9. Waltz, *Theory*, pp. 40, 79.
10. Ibid., p. 66.
11. Waltz, "Balance of Power", p. 59.
12. Ibid., p. 59.
13. Waltz, *Theory*, p. 72.
14. Ibid., p. 73.
15. Ibid., pp. 163–4.
16. Ibid., pp. 134–8.
17. For a discussion of neo-realism see Robert G. Gilpin, "The richness of the tradition of political realism," *International Organization*, vol. 38, no. 2, Spring 1984, pp. 287–304; Joseph S. Nye, Jr., "Neorealism and Neoliberalism," *World Politics*, vol. 40, January 1988, pp. 235–51.
18. Waltz, *Theory*, p. 170.
19. Ibid., p. 174.
20. Ibid., p. 204.
21. Ibid., p. 204.
22. Ibid., p. 97.
23. Waltz, *Man, the State and War*, pp. 14, 160.
24. Some scholars raise these questions. See, for instance, Bruce Russett, *Controlling the Sword: The Democratic Governance of National Security*; Harvard University Press, Cambridge, MA 1990.
25. Waltz, *Theory*, p. 158.
26. Ibid., p. 159.
27. Ibid. p. 204.
28. For an excellent account of the precarious nature of the European balance see Ludwig Dehio, *The Precarious Balance; Four Centuries of the European Balance of Power*, Knopf, New York 1962. The German title of the study is also very suggestive: Ludwig Dehio, *Gleichgewicht oder Hegemonie: Betrachtungen über ein Grundproblem der neueren Staatengeschichte*, Scherpe Verlag, Krefeld 1985.

29. See for instance Glenn H. Snyder, "The Balance of Power and the Balance of Terror," in Dean G. Pruitt and Richard C. Snyder (eds.), *Theory and Research on the Causes of War*, Prentice-Hall, Englewood Cliffs, NJ 1969, pp. 114–26.
30. Robert Gilpin, *War and Change in World Politics*, Cambridge University Press, Cambridge, MA 1981; see also Robert Gilpin, *U.S. Power and the Multinational Corporation, The Political Economy of Foreign Direct Investment*, Basic Books, New York 1975; Robert Gilpin, *The Political Economy of International Relations*, Princeton University Press, Princeton, NJ 1987.
31. Other authors have also produced theories about hegemonic change. The most prominent are Paul Kennedy and Mancur Olson. I have decided to choose Gilpin because he states his case more systematically than Kennedy and because he is more of a political scientist than Olson. See Paul Kennedy, *The Rise and Fall of the Great Powers: Economic Change and Military Conflict from 1500 to 2000*, Fontana Press, London 1988; Mancur Olson, *The Rise and Decline of Nations, Economic Growth, Stagflation, and Social Rigidities*, Yale University Press, New Haven, Conn. 1982.
32. Robert G. Gilpin, "The richness of the tradition of political realism," *International Organization*, vol. 38, no. 2, Spring 1984, p. 288.
33. For other theories of cyclical and hegemonic change see George Modelski, "The Long Cycle of Global Politics and the Nation-State," *Comparative Studies In Society and History*, vol. 20, April 1978, pp. 214–35; Immanuel M. Wallerstein, *The Modern World-System*, Academic Press, New York 1974 (two vols); Charles Doran and Wes Parsons, "War and the Cycle of Relative Power," *American Political Science Review*, vol. 74, December 1980, pp. 947–65; Richard Rosecrance, "Long Cycle Theory and International Relations," *International Organization*, vol. 41, no. 2, Spring 1987, pp. 283–301.
34. Gilpin, *War and Change*, pp. 10–11.
35. Ibid., p. 12.
36. Ibid., p. 15.
37. Ibid., pp. 52–105.
38. Ibid., p. 105. The fact that no law-like statement can be deduced about the mechanism of the "factors determining change" distinguishes, according to Gilpin, his approach from that of Modelski or other theorists of historic cycles. For a more detailed discussion see Gilpin, *War and Change*, p. 205.
39. Ibid., pp. 116–44.
40. Ibid., p. 145.
41. Ibid., p. 156.
42. Ibid., pp. 159–68.
43. Ibid., pp. 168–85.
44. Ibid., p. 185.
45. Ibid., pp. 191–6.
46. Ibid., p. 197.
47. Ibid., pp. 199–200.
48. Ibid., p. 185.
49. Ibid., p. 210.
50. Ibid., p. 229.
51. Ibid., p. 230.
52. Gilpin, "Richness of the tradition," p. 290.

53. Ibid., p. 290.
54. Gilpin, *War and Change*, pp. 89–95.
55. See William T. R. Fox, *Political Science Quarterly*, vol. 97, no. 4, Winter 1982–83, p. 685 (book reviews).
56. Hedley Bull, *The Anarchical Society, A Study of Order in World Politics*, Macmillan, London 1977, pp. 200–29. Johan Galtung, on the other hand, has a tendency to identify any situation of inequality and predominance as an imperialistic one and thereby to confuse the concept; see Johan Galtung, "Eine strukturelle Theorie des Imperialismus," in Dieter Senghaas (Hrsg.), *Imperialismus und strukturelle Gewalt: Analysen über abhängige Reproduktion*, Suhrkamp, Frankfurt a/Main 1972, pp. 29–104. Duncan Snidal, in a discussion of Gilpin's work, distinguishes between "benevolent" and "coercive" hegemony, which seems quite useful; see Duncan Snidal, "The Limits of Hegemonic Stability Theory," *International Organization*, vol. 39, no. 4, Autumn 1985, p. 588.
57. The difference between hegemony and empire can, of course, also be explained with other terms. Empire is closely tied to zero-sum reasoning and exploitation, whereas hegemony can coincide with nonzero-sum reasoning and mutual benefit.
58. Gilpin, "Richness of the tradition," p. 290.
59. Gilpin, *War and Change*, pp. 186–210.
60. Herman Kahn, *Thinking About the Unthinkable*, Horizon Press, New York 1962; see also Thomas C. Schelling, *The Strategy of Conflict*, Oxford University Press, New York 1963; Thomas C. Schelling, *Arms and Influence*, Yale University Press, New Haven, Conn. 1966; Albert Wohlstetter, "The Delicate Balance of Terror," *Foreign Affairs*, vol. 37, no. 2, 1958, pp. 211–34.
61. For an interesting discussion of this dilemma see Scott Sagan, *Moving Targets, Nuclear Strategy and National Security*, Princeton University Press, Princeton, NJ 1989.
62. For a detailed discussion of some of the basic terms and of the history of deterrence see: Alexander L. George and Richard Smoke, *Deterrence in American Foreign Policy: Theory and Practice*, Columbia University Press, New York 1974, pp. 38–45; Richard Smoke, *National Security and the Nuclear Dilemma*, Random House, New York 1984; Charles Kegley and Eugene Wittkopf, *The Nuclear Reader*, St. Martin's Press, New York 1989; Y. Harkabi, *Nuclear War and Nuclear Deterrence*, Israel Program for Scientific Translations, Jersualem 1966; Raymond Aron, *The Great Debate, Theories of Nuclear Strategy*, Doubleday, Garden City, NJ 1965.
63. Fred Kaplan, *The Wizards of Armageddon*, Simon & Schuster, New York 1983; Bernard Brodie, *Strategy in the Missile Age*, Princeton University Press, Princeton, NJ 1959.
64. Herman Kahn, *On Thermonuclear War*, Princeton University Press, Princeton NJ 1960.
65. Kahn, *Thinking*, p. 11.
66. Ibid., p. 27.
67. Ibid., p. 40.
68. Ibid., p. 44.
69. Ibid., p. 51.
70. Ibid., p. 57.

71. Ibid., p. 82.
72. Ibid., p. 100.
73. Ibid., p. 109.
74. George and Smoke, *Deterrence*, pp. 39–40.
75. Ibid., pp. 41–55.
76. Schelling, *Strategy of Conflict*, (see note 60).
77. Kahn, *Thinking*, p. 45.
78. Ibid., p. 45.
79. Ibid., p. 185.
80. Ibid., p. 200.
81. Ibid., p. 207.
82. Ibid., p. 206.
83. Richard Ned Lebow, *Between Peace and War: The Nature of International Crisis*, Johns Hopkins University Press, Baltimore, MD 1981; Richard Ned Lebow, *Nuclear Crisis Management: A Dangerous Illusion*, Cornell University Press, Ithaca, NY 1987; *Journal of Social Issues*, vol. 43, no. 4, 1987 (*Beyond Deterrence*); Robert Jervis, *The Illogic of American Nuclear Strategy*, Cornell University Press, Ithaca, NY 1984; Robert Jervis, *Perception and Misperception in International Politics*, Princeton University Press, Princeton, NJ 1976.
84. Raymond Aron, *Clausewitz. Den Krieg denken*, Propyläen, Frankfurt a/Main 1980; Bernard Brodie wrote a lengthy introduction to one of the more recent issues of *On War: Carl von Clausewitz, On War* (edited and translated by Michael Howard and Peter Paret, introduction by B. Brodie), Princeton University Press, Princeton, NJ 1976; Anatol Rapoport, a critic of the Neo-Clausewitzians, wrote a long introduction to an earlier issue of *On War: Carl von Clausewitz, On War* (edited with an introduction by Anatol Rapoport), Penguin Books, Baltimore, MD 1968.
85. Halford Mackinder, *Democratic Ideals and Reality*, Norton, New York 1962. This book contains the major publications of Mackinder, including the often quoted articles "The Geographical Pivot of History" (1904) and "The Round World and the Winning of the Peace" (1943). See also W. H. Parker, *Mackinder: Geography as an Aid to Statecraft*, Clarendon Press, Oxford 1982.
86. Colin S. Gray, *The Geopolitics of Super Power*, University Press of Kentucky, Lexington, KY 1988. See also Colin S. Gray, *The Geopolitics of the Nuclear Era: Heartlands, Rimlands, and the Technological Revolution*, Crance, Russak, New York 1977; Colin S. Gray, *Nuclear Strategy and National Style*, Hamilton Press, Lanham, MD 1986; Colin S. Gray, "Keeping the Soviets Landlocked: Geostrategy for a Maritime America," *The National Interest*, no. 4, Summer 1986, pp. 24–36.
87. Gray, *Geopolitics of Superpower*, p. 9.
88. Ibid., pp. 30, 31.
89. Ibid., pp. 103, 36.
90. Ibid., p. 38.
91. Ibid., p. 44.
92. Ibid., p. 109.
93. Ibid., p. 110.
94. Ibid., p. 110.
95. Ibid., p. 108.
96. Ibid., p. 56.

97. Ibid., p. 75.
98. Ibid., p. 118.
99. Ibid., p. 123.
100. Ibid., p. 124.
101. James Burnham, *Containment or Liberation?* Day, New York 1953; James Burnham, *The Struggle for the World*, Day, New York 1947; James Burnham, *The Coming Defeat of Communism*, Day, New York 1950; James Burnham, *Suicide of the West*, Day, New York 1964.
102. Gray, *Geopolitics of Superpower*, p. 183.
103. Ibid., p. 184.
104. Ibid., pp. 184–5.
105. Ibid., p. 186.
106. Ibid., pp. 58–63.
107. Ibid., pp. 93, 101.
108. Ibid., pp. 99–100.
109. Richard Rosecrance, *The Rise of the Trading State, Commerce and Conquest in the Modern World*, Basic Books, New York 1986.
110. The argument that capitalism is inherently peaceful is intimately related to this view. See Joseph A. Schumpteter, *Imperialism and Social Classes*, Augustus M. Kelley, New York 1951.
111. Rosecrance, *Rise of the Trading State*, p. 44.
112. Ibid., p. xi.
113. Ibid., p. 62.
114. Ibid., p. 172.
115. Ibid., p. 31.
116. Ibid., p. 20.
117. Ibid., p. 155.
118. Ibid., p. 158.
119. Ibid., p. 38.
120. Ibid., pp. 161, 38.
121. Ibid., p. 158.
122. Ibid., p. 161.
123. Ibid., p. 28.
124. Ibid., p. 140.
125. Ibid., p. 139, 15.
126. Ibid., p. 139.
127. Ibid., p. 210.
128. Ibid., p. 23.
129. Ibid., p. 23.
130. Ibid., p. 57.
131. Ibid., p. ix.
132. Ibid., p. 25.
133. Ibid., pp. 56–8.
134. Ibid., p. 61
135. Ibid., p. 168.
136. Ibid., p. 60.
137. For a modern treatment of Kant see Michael Doyle, "Kant, Liberal Legacies, and Foreign Affairs," *Philosophy and Public Affairs*, vol. 12, no. 3, Summer

1983, pp. 205–35; Michael Doyle, "Liberalism and World Politics," *APSR Review*, vol. 80, no. 4, December 1986, pp. 1151–69.
138. Rosecrance, *Rise of the Trading State*, p. 27.
139. Joseph S. Nye, Jr., "Neorealism and Neoliberalism," *World Politics*, vol. XL, no. 2, January 1988, pp. 240, 246.
140. Adam Smith, *An Inquiry into the Nature and Causes of the Wealth of Nations*, Clarendon Press, Oxford 1976 (Book IV deals with mercantilism); *Richard Cobden: Speeches on Questions of Public Policy*, edited by John Bright and J. E. T. Rogers, Fisher Unwin, London 1909, (2 vols), pp. 479–96. Arnold Wolfers and Laurence W. Martin, *The Anglo-American Tradition in Foreign Affairs*, Yale University Press, New Haven, Conn. 1956. For an excellent survey of economic theories of war and peace see Edmond Silberner, *La guerre dans la pensée économique du XVIe au XVIIIe siècle*, Sirey, Paris 1939, pp. 247–61; Edmond Silberner, *La guerre et la paix dans l'histoire des doctrines économiques*, Sirey, Paris 1957.
141. Rosecrance, *Rise of the Trading State*, p. 31.
142. Robert O. Keohane, *After Hegemony, Cooperation and Discord in the World Political Economy*, Princeton University Press, Princeton, NJ 1984. See also Robert O. Keohane, *International Institutions and State Power: Essays in International Relations Theory*, Westview Press, Boulder, CO 1989; Robert O. Keohane and Joseph S. Nye, *Power and Interdependence: World Politics in Transition*, Little, Brown, Boston, MA 1977; Robert O. Keohane and Joseph S. Nye (eds.), *Transnational Relations and World Politics*, Harvard University Press, Cambridge, MA 1972.
143. There is a voluminous literature on regimes. The following publications are among the more important: Stephen D. Krasner (ed.), *International Regimes*, Cornell University Press, Ithaca, NY 1983; Kenneth A. Oye (ed.), *Cooperation under Anarchy*, Princeton University Press, Princeton, NJ 1985; Oran Young, "International Regimes: Toward a New Theory of Institutions," *World Politics*, vol. 39, October 1986, pp. 104–22; *International Organization*, vol. 36, no. 2, Spring 1982: issue dedicated to International Regimes.
144. For a discussion of hegemonic stability theory see Charles P. Kindleberger, *The World in Depression, 1929–1939*, University of California Press, Berkeley, CA 1973.
145. Keohane, *After Hegemony*, p. 31.
146. Ibid., pp. 31–2.
147. Ibid., p. 67. See also p. 84.
148. Ibid., p. 244.
149. Ibid., p. 7.
150. Ibid., p. 22.
151. Ibid., p. 7. See also David Mitrany, *A Working Peace System*, Quadrangle Books, Chicago, Ill. 1966; David Mitrany, *The Functional Theory of Politics*, St. Martin's Press, New York 1976.
152. Ibid., p. 8.
153. Ibid., p. 5.
154. Ibid., p. 54.
155. Ibid., p. 52.
156. Ibid., p. 57.

157. There is disagreement over how useful a step it was and, more generally, over how useful the concept is in general. For a critique of the concept see J. Martin Rochester, "The rise and fall of international organization as a field of study," *International Organization*, vol. 40. no. 4, Autumn 1986, p. 800; Oran R. Young, "International Regimes: Toward a New Theory of Institutions," in *World Politics*, vol. 39, no. 1, October 1986, p. 107.
158. Keohane, *After Hegemony*, p. 57.
159. Ibid., p. 59.
160. For a lucid presentation and explanation of the Prisoners' Dilemma and related questions see Karl W. Deutsch, *The Analysis of International Relations*, Prentice-Hall, Englewood Cliffs, NJ 1968, pp. 112–32.
161. Keohane, *After Hegemony*, p. 69.
162. Ibid., pp. 76–7.
163. Ibid., p. 79.
164. Ibid., pp. 80–3, 97–101.
165. Ibid., pp. 85–95.
166. Ibid., p. 101.
167. Ibid., pp. 110–32.
168. Ibid., pp. 135–240.
169. Ibid., p. 67.
170. James M. Buchanan, *The Limits of Liberty: Between Anarchy and the Leviathan*, University of Chicago Press, Chicago, IL 1975; G. Brennan and James M. Buchanan, *The Reason of Rules: Constitutional Political Economy*, Cambridge University Press, Cambridge, MA 1985.
171. For an excellent critique of Keohane that comes to identical conclusions on this point see Joseph M. Grieco, *Cooperation among Nations; Europe, America, and Non-Tariff Barriers to Trade*, Cornell University Press, Ithaca, NY 1990, p. 217.
172. Keohane, *After Hegemony*, p. 55.
173. Ibid., p. 107.
174. Ibid., p. 259.
175. Ibid., p. 56.
176. Charles E. Osgood, *An Alternative to War or Surrender*, University of Illinois Press, Urbana, IL 1962.
177. William M. Evan and Stephen Hilgartner (eds.), *The Arms Race and Nuclear War*, Prentice-Hall, Englewood Cliffs, NJ 1987; Dean G. Pruitt and Richard C. Snyder, *Theory and Research of the Causes of War*, Prentice-Hall, Englewood Cliffs, NJ 1969; Melvin Small and J. David Singer, *International War, An Anthology*, Dorsey Press, Chicago, IL 1985.
178. For a very useful survey see Robert Mandel, "Psychological Approaches to International Relations," In Margaret G. Hermann (ed.), *Political Psychology*, Jossey-Bass, London 1986, pp. 251–78.
179. Stanley Hoffmann, "On the Political Psychology of Peace and War: A Critique and an Agenda," *Political Psychology*, vol. 7, no. 1, 1986, p. 4.
180. Osgood, *Alternative*, p. 88.
181. Ibid., p. 87.
182. Ibid., pp. 89–134.
183. Ibid., pp. 25–6, 69–70.
184. Ibid., pp. 136–7.

185. Ibid., p. 126.
186. Ibid., p. 128.
187. Ibid., p. 129.
188. Ibid., pp. 136–7.
189. Joseph B. Board, Jr., "An Alternative to War or Surrender," *Midwest Journal of Political Science*, vol. VII, no. 2, May 1963, p. 184.
190. Fred A. Sondermann, "Peace initiatives; the literature of possibilities: a review," *The Journal of Conflict Resolution*, vol. VII, No. 2, June 1963, p. 148.
191. Grenville Clark and Louis B. Sohn, *World Peace Through World Law*, Harvard University Press, Cambridge, MA 1958.
192. Ali Mazrui, *A World Federation of Cultures*, Free Press, New York 1975; Gustavo Lagos and Oracio Godoy, *Revolution of Being: A Latin American View of the Future*, Free Press, New York 1977; Johan Galtung, *The True Worlds: A Transnational Perspective*, Free Press, New York 1980; Richard A. Falk, *A Study of Future Worlds*, Free Press, New York 1975; also Saul H. Mendlovitz (ed.), *On the Creation of a Just World Order*, Free Press, New York 1975.
193. Falk, *A Study*, p. 161.
194. Ibid., p. 185.
195. Ibid., p. 185.
196. Ibid., pp. 188–9
197. Ibid., p. 194.
198. Ibid., p. 224.
199. Ibid., p. 226.
200. Ibid., p. 234.
201. Ibid., pp. 237–8.
202. Ibid., p. 238.
203. Ibid., pp. 238–9.
204. Ibid., pp. 242–6.
205. Ibid., p. 283.
206. Ibid., p. 290.
207. Ibid., p. 220.
208. Richard Falk, *Revitalizing International Law*, Iowa State University Press, Ames, IA 1989, pp. 27–43.
209. Falk, *A Study*, pp. 289, 295.
210. Ibid., p. 277.
211. Ibid., p. 312.
212. Ibid., p. 278.
213. Ibid., p. 413.
214. Reinhold Niebuhr, *The Children of Light and the Children of Darkness*, Charles Scribner's Sons, New York 1960; Reinhold Niebuhr, *The Irony of American History*, Charles Scribner's Sons, New York 1962.
215. Falk, *A Study*, p. 220.
216. Ibid., p. 178.
217. Ibid., p. 68.
218. Ibid., p. 64.
219. Ibid., p. 17.
220. Ibid., p. 184.
221. Ibid., p. 185.

4 Worldviews: A Summary

1. For a useful essay on some of the idealist conceptions that follow see John H. Herz, "Idealist Internationalism and the Security Dilemma," *World Politics*, vol. 2, no. 2, January 1950, pp. 157–80.
2. Thomas Paine, *Rights of Man*, Penguin Books, Baltimore, MD 1969.
3. John Locke, *Two Treatises of Government*, Cambridge University Press, London 1988.
4. Max Beloff, *Thomas Jefferson and American Democracy*, Penguin Books, Baltimore, MD 1972.
5. For an excellent discussion of the various aspects of individualism see Steven Lukes, *Individualism*, Basil Blackwell, Cambridge, MA 1973.
6. Adam Smith, *The Wealth of Nations*, Penguin Books, Baltimore, MD 1970.
7. For a lucid presentation of game theory see Karl W. Deutsch, *The Analysis of International Relations*, Prentice-Hall, Englewood Cliffs, NJ 1968, pp. 112–32. For a general treatment of the idea of games see Anatol Rapoport, *Fights, Games and Debates*, University of Michigan Press, Ann Arbor, Mich. 1960.
8. Jeremy Bentham, "Emancipate Your Colonies! An Appeal to the National Convention of France in January 1793," Effingham Wilson, London 1838.
9. Herbert Spencer, *The Principles of Sociology*, Appleton & Co., New York 1897; Herbert Spencer, *Illustrations of Universal Progress*, Appleton & Co., New York 1889.
10. James N. Rosenau, *Turbulence in World Politics, A Theory of Change and Continuity*, Princeton University Press, Princeton, NJ 1990.
11. Anatol Rapoport also speaks of "eschatological" or "messianic" wars. See his introduction to *Clausewitz, On War*, Penguin Books, Baltimore, MD 1968, pp. 15–17.
12. Michael Doyle, "Liberalism and World Politics," *APSR Review*, vol. 80, no. 4, December 1986, pp. 1151–69; Michael Doyle, "Kant, Liberal Legacies, and Foreign Affairs," *Philosophy and Public Affairs*, vol. 12, no. 3, Summer 1983, pp. 205–35, and no. 4, pp. 323–53.
13. William Godwin, *Enquiry Concerning Political Justice*, Penguin Books, Baltimore, MD 1976; Gene Sharp, *The Politics of Nonviolent Action*, Porter Sargent, Boston, MA 1973.
14. Karl Marx, *Capital*, Random House, New York 1977.
15. Wilhelm Röpke, *Economic Order and International Law*, Recueil des Cours, Académie de droit international, A. W. Sijthoff, Leiden 1955, pp. 217–50.
16. John Maynard Keynes, *The Economic Consequences of the Peace*, Macmillan, London 1971; Richard Cooper, *Economic Policy in an Interdependent World*, MIT Press, Boston, MA 1986.
17. Thomas Hobbes, *Leviathan*, Washington Square Press, New York 1964; Niccolo Machiavelli, *The Prince and Selected Discourses*, Bantam Books, New York 1966.
18. Reinhold Niebuhr, *The Children of Light and the Children of Darkness*, Charles Scribner's Sons, New York 1960.

19. Edward Hallett Carr, *The Twenty Years' Crisis, 1919–1939*, Harper & Row, New York 1964; Hans J. Morgenthau, *Politics Among Nations: The Struggle for Power and Peace*, Alfred A. Knopf, New York 1967, pp. 25–35.
20. G. W. F. Hegel, *Reason in History: A General Introduction to the Philsophy of History*, Bobbs-Merrill, New York 1953; see also Karl R. Popper, *The Open Society and its Enemies*, vol. II, Harper & Row, New York 1962.
21. Edmund Burke, *Reflections on the Revolution in France*, Penguin Books, Baltimore, MD 1969; *Selections from Treitschke's Lectures on Politics*, translated by Adam L. Gowans, Gowans & Gray, London 1914, pp. 9–46.
22. George F. Kennan, *Memoirs 1925–1950*, and *Memoirs 1950–1963*, Pantheon Books, New York 1967 and 1972; Michael Joseph Smith, *Realist Thought from Weber to Kissinger*, Louisiana State University Press, Baton Rouge, LA 1986, pp. 165–217.
23. Antoyne de Montchrétien, *Traité de l'économie politique*, Slatkine Reprints, Geneva 1970; Friedrich List, *Das nationale System der politischen Oekonomie*, Gotta'sche Buchhandlung, Stuttgart 1925; see also Edmond Silberner, *La guerre et la paix dans l'histoire des doctrines économiques*, Sirey, Paris 1957.
24. Stephen Krasner, *Defending the National Interest, Raw Materials Investments and U.S. Foreign Policy*, Princeton University Press, Princeton, NJ 1978; Stephen Krasner, "State Power and the Structure of International Trade," *World Politics*, vol. 28, no. 3, April 1976, pp. 317–47; Jeffry A. Frieden and David A. Lake (eds), *International Political Economy, Perspectives on Global Power and Wealth*, St. Martin's Press, New York 1991.
25. Joseph M. Grieco, *Cooperation among Nations: Europe, America, and Non-Tariff Barriers to Trade*, Cornell University Press, Ithaca, NY 1990.
26. Hedley Bull, *The Anarchical Society: A Study of Order in World Politics*, Macmillan, London 1977.
27. Immanuel M. Wallerstein, *The Modern World-System*, Academic Press, New York 1974.
28. V. I. Lenin, *Imperialism, the Highest State of Capitalism*, International Publishers, New York 1988; Paul Leroy-Beaulieu, *De la colonisation chez le peuples modernes*, Guillaumin, Paris 1882.
29. Johan Galtung, "Eine strukturelle Theorie des Imperialismus," in Dieter Senghaas, *Imperialismus und strukturelle Gewalt: Analysen über abhängige Reproduktion*, Suhrkamp, Frankfurt a/Main 1978, pp. 29–104; Dieter Senghass, *Weltwirtschaftsordnung und Entwicklungspolitik: Plädoyer für Dissoziation*, Suhrkamp, Frankfurt a/Main 1977.
30. Benjamin Disraeli, "Speech on Calling out Reserve Forces," and "Speech on the Berlin Treaty," in T. F. Kebbel (ed.), *Selected Speeches of the Late Benjamin Disraeli*, Longmans, Green & Co., London 1882.

Index

anarchy
  anarchic idealist worldview 14, 16, 58, 63, 116, 120, 129–30
  anarchic realist worldview 14–15, 29, 84, 119
Angell, Norman 4, 14, 23, 59, 65–71, 78–9, 120, 123, 135–6, 147, 149–54
Aron, Raymond 2–3, 21–2, 98, 106

balance of power 3–4, 8, 10, 12–13, 15–17, 29–36, 39–42, 48–50, 62, 75, 81–8, 105–13, 119–20
bellum iustum 54, 79
Bentham, Jeremy 9, 57–8, 123, 152
Bernhardi, Friedrich von 3, 9, 16–17, 42–50, 87, 93, 113, 158–60, 162–5
Bismarck, Otto von 40–2, 46, 48, 113
Bonaparte, Napoléon 51
Brodie, Bernard 36, 40, 97
Bull, Hedley 95, 161–2

capitalism 17, 59, 94
Carr, Edward Hallett 71, 158
Clausewitz, Carl von 3–4, 23, 36–42, 88, 98, 106, 113, 159, 161
Cobden, Richard 123
Cold War 1, 5, 16, 17, 82–3, 95, 107–10, 112, 130–4, 136
collective security 2, 11, 15, 65, 71, 72, 78, 135, 154
Congress of Vienna 12, 32, 42, 48, 75, 93
conservatism 9, 11, 58
containment 108, 110–11
Cuban missile crisis 83, 104

Darwin, Charles 43
democracy 4, 55, 59, 62, 64, 73–6, 115, 121, 153
détente 113
deterrence 96, 100–1
Doyle, Michael 58, 153
Dulles, John Foster 111

European Community 9, 12, 126

Falk, Richard A. 5, 15, 135, 137–48, 149–57
federation 4, 14, 31, 48, 56–7, 62, 87
first-, second-, and third-image thinker 10, 71
flexible response 110–11

France 32, 48–9, 51, 57, 60, 67, 115
  French Revolution 33, 51
free trade 4–5, 12, 14, 57, 60, 63, 76, 87, 89, 115–16, 120–4, 147

Galtung, Johan 63, 82, 163
GATT 9, 89, 95, 120, 126, 141
Geneva Conventions 54
Gentz, Friedrich von 3, 8, 15–17, 29–36, 41, 49–50, 86–8, 93, 105, 113, 158–62
Germany 17, 31, 42–4, 46–9, 60, 66–9, 72, 77, 91, 93
Gilpin, Robert 4–5, 9, 16, 24, 88–96, 116, 120–4, 159–65
Godwin, William 13, 153–4
Gray, Colin 4–5, 7, 24, 106–15, 122, 158–60, 162
Great Britain 44, 47–9, 61, 64, 66–8, 115, 120
GRIT 131, 136

Hegel, Georg Wilhelm Friedrich 41–2, 50–1, 58, 149, 158, 162
hegemony 1–5, 9, 12, 15, 30–3, 42, 49, 84, 87–90, 93–5, 105, 109, 113, 119–27, 160, 165
hierarchy
  hierarchic idealist worldview 14–15
  hierarchic realism 5, 16, 93, 163
  hierarchic realist worldview 14, 42, 50, 60, 63, 103, 163
  hierarchical world order 4, 13, 15, 147, 164
Hitler, Adolf 41, 113
Hobbes, Thomas 13, 58, 59, 94, 149, 157–8
Hobson, John A. 4, 16, 59–65, 70, 78, 82, 120–1, 135, 150–4
human rights 49, 58, 86, 137, 141, 150–3, 160

idealism 4, 11, 16, 43–4, 46, 60, 65, 78, 92, 124, 127–30, 136, 155–6
imperialism 2, 4, 8–9, 13, 16–17, 28–9, 42, 50, 57–65, 95, 114, 123, 152, 160
Industrial Revolution 69–70
integration 1–4, 12–14, 70, 120, 125, 140, 149, 154, 157
internationalism 60, 62, 64, 78
intervention 29, 32, 53, 110, 138, 156

190

Index

ius in bello 54

Japan 91, 93, 107, 115–6, 126

Kahn, Herman 4, 7, 96–106, 114, 122, 158–9, 162
Kant, Immanuel 4, 9, 14, 24, 41–3, 51–9, 70, 77–8, 86, 121, 135, 149, 151–5
Kaplan, Morton 21–2, 82
Kennedy, John F. 83, 97, 102–5
Keohane, Robert 5, 7, 15, 89, 95, 123–30, 136–7, 147, 150, 156
Keynes, John Maynard 9, 59, 71, 156
Khrushchev, Nikita S. 83, 102
Kissinger, Henry A. 106, 113, 159–60
Krasner, Stephen D. 125, 159–60

law of uneven growth 16, 24, 92–6, 165
law of pure passion 24
law of pure reason 23–4
League of Nations 4, 56, 65, 72, 75, 77, 79, 129
Lenin, V.I. 16–17, 59, 63, 65, 82, 109, 149, 163
Leroy-Beaulieu, Paul 163–4
liberalism 9, 11, 45, 58, 115, 121, 123, 150
Locke, John 9, 149–51

Machiavelli, Niccolò 157, 159–60
Mackinder, Halford 5, 107–8, 114
Marx, Karl 65, 149, 154
Marxism 9, 65
mercantilism 69, 123, 152
Metternich, Clemens von 29, 32, 48, 93, 113
Morgenthau, Hans J. 4, 10–11, 81, 158, 161

nation-state 8, 14, 17, 70, 90, 135
national interest 29, 31, 35, 50, 79, 87, 110, 114, 161
nationalism 60, 62, 64, 118
NATO 101, 103, 110
neutrality 161, 163

optimism 1, 59, 96, 112–113, 124
Osgood, Charles E. 5, 7, 104, 130–6, 146, 148–50, 155–7

pacifism 53, 69
Paine, Thomas 58, 149
pessimism 92, 124
pluralism 7, 9, 74, 140, 151
powers
  great powers 30, 48, 62, 83–8, 105, 108, 122, 135, 162

land powers 30, 107
sea-powers 30, 107
small powers 30, 83, 122, 138, 162
Prisoners' Dilemma 7–8, 35, 58, 64, 79, 125–8, 136, 147, 150, 156
progressivism 72–3

raison d'état 45, 158
rational choice 5, 88–9, 93, 116–17, 124–9, 136
Reagan Doctrine 111
realism
  neo-realism 4, 81, 83–84, 86, 88
  Realpolitik 3, 16, 108, 113
  structural realism 4
regimes 2, 5–8, 15, 32–3, 58, 62, 89, 95, 120, 123–30, 147, 154, 156
republicanism 55, 58, 121
rollback 111
Röpke, Wilhelm 154–5
Rosecrance, Richard 5, 14–15, 24, 82, 89, 115–24, 130, 135–6, 147, 150–4
Rousseau, Jean-Jacques 9–10
rule of law 55, 78, 153, 155, 157
Russia 32, 48–9, 60, 108, 115

Saint Pierre, Abbé de 51, 56
sanctions 80, 155–6
Schelling, Thomas 96, 101
self-fulfilling prophecy 98, 104
self-help 4, 7–8, 15, 78, 83–6, 119–20, 147, 154–7, 160–1
self-interest 29, 31–5, 44, 48, 66, 84–8, 105, 124, 129, 136, 150, 160
Senghaas, Dieter 63, 163
Sharp, Gene 153–4
Smith, Adam 9, 57, 120, 123, 149–50, 154
Social Darwinism 50, 62, 93
socialism 9, 61
stability 1, 7, 14, 33, 83, 89, 100–5, 112, 120–7, 156–64
START 46, 65, 89, 99, 115, 131, 137
state
  state-power 85, 151, 159
  trading-state 1, 5, 14, 115–17, 120, 122
structuralism 7, 9
subjectivity 25–6, 130
supranationality 8–9, 12, 70, 79

Treitschke, Heinrich von 42, 45, 51, 158–60, 163

United Nations 4, 79, 134, 137, 141

United States 11, 57, 60, 68, 72, 86, 94, 96–100, 102–4, 107–15, 120, 132, 134–5, 146

Versailles Treaty 71
Vietnam 101, 106, 146

Wallerstein, Immanuel 63, 162
Waltz, Kenneth 2–4, 8–11, 13, 16, 17, 21, 24, 27, 71, 81–9, 93–5, 105, 114–15, 124, 158–61
war
 by calculation 99
 by miscalculation 99
 catalytic war 99
 hegemonic war 47, 90, 92
 preventive war 92, 96
Westphalia, Treaty of 12, 90, 94
William II 41–2, 113
Wilson, Woodrow 4, 9–11, 15–16, 57, 71–9, 121–2, 129, 135–6, 146, 149–53, 155–7
Wohlstetter, Albert 97
WOMP 137, 144, 146
world government 5, 10, 15, 120, 134–8, 141, 147–8, 154
World Order System 138, 140
World Polity Association 141–3, 147–8
World War I 14, 16–17, 40, 42, 65, 83
World War II 40, 103, 108, 118, 121

zero-sum game 35, 49, 58, 64, 69, 119, 136, 147, 150, 156, 161, 163